D0279419

DEVISING THEATRE

Devising Theatre is a practical handbook that combines a critical analysis of contemporary devised theatre practice, with descriptions of selected companies, and suggestions for any group devising theatre from scratch. It was written because of a perceived need for information about the subject, and is the first book to propose a general theory of devised theatre.

After introducing devised theatre, and identifying the unique nature of this type of performance, the author goes on to examine how devised theatre is perceived by professional practitioners, and considers the potential processes of creating a devised performance. The author looks at the particular working practice and products of a number of professional companies, including a Reminiscence theatre for the elderly, a company at the cutting edge of the contemporary, experimental scene, a theatre-in-education group, and site-specific work that is community or visually performance based. The author also offers ideas and exercises for exploration and experimentation.

Alison Oddey is a lecturer in Drama and Theatre Studies at the University of Kent. Since 1977, she has devised theatre with young people, professional actors, teachers in training and undergraduate students. She has published articles in theatre journals and taught a series of practical workshops on devising theatre at the Universities of Amsterdam, Utrecht, and Antwerp.

DEVISING THEATRE

A practical and theoretical handbook

Alison Oddey

London and New York

First published 1994
by Routledge
11 New Fetter Lane, London EC4P 4EE

Simultaneously published in the USA and Canada
by Routledge
29 West 35th Street, New York, NY 10001

First published in paperback 1996

Reprinted 1997 and 1999

Typeset in Palatino by EXCEPT*detail* Ltd, Southport

Printed and bound in Great Britain by Biddles Ltd,
Guildford and King's Lynn

British Library Cataloguing in Publication Data
A catalogue record for this book is available from the British Library

Library of Congress Cataloguing in Publication Data
Oddey, Alison
Devising Theatre: A practical and theoretical handbook/Alison Oddey.
p. cm.
Includes bibliographical references and index.
1. Experimental theater – Great Britain.
2. Improvisation (Acting)
I. Title.
PN2595.13.E97O33 1994
792'.022—dc20 93–50888

ISBN 0–415–04899–0 (hbk)
ISBN 0–415–04900–8 (pbk)

In loving memory of my father,

to my mother,

for Ben,

but most of all for myself.

In my beginning is my end.

('East Coker', *Four Quartets*, T.S. Eliot)

CONTENTS

ILLUSTRATIONS

PREFACE

I wrote this book for several reasons, the main one being that I felt there was a lack of information on the subject of devising theatre. When asked to recommend reading material to students on this particular subject, I was unaware of any publication that addressed a general theory and practice of contemporary British devised theatre or that included a diversity of devising processes and devised products from different professional companies within one book. At the same time, I wanted to enjoy researching and writing this book; my starting point was a strong, passionate interest in the subject matter, based on sixteen years' personal experience of devising theatre with young people, actors, training teachers, and students in higher education.

This handbook is written for students in higher education, professional companies, or any group wanting to devise theatre from scratch. It provides a general theory of devising theatre, supported and illustrated by selected examples from contemporary British devised theatre practice. It includes description, critical evaluation and analysis of specific work processes and theatre performances. It can be dipped into and used in various ways that will point the reader in a number of different directions. The book is intended as a practical and theoretical guide to devising theatre that will offer the reader an insight into the specific challenges and processes of devising, the sub-genre of devised theatre, as well as the infinite possibilities of working as a group or a devising theatre company.

One of the difficulties in writing this book has concerned contradictions and ambiguity. What I most enjoy about devising theatre is being with a group of people, exploring and experimenting with the nature of performance. What originally attracted me to devising theatre still remains: first, the thrill and excitement of being part of the developing, original product to be performed; and second, the collaborative, sharing experience of making theatre with others. Its strength of appeal is in the multifarious aspects of the process (whether as a performer/deviser, director/deviser, or teacher), from the practical 'on the floor' work, which allows me to be instinctive and spontaneous, to the more theoretical aspects of research, discussion, planning, and construction. However, it is through the solitary occupation of writing that I must capture the essence of devising theatre.

This book is the beginnings of a dialogue to be shared with others. It is neither definitive nor prescriptive, but sets up a conversation about devising theatre. It is a partial map that charts some of the working methods and ideologies informing current practice. There is an urgent need for dissemination of both theoretical and practical information about contemporary practice, not only within educational institutions but also within the theatre profession generally. It is important to document the diverse work of professional companies devising theatre in order to improve the profile and status of the subject. What delighted me most about the research period was the opportunity to discuss the subject with so many professional practitioners, exchanging knowledge and opinions whilst acknowledging both educational and theatrical viewpoints at the same time. The research material formed the basis for an examination of the subject from a personal, empirical perspective within the social and cultural context of devised theatre practice in the late 1980s and into the early 1990s.

I started my personal investigation with a number of questions to be answered; I end with even more to be resolved! I am laying down the foundations of a sprawling, fragmentary, process-based subject, which demands other, more critically analytical, works to be written. I hope this book stimulates further enquiry, interest and pleasure when devising theatre, and that many more conversations follow. . . .

Alison Oddey
May 1993

ACKNOWLEDGEMENTS

My thanks to all those who have participated in the ongoing debate about devising theatre, analysing their own work processes and practice within the contemporary context of the early 1990s. This, particularly, includes all the companies and individuals who were interviewed as part of my research for this book, which was generously supported by two research grants from the University of Kent in 1989 and 1990. I should also like to thank Bernard Holmes and Silcock Express Holdings Limited for private sponsorship, which enabled me to take a study leave from the University of Kent in Michaelmas term 1990. I also wish to acknowledge Faber & Faber Ltd and Harcourt Brace Jovanovich for allowing me to use extracts from 'East Coker' from *Four Quartets* in *The Complete Poems and Plays* by T.S. Eliot.

Special thanks also to all those who taught and inspired me in the Drama Department at Exeter University; to Professor Peter Thomson, Professor Martin Banham, and Professor David Bradby, who encouraged me to write in the first place; to Augusto Boal for his courage and creativity; to editors Helena Reckitt and Talia Rodgers of Routledge for trusting and believing in me, shown through their continual encouragement, time, support and sharp, perceptive comments; and to Professor Lyn Innes for her understanding and expert advice.

Last, but not least, I want to thank all those who encouraged, listened, and supported in a number of ways, particularly my dearest sister Caroline and my brother Michael, who are both extraordinarily talented in their own fields, my godmother Betty Rennie, Vivien Hale, and my closest friends Alison Kirkpatrick, Alyson Bowhay, Carol Graham, Hilary Taylor, and

Terry O'Connor. And my thanks to all those students over the years who have allowed me to learn with them, particularly the 'Out of Order' and 'Antic Theatre' devising companies of 1989–90 and 1992–93 who contributed a great deal to my thinking about devised theatre. Finally, my love and appreciation to Ben, for all his in-house support, patience, love, wisdom, and invaluable advice.

1

AN INTRODUCTION TO DEVISED THEATRE

Devised theatre can start from anything. It is determined and defined by a group of people who set up an initial framework or structure to explore and experiment with ideas, images, concepts, themes, or specific stimuli that might include music, text, objects, paintings, or movement. A devised theatrical performance originates with the group while making the performance, rather than starting from a play text that someone else has written to be interpreted. A devised theatre product is work that has emerged from and been generated by a group of people working in collaboration.

Devising is a process of making theatre that enables a group of performers to be physically and practically creative in the sharing and shaping of an original product that directly emanates from assembling, editing, and re-shaping individuals' contradictory experiences of the world. There is a freedom of possibilities for all those involved to discover; an emphasis on a way of working that supports intuition, spontaneity, and an accumulation of ideas. The process of devising is about the fragmentary experience of understanding ourselves, our culture, and the world we inhabit. The process reflects a multi-vision made up of each group member's individual perception of that world as received in a series of images, then interpreted and defined as a product. Participants make sense of themselves within their own cultural and social context, investigating, integrating, and transforming their personal experiences, dreams, research, improvisation, and experimentation. Devising is about thinking, conceiving, and forming ideas, being imaginative and spontaneous, as well as planning. It is about inventing, adapting, and creating what you do as a group.

Contemporary British devised theatre practice embraces a broad diversification of professional companies. They include The People Show, Trestle Theatre, Belgrade Theatre-in-Education Company, Red Ladder, and Welfare State International, all of whose artistic, educational, or political intentions initiate, shape, and realise the making of very different kinds of theatre products. Their work includes experimental visual performances integrating various art forms, physical mask theatre, participatory theatre-in-education programmes for primary schoolchildren with severe learning difficulties, shows for young people that encourage the exploration of difficult questions facing them as young adults, and celebratory, community-based large-scale spectacles or site-specific theatrical events. Initially, I chose thirteen professional devising companies for detailed research purposes, whose work interested me for various reasons. (See Appendix I for a brief description of these companies.) There was no scientific approach to selecting them, and I could have easily made an alternative list of companies, equally impressive and worthy of attention.

Companies devising theatre constantly have to address the changes brought about by the socio-political and cultural climate of the time. The preoccupations and changes in attitudes of contemporary society are reflected in the themes, content and form of devised theatre products. A group cannot devise in a vacuum; work originates and progresses within the broadest context of culture and society, the changing world and all its events.

VIRTUE IN ECLECTISM?

What identifies and defines devised theatre as a separate form worthy of consideration is the uniqueness of process and product for every group concerned. The significance of this form of theatre is in the emphasis it places on an eclectic process requiring innovation, invention, imagination, risk, and above all, an overall group commitment to the developing work. However, it is the very nature and eclecticism of the devising experience that makes it impossible to articulate any single theory of how theatre is devised, when every professional company or group works in a unique way with different

2

intentions, interests, and concerns. What makes devising so special is the potential freedom or opportunity to move in a number of different directions through a collaborative work process, developing an original theatre product to be performed. It can produce more creative solutions than other forms of theatre, although this is fundamentally determined by group dynamics and interaction.

Any definition of devised theatre must include process (finding the ways and means to share an artistic journey together), collaboration (working with others), multi-vision (integrating various views, beliefs, life experiences, and attitudes to changing world events), and the creation of an artistic product. Sometimes devised theatre is made for, with, or from a particular audience. However, there are some unclear boundaries within the subject of devised theatre, around which there are many areas of disagreement amongst theatre practitioners. Must devised theatre always be considered as a group activity, for instance, if a solo performer collaborates with another artist but is not part of a company? How do we define a devised play script in terms of authorship and ownership between a writer and company? What is the value and relationship of process to product, and the significance of the process in relation to accessibility and the creation of a performance?

Devised theatre also raises some fascinating questions for other forms of theatre, which are ultimately concerned with areas of content, form, or audience, as well as preliminary aims and objectives. I am intrigued by the differences and similarities in methodologies of devising theatre; how the process of making theatre relates to a particular working practice, ideology, and product; how a company's intentions or objectives influence and determine significant decisions of content, form, and audience; and why the process of devising, or the creation of a unique form of theatre product appeals to such a variety of companies devising theatre in Britain today.

TRADITION

It is important to record the work of devised theatre as evidence of our ever-changing culture and society. The People Show, for instance, is a company that has devised theatre for over twenty-seven years, and witnessed numerous performers proceed into the various traditional roles of conventional theatre. Devised theatre is an alternative to the dominant literary theatre tradition, which is the conventionally accepted form of theatre dominated by the often patriarchal, hierarchical relationship of playwright and director. This dominant tradition revolves around and focuses on the interpretation of the playwright's text by a director, culminating in a performance which is realised through a production process (within a prescribed period of time and means) in a theatre building. British post-war theatre has almost always been text-led, originating with the playwright and emphasising the written word. The written play script has been the starting point and basis of British theatre production. Therefore, the dominant tradition of theatre and criticism has always been about the relationship of writing and performance. Conventional or text-based theatre is a large, diverse category of theatre. When I refer to the dominant form, I am not suggesting a homogenisation of traditional forms of theatre into one, nor am I promoting devised theatre as a form in opposition.

Devised theatre is not always in contradistinction to 'straight' theatre. Devised work is a response and a reaction to the playwright–director relationship, to text-based theatre, and to naturalism, and challenges the prevailing ideology of one person's text under another person's direction. Devised theatre is concerned with the collective creation of art (not the single vision of the playwright), and it is here that the emphasis has shifted from the writer to the creative artist. Thus, all too often, a devised performance is perceived as a sub-genre of theatre in the sense that it is not constructed in the established, accepted way of making theatre – from playwright, via director and actors, to performance. In the late 1960s and early 1970s, numerous companies were evolving with the common desire of considering different ways of creating a theatrical performance. This was the birth of new forms or styles of theatre, including the start of the theatre-in-education movement in 1965 with the founding of the first British theatre-in-education team at the Belgrade Theatre, Coventry;[1] the beginnings of community theatre, exemplified by Red Ladder Theatre Company, who started in 1968 as a political theatre group – the Agitprop Street Players;[2] the development of performance art, as evident in Welfare State

4

International's celebratory, theatrical spectacles originating in 1968;[3] and experimental multi-disciplinary visual theatre.[4]

With changes in attitudes towards sexuality, the existing political and social climate in Britain, and censorship of the stage abolished, it is hardly surprising that theatrical expression found new ways of reflecting political upheaval and discontent. Devised theatre offered the opportunity to groups of artists to try out ideas or notions that were not text-led. It provided the potential for a designer, choreographer, or performer to initiate a concept or starting point for performance. In turn, this encouraged the development of a performance language that included non-verbal forms.

An example

The company claiming to be in at the start is The People Show, a group of artists (not actors) who came together in 1966 to work collaboratively towards devising a visual theatre product in performance. A touring performing group, The People Show offered an alternative to text-based theatre, in terms of providing experimental visual performance rather than productions of new plays and writing. The company's early work experimented with various aspects of both visual and performing arts, combining written words, music, improvisation, and environmental settings. By 1971, their shows had developed a more image-based, visual emphasis, described here by founder member Mark Long as:

> Now the shows are not so loose as they were, but they don't depend on word structures, or script structures, or plots. We are working around visual structures. A series of visual images is worked on beforehand and then we embroider these – with our bodies, with our words and with our reactions – to enlarge the images for the audience. In the last year, we've done six entirely different shows, all quite structured visually.[5]

David Gale, a founder member of Lumiere & Son in 1973, describes The People Show in the 1970s as 'turning out consistently impressive, surreal, poetic work that derived from the most daring devising process I have ever come across'.[6] The People Show's method of working relied on the differences and conflict between individual artists within the group, which changed with every new show's situation, conditions and circumstances. Every show was a unique devising experience, resulting in an original product that changed with every performance. The relationship of process to product was determined by the individual artists' interests and interpretation of ideas, rather than an agreed group vision of a show. A key characteristic of their working method was to place great emphasis on the relationship between actor and audience, which meant that the 'first night' was simply the beginning of a show. Long observes:

> The presence of the audience is one of the biggest factors in the creative process itself. When an audience sees the show, your feeling and understanding for the show is inevitably altered. The audience reaction offers that feeling or understanding. It's part of the process, as is the performance as much part of the process as the rehearsal.[7]

The People Show is illustrative of a group of individual artists in collaboration with each other, taking risks, having a sense of the unknown at the start of the devising process, exploring and experimenting with ideas, form, structure, and the nature of visual performance. This company has established a particular approach to making visual theatre that uses lighting, sound, music, and technical resources to discover the possibilities of image and spectacle within the performance space. The exploration and experimentation with technical facilities in the theatre are an important part of the group's work. In a 1982 article, Long comments:

> The other thing which I think is very important, which we try to do with all new members of the group, not always very successfully, but which I think is absolutely vital, is that everybody in the group has to have an understanding of lighting, an understanding of building and a definite visual comprehension of costume.[8]

Since 1966, The People Show has developed a unique visual and aural style of theatre, recruiting members from a multidisciplinary background with interests in the visual arts, music, and technical theatre. The People Show and its early shows were significant in establishing a unique working process of

6

individual artists in collaboration with each other, using the resources within the group to make, construct, and continually develop a theatre product in performance. This particular process of devising embraces the use of images, a structured environment, the contribution of individual artists' ideas, and a conscious awareness of the interaction with the audience in performance.

In order to examine in later chapters the nature of a devised performance, the actor–spectator relationship, and the desire to create theatre for a particular audience, community, or site-specific location, I intend to identify and establish the specific challenges of the subject of devising theatre by asking what differentiates devised theatre from the dominant literary theatre tradition, and why do people want to devise theatre? I want to suggest the distinguishing characteristics of devised theatre, as well as speculate about some of the reasons why companies or groups evolve to pursue this alternative form of theatre.

BEGINNINGS

What initially identifies devised theatre is that the creative process originates in ways different from traditional theatre. Questions arise about where and how to start making a performance, and what kind of product is to be created. Devised theatre can start from an infinite number of possibilities, such as an idea, image, concept, object, poem, piece of music, or painting, and the precise nature of the end product is unknown. In conventional theatre, however, everyone knows the production is, for example, Shakespeare's *Hamlet* from the outset. The script dictates the plot or narrative line, the number of characters, the setting, the scene directions, and the length of the piece. In devised theatre, at one end of the spectrum is an open book with only unmarked pages, whilst at the other end is a skeletal outline of the proposed piece to be devised. It may be a large-scale community event with local participants in Bradford, a participatory secondary theatre-in-education programme, a piece of reminiscence theatre for the elderly in south London, or a performance piece exploring the notion of reality, fiction, and contemporary culture.

Devised theatre demands decisions about how and where to begin. This is different from text-based theatre, where the play script defines and determines the parameters of the performance, however abstract the content might be. In chapter two, I look at how and where a group begins to devise theatre, and the kind of stimuli or starting points that may initiate a devised theatrical product, arguing that form, content, or audience (in any number of combinations) determine the devising route to be taken.

Value in democracy?

The way a group or company operates, is organised structurally, identifies roles or responsibilities, and works together differs from traditional theatre. A central reason for the large number of companies devising theatre in the 1970s was the strong desire to work in an artistically democratic way. The 'collective' grew out of a socio-political climate that emphasised democracy, so that many groups were interested in breaking down the patriarchal and hierarchical divisions of the traditional theatre company. The growth of collectives in the British alternative theatre since 1970 has been written about in various books, such as Catherine Itzin's *Stages in the Revolution* or Michelene Wandor's *Carry on Understudies, Theatre and Sexual Politics*, and Rob Ritchie's *The Joint Stock Book*[9] provides important documentation of one successful model of collective theatre. This book illustrates the various approaches taken to redefining the relationship of writer, director, and actor, and how they differ from the hierarchy of conventional theatre.

The influence of the Women's Liberation Movement and feminism in the 1970s encouraged a change of attitudes, gave women an improved position as theatre workers, and supported the development of experimental theatre to explore the social and sexual attitudes of society. The introduction to *Monstrous Regiment, A Collective Celebration*, edited by Gillian Hanna,[10] provides a useful insight into how this women's collective operated from the mid-1970s, initially as a democratic collective, and later as a more skills-specialised division of roles within the group. Companies founded in the 1970s established different ways of devising theatre, which are illustrated in the diverse examples of Forkbeard Fantasy (1974), Gay Sweatshop (1975), and IOU (who broke away from Welfare State International in 1976 to work as a collective).

In the 1970s devising companies chose artistic democracy in favour of the hierarchical structures of power linked to text-based theatre, and yet within the last twenty years or so there has been a move from this standpoint to more hierarchical structures within many companies in response to an ever-changing economic and artistic climate. In the cultural climate of the early 1990s, the term 'devising' has less radical impli-cations, placing greater emphasis on skill sharing, specialisa-tion, specific roles, increasing division of responsibilities, such as the role of the director/deviser or the administrator, and more hierarchical company structures. This is evident from the changing practice of those professional companies who began devising theatre in the early or mid-1970s, and have altered the nature of their work for a number of different reasons. Variable economic conditions have prevented some companies from working as a permanent ensemble throughout the year, with the effect that they now employ a smaller core of permanent staff, using freelance artists from project to project. Companies must decide how to organise a power infra-structure, which is exemplified by the roles or responsibilities chosen by the group, and how decision-making takes place.

Politics

Group dynamics, relationships, and interaction between people are a distinguishing feature of devising theatre. The relation-ships between individual specialist members are different from the production hierarchy of a text-based theatre. In a conven-tional play producing company, people are selected for specific tasks or roles, rather than for political, pedagogical, or artistic beliefs. Implicit in devised theatre are questions about personal politics in relation to group politics, which are reflected in the making of a company statement or policy. The participants and their life experiences contribute to both process and product. A group statement or policy identifies a particular style, a unique language or vocabulary, shared beliefs, or a commitment to why a company wishes to make a specific theatrical product. A devising company offers the opportunity for flexibility between group members, in both the integration and exchange of ideas or roles within a project.

This form of theatre provides wider opportunities and

possibilities for all the members of a group. It encourages and enables new working relationships between the roles of writer, director, designer, technician, musician, and performer. Roles and responsibilities are not necessarily restricted or defined by text-based theatre, where there are clear divisions or parameters for job specification. Traditional theatre is compartmentalised into single tasks, such as acting or lighting the stage, whereas devised theatre demands a group of people who are versatile and multi-talented.

In conventional play production, an actor is only expected to play a specific part, working from the playwright's original vision through the director's interpretation to the final creation of the role. In devised theatre, a performing company member may take aspects of administrative work or developmental research work with a particular audience. In most devising companies, everyone is expected to 'muck in' or pull together, regardless of their allocated roles. This includes the company striking a set after a performance, a performer driving a van whilst on tour, or everyone helping to complete the set. I reiterate, however, that I am not suggesting that devised theatre is in diametrical opposition to traditional theatre. Indeed, many conventional, small-scale touring companies of text-based theatre will totally identify with striking the set and driving the van as being shared tasks!

Changing needs of the performer

One reason for the emergence of so many companies devising theatre from the mid-1960s onwards was as a response to changes in education, actor training, and the development of the performer. Historically, the drama schools focused on voice production, and training the actor's voice as an instrument to speak text. The influence of 'method' acting, with its emphasis on investigating the psychological nature of a character and detailed realistic portrayal, has encouraged the actor to study a role in far greater depth. It is also true that the development of film and television has meant that the actor has had to become a more thinking, feeling, truthful being, able to realise roles through both verbal and non-verbal skills. These developments in actor training, combined with increased opportunities to study drama on degree courses, have produced actors who wish to engage intellectually in the discussion of work, or practically in the creative process of making a performance. Although traditional literary theatre provides an actor with more opportunity for creative expression than previously, devised theatre offers a different route for the actor, which is often associated with having greater status and input within the overall creation of the theatrical product.

Devised theatre offers the performer the chance to explore and express personal politics or beliefs in the formation and shaping of the piece. This is illustrated by some women performers who feel confined by female stereotypes produced by male playwrights, and wish to experiment with creating roles that reflect their own experiences as women. Annie Griffin (formerly of Gloria, and now with Pirate Productions) devises theatre because of her interests in feminism and the politics of self-presentation, combined with her desire as a performer to engage with an audience and creatively decide how she wants to *be* in performance. A performer/deviser has a personal input and commitment to the making of the product from the start, which consequently means that the needs of the performer/deviser are recognised, and are therefore different from the actor in text-based theatre. In the traditional literary form, the actor is awarded a part or role based on external appearance and previous work so far, whereas a devising company offers the performer the opportunity and challenge of creating or developing work from an initial brief, against traditional expectations or stereotyping.

METHODOLOGY

A strong need of many new groups or companies devising theatre is to make original theatrical products through a variety of processes and methods of working. There is no one accepted way of devising a performance, whilst a conventional play production tends to follow a particular route. The process of making or creating sets devised theatre apart from traditional forms of theatre, and is its distinctive hallmark. The significance of the process is that it determines the product, and is a unique experience for every different group of people working together. The devising process is about the ways and means of

11

making a theatrical performance: a company chooses how the product is to be created, which involves decisions about the most appropriate process in light of the intended product. This may include methods of research, discussion, 'workshopping' material, improvisation, the use of a writer, or visual experimentation.

A devising process can mean a specific method of working, which employs the traditional roles from text-based theatre in an alternative way. For instance, Ann Jellicoe has a particular method of making a community play that uses the writer in a different way than simply being a playwright.[11] The commissioned playwright must respond to the precise needs of the community, writing for a town and contributing to the creation of a unique community event. The role of a writer in relation to the devising process may mean re-working or re-writing text during this developmental period, and can be approached from a number of different directions. In chapter three, I describe and examine how other conventional roles are defined by various devising companies, such as director, writer, or designer, whilst identifying some of the processes used when devising theatre.

Time

One important reason why groups devise theatre is to communicate and express particular interests or concerns – to say something about their specific situation. In order to do this, fundamental decisions about the use of time and finance have to be made for each project. Devised theatre has the potential to choose a time span for the making of the product, which is governed or determined by resources and budget. In conventional theatre, there is an accepted pattern of prescribed time for the production process of a play. This is evident in the repertory system of text-based theatre, where three weeks is an accepted timescale for rehearsing each script.

Each devising company chooses the period of time to be allocated to both process and product. This involves balancing initial planning, research, and preliminary workshops against how time is scheduled for the making of the product, for rehearsal, and in performance. Decisions about time are specifically related to the nature of the devised piece, the purpose and intention of the work. A company is concerned with the length and duration of a performance, work in progress, and touring arrangements: a participatory theatre-in-education programme can last a day, or an outdoor site-specific celebration may not commence until late evening. Some companies place a limited time structure on the devising process, whilst others work within a much longer period despite financial restrictions. What is essentially different for devised theatre is the company's need to plan and schedule its own timescale according to the development of the work, and in relation to a flexible structure of potential change, shift of focus, and spontaneous decision-making.

Time is needed for the trying out of ideas, the experimentation of work, the development of a process, and subsequently to create deadlines out of that work. There are not the time constraints normally allocated to specific roles or responsibilities in text-based theatre, where, for example, the musician employed to play music in a theatre production usually comes in at the end of the rehearsal period, or a lighting designer might expect to have about twelve hours to light a musical or complex play in a five-hundred-seat theatre. In a devising company, such as IOU or Lumiere & Son, a musician can suggest the time needed to make a contribution to the developing piece at the start. However, a difficulty arises for some companies devising innovative, experimental work when a good idea can develop over a number of years, such as Station House Opera's series of works using breeze blocks in performance over a period of four to five years. This raises the question of different levels of funding needed to accommodate planning or preparation time, a devising period of workshops and discussion, as well as rehearsal or touring timescales. The notion of producing more than one show out of a time-related budget is not relevant to a system of funding based on established conventions of touring the traditional play in Britain. Within the broad spectrum of contemporary British devised theatre practice, the overall length of time used to devise a theatrical product or performance varies greatly with every company's internal planning and organisation. This is illustrated by the examples of Trestle Theatre's 'Top Storey' (1990), which took ten weeks to devise (including one month's research and development), and 'Crime of Love' (1991), which was completed within six weeks.

Devising theatre demands decisions about the organisation and structuring of time, whether it be a three-week residency, a ten-day site-specific piece, or a three-month tour. Apart from the making of the artistic product, there are time decisions related to the administration of the product, publicity, company business, and evaluating the work. In devised theatre there is always a sense of never having enough time to work. This is particularly true of those roles from traditional text-based theatre, which have different functions within the devising company; for instance, the set designer cannot design the set at the start and know that the task is complete. A designer in a theatre-in-education company may have little time to create a visually satisfying space if the process is fraught with difficulties and subject to constant change.

Resources

Finance and budget for a devised show are inextricably linked to decisions about time. The 1970s saw increases in Arts Council subsidies, which helped the expansion of alternative theatre. Thus, Joint Stock had funding for four-week workshops, five to six weeks of rehearsal, and three months of touring. The communal way of working was respected in terms of both temporal and financial requirements. However, the 1980s saw a preoccupation with fund-raising and sponsorship to the extent that many companies felt their creativity stifled, the artistic side of the work devalued, and experienced a need to become multi-faceted. For some companies this meant developing workshops, residencies, or touring projects, in order to survive. Gillian Hanna, a founder member of Monstrous Regiment, compares the company's situation in 1978 to 1989 in an article, 'Waiting for Spring to Come Again: Feminist Theatre 1978 and 1989',[12] which states that its original revenue funding grant paid for eleven people to work full-time over a year, whilst its current grant covers an administrator only.

In the early 1990s, devised theatre receives less Arts Council funding generally than traditional play production that is based in a theatre building.[13] Theatre buildings need income to survive and be maintained. The building provides a potential artistic continuity in a specific community or region, whether by maintaining the particular operation or transforming it. Thus, the Arts Council will withdraw funding from a building-based company whose artistic quality is not adequate. Indeed, I found when I was a member of South East Arts Drama Panel (1988–92), decisions about financial applications for non-theatre building-based companies were heavily restricted by the fact that there were three repertory theatres in the region requiring a significant part of the budget in order to be maintained.

Those devising companies linked to particular theatre buildings are partly resourced for this reason, such as Belgrade Theatre-in-Education Company in Coventry, which receives some Arts Council funding under the auspices of Belgrade Theatre Trust, in addition to central funding from Coventry City Council.[14] For devising companies based in buildings which are not part of an existing theatre structure or designed specifically to accommodate an audience, there are still additional costs of rehearsal space, administrative work, storage, and the needs of a particular project.

This alternative form of theatre is often specifically 'Project' funded, although there are some companies devising theatre who are 'Annual Clients' or 'Three year franchise clients (touring)'.[15] Unless a company is franchise funded over three years, it must make applications for individual projects to the Arts Council. Subsequently, many devising companies have to prove the value and significance of their particular products with every application, rather than developing the work in a financially secure situation over several years. One of the real problems for newer companies devising live art, performance theatre, or experimental work is working within a category of theatrical form that is still relatively unacknowledged. Despite the Arts Council's attempt to maintain up-to-date information on such companies, one cannot ignore the fact that ultimately all individual views or opinions of officers, advisers, or panel members are subjective responses to the work. Consequently, devised theatre is often dependent upon a variety of financial resources linked to a proposed project, which has no guaranteed future funding. For some companies, this becomes a debate about basic living standards versus how much budget to afford to the making of the devised product. Therefore, members of a group choose how to use its budget, which may include the decision to pay themselves less money (to enable a longer devising period) rather than receiving the basic salary for a specific responsibility, as in conventional theatre.

Each devising company determines how money is spent in relation to the intended theatrical product, with the flexibility of re-distributing costs arising out of changes and decisions made during the devising process. In text-based theatre, a play production budget is easily categorised into costumes, set, lighting, stage management, properties, and so on. In devised theatre, the priorities of allocating resources will be different every time. In a theatre-in-education participatory programme where the play is only a tiny part of the whole day's proceedings, the focus may be on spending money to resource the development of workshops, teaching materials, or time spent in schools. Equally, if the intention is to explore the technical or visual possibilities of the space, then money is invested here rather than in other areas of performance-making.

In devised theatre, money is used to experiment, try out, or explore possibilities, which may eventually bring failure with the final product. Britain is far less willing to subsidise new forms of alternative or innovative theatre than some European countries, such as Holland or Germany, who prioritise the need for constant experimentation and artistic discovery. In chapter four, I examine two company working practices and different devised products. 'Christmas at War' (1989) was created by Age Exchange over a period of four weeks on a budget of approximately £1,000, which represented the total amount available to pay the actors and production costs, as well as research and development.[16] 'Some Confusions in the Law about Love' (1989–90) was devised by Forced Entertainment Theatre Co-operative in three months up to a work-in-progress preview, and five months overall until the first acknowledged public performance, involving a production budget of £4,040.[17] In chapter five, I provide a detailed account of the developing process to produce a participatory theatre-in-education programme, exemplified in Greenwich Young People's Theatre's 'The Edge of Reason' (1989–90), which was devised over a period of ten four-day weeks (including re-work time of two days) on a production budget of £800, and an educational pack budget of £250.[18]

Space

A fundamental reason why groups evolve and devise theatre is to explore and experiment with the form or nature of performance. Devised theatre uses space in a significantly different way from text-based theatre. Choosing a space or location to perform in is a preliminary consideration for a group, and may be the core reason for devising a particular product. How the space is organised and structured for performance is part of the developing process, which is signicantly different to conventional play production. Traditional theatre employs a set designer to design the pre-ordained space at the start, according to instructions from both playwright and director, and allows actors a limited time to inhabit the designer's created world of the script. Decisions about space in the alternative theatrical form are ongoing, unless space defines the reason for a devised theatre project. The creation of a site-specific performance demands different considerations to be taken into account in terms of the actor–spectator relationship, planning and preparation, as well as technical concerns.

In the literary tradition, a play is normally presented inside a theatre building on a stage (whether it be proscenium, thrust, apron, or other), or in an acknowledged 'acting' area in relation to the audience. Devised theatre can also be performed inside a theatre building, but often is conceived and made outside this accepted setting. Many devising companies are concerned with making a performance away from the conventional space; for example, theatre-in-education programmes are often devised to tour in schools, large-scale spectacles or events are site-specific (that is, they are devised out of a particular chosen location or environment), and reminiscence theatre may be performed in community halls or hospitals. Devised theatre, therefore, is often concerned with the non-theatrical space, and consequently with decisions related to choice, use, or organisation of the space.

The visual concept is often a starting point for a devised performance, which is different to conventional theatre. A company may work out of and inside a defined, constructed space in order to discover the form or structure of the piece. As the performer negotiates the space, experimenting and trying out ideas, the product evolves and progresses from the developing process of discovery. It is the relationship between performers and fictional space that is significant, and an important reason why Forced Entertainment Theatre Co-operative always devise in a set, or a provisional set mock-up, constructing it physically from the beginning. It is rare for traditional text-based theatre to provide actors with a fully created visual world during the rehearsal period, and convention dictates that the 'set' is constructed several days prior to performance.

Technology

Devising empowers the technical side of theatre from the start, in that it can become an important reason for making a theatrical performance in a space. This is significantly different to the traditional form, where technical theatre serves to illustrate, illuminate, or describe the play product. In devised theatre, technical areas of expertise can contribute to the making process, developing with the product in its evolution. For this reason, I have chosen to look at how video, film, slide projections, lighting and sound are employed by some devising companies in a chosen space, and at how these technical resources are used to create a performance. Devised theatre allows the opportunity for the integration of technology, and enables the acknowledgement of technical innovation, television, and the growth of leisure activity in contemporary culture.

Devised theatre addresses questions of how to utilise a non-theatrical space in terms of the actor–spectator relationship, and visual use of the playing environment. The created space or use of visual metaphor is important in terms of reflecting the company's intentions or reasons for making theatre, and offers the possibility of a multi-disciplined arts approach. This particular form of theatre is often concerned with varying combinations of mixed art forms. One reason why many companies came together in the late 1960s or early 1970s was to initiate collaboration between performance artists interested in music, dance, and visual or technical arts. The integration and use of video, film, sculpture, music, or the visual arts brings a re-vitalisation to the devising process and product. This is particularly apparent in the area of devised performance art products, or in site-specific spectacles or events.

18

Integration of arts

For some performers the appeal of devising lies in the opportunity to work with people in inter-disciplinary art forms. Devised theatre often uses music, dance, or art in an integrated form, or in a new relationship. This kind of performance theatre enables a performer to engage in the creation of a visual or physical language, which is not present in conventional theatre based on words. Devised theatre may involve the deconstruction of words, as it is a form of theatre that often veers away from written text, or emphasis on the spoken word. It is a form of theatre that analyses culture and society in a different way to the dominant traditional form, bringing an awareness of contemporary culture through a medium that is not the 'norm' of theatre, that is, the play text. By integrating video, soundtrack, visual and physical imagery together as performance text, one is presented with a multifarious vision from which the audience can choose how to experience the work.

Artistically, there has been a move away from devising issue-based or politically orientated work as in the 1970s, to theatre that is more visually, physically, or performance-based. Some companies have wanted to interact with other artists, being open to influences outside the core. Companies have become multi-faceted in the sense that they may tour professional work in tandem with offering residencies, interactive events with communities, or educational and outreach work. In chapter six, I look at a range of devised theatre work, which utilises a combination of different art forms in relation to site-specific products or residencies. I examine the detailed performance work of IOU, Major Road's large-scale events for local communities, Forkbeard Fantasy's visual interactive use of film and live performance, and Lumiere & Son's use of location in relation to the company's particular working practice.

AUDIENCE

The nature of a devised performance is different to conventional theatre in the sense that it explores the dynamics in the relationship between performer and spectator in the chosen space, developing through process to product. The devising process is able to define a relationship with an intended audience or community from the start, providing an opportunity for audience contribution or participation in the work. Theatre that is devised for a community has specific objectives, which may place greater or lesser emphasis on the process itself, or on the final theatrical product. The devised performance may be a procession involving local participants, which is viewed both as spectacle, celebration, and event. Devised theatre has the potential to address specific issues with a community, or to create performances for a non-theatre-going audience.

An important reason why groups evolve and devise is to create theatre for a particular audience. This may be a primary reason for a company's existence, such as Greenwich Young People's Theatre, a theatre-in-education company for young people, or it may contribute to a general philosophy of making theatre for a non-theatre-going audience in a non-theatrical space, such as street theatre or performance art installations in public places. This is well illustrated in examples of community-devised theatre, residencies, or theatre-in-education work. Groups devise theatre for, with, or from a specific audience, and therefore the nature of the spectator-actor relationship is a very particular one.

When the audience is the primary reason for devising a theatrical performance, such as in a residency involving local people, a theatre-in-education programme for secondary school pupils, or an elderly community, a company considers the needs, concerns or interests, and active involvement of that specific audience. A company's initial intentions or objectives for devising theatre are crucial to how the performer–spectator relationship is set up, and to the function or purpose of devising a theatrical product, spectacle, or event. Devised theatre provides the intended spectators with access to the process of creativity, as well as an alternative experience to the traditional theatre venue and product.

How to evaluate?

How much involvement is the intended audience to have with the process of creating the product? The extent to which an audience is integrated into the decision-making process varies with every project. An audience can become part of a research process, actively involved in rehearsals, or in diverse aspects of the production process. Both spectator and performer engage in a devised performance in a different way to traditional text-based theatre, because of their direct, personal involvement with the process. A company has to find a way to monitor the process in relation to the developing product, in order to evaluate the progress of the work. What is the value of the devising process? How can it be measured in terms of the final product seen by the spectator? This is particularly pertinent for companies devising theatre with a specific audience in mind. When devising a community piece of art that encourages twenty-five local people to participate and become involved in the process of making, how do you judge or evaluate the product? What is the context for comparison, and what are the criteria for judging the work? Devised theatre should not be assessed by the same criteria used to judge conventional theatre, providing an evaluation rooted in pre-determined standards of excellence based on a literary tradition. Such evaluation has wider implications about the allocation of theatre funding in relation to issues of access and availability, as well as the function or purpose of theatre.

RECORDING AND REPRESENTATION

Devised theatre is transient and ephemeral, which makes the documentation of the form difficult. In turn, this does not encourage the promotion, status, or existence of the work, unless it can be recorded in some way or another. In text-based theatre, not only does the play script initiate the work, but it also documents it too. The published play script is a record of that production, even though it cannot differentiate between the latest Royal Shakespeare Company or Royal National Theatre production's interpretation of 'Hamlet'. There is a paradox here too. Why would any theatre company want to reproduce a devised play script when it was pertinent and personal to a particular group of people? Why should we want to document devised theatre, if its purpose is to be a unique experience for the group concerned? If we wish to study and develop this alternative theatre form we must document the existing work in one way or another.

21

How does one document a form whose manifestations are so radically different in intention, content, form and audience? Certainly, it is easy to produce published play scripts of participatory theatre-in-education programmes, or community plays, but how do you represent a large-scale spectacle or a performance text which is made up of visual imagery, physical language, and soundtrack? Much devised work is videoed, but problems arise with access and availability, or with how shots are chosen to represent a live performance. As a predominantly verbal culture, there is a strong existing tradition of analysing and criticising the meaning of art through the spoken or written word.

What are the ways of recording a performance text that is not concerned with verbal narrative, but which is ultimately a form of physical or visual theatre constructed in images or movement? What is the value in documenting the process of a devised piece of theatre? For students of theatre, practitioners, and all those interested in the subject, access to such information is invaluable. Documentation provides research material for considering and evaluating a process of devising in relation to a company's particular set of objectives or intentions. It enables the observer to understand how and why a specific performance was created. It also gives insight into the various concerns or preoccupations of multifarious groups of people in contemporary society. In chapter seven, I discuss more fully the issues of devising and documentation: how we need to find alternative forms of assessment or critical evaluation of the devised product; education and training; and I address the access and excellence debate.

CHOICE AND RESOLUTION

Central to the devising process is problem-solving. Questions are raised about form, content, or audience, whilst deciding on a preliminary structure that works. Who is it for? What is the function or purpose of the product? Devising demands decisions about how to proceed, how to operate as a company, how to manage time, money, and space, how to activate a decision-making process, how to move forward, and how to use relevant methods of working during the process in order to reach the end goal of the devised performance. In chapter eight

I offer some practical suggestions, approaches, ideas, or introductory exercises for any new group wanting to initiate a preliminary process of working, as well as referring to problems or difficulties encountered by groups in the devising process.

Traditional theatre is centrally concerned with the reproduction and interpretation of written texts, which may include the adaptation of a Shakespeare play into a contemporary production that reflects modern concerns. Whilst the dominant literary form of theatre addresses current cultural and societal preoccupations, as illustrated in new plays or theatre writing, the alternative devised form is essentially involved with the here and now of group concerns. The 1990s have seen the development of the individual artist forming a company to devise a particular show or project. The production company Gloria was founded in June 1988 to promote the work of five associated but independent artists to work in this way, but not as a permanent ensemble. This method of working is also reflected in those individual performers who have initiated a collaboration with other chosen artists, in order to work on a particular idea as a collective intelligence towards the creation of a performance. This is illustrated by the work of several ex-members of Impact Theatre (1979–86),[19] such as Graeme Miller, who devised the successful 'A Girl Skipping' (1991) in this way.

Devised theatre is a contemporary reflection of culture and society. It is continually addressing new theatrical forms, making original contributions out of the existing interests and considerations of the time. It is about the relationship of a group of people to their culture, the socio-political, artistic and economic climate, as well as issues or events surrounding them. Devising allows for a constant re-definition of theatrical performance, and for work to begin from any starting point. Choice, opportunity and infinite possibility set devised theatre apart from conventional play text production.

2

BEGINNINGS
How and where to start

. . . people probably learn that the creation of a work of art
is not hacking away at a block of wood and hoping that it
turns out to be the image you want. It actually has to be
well thought through; you have to have so many per-
imeters and some inspiration. It's a lot of hard work and
requires technical skill creating what it is you know you
want.

(John Wood, Writer-in-Residence,
Greenwich Young People's Theatre)

Devising begins with the interaction between the members of a
group and the starting point or stimulus chosen. The group
absorbs the source material, responds to it, and then generates
a method of working appropriate to the initial aims of the
company and project. The devising process challenges every
group member to confront the work, engage with it individually at different levels, as well as developing a sense of group
cooperation, affiliation and unity at the same time. All groups
are different as personalities change the group dynamics and
impetus of the work. Working in unison becomes difficult
when individuals conflict with each other, but is also an
intrinsic part of establishing a collective group identity. Ultimately, it is about the group discovering a relationship between
itself and the product it produces.

Members of a group beginning to devise theatre must be
open to each other, building and developing honesty, trust, and,
crucially, diplomacy! It is essential for each member to be able
to reveal the personal, knowing that there is sensitivity and
support within the group. Every individual must invest something of his or her person if the group is to communicate fully.

Respect and trust in each other permits criticism, enabling individuals to give up personal interests in particular areas of investigation in favour of decisions that may benefit the group to explore new directions. Mark Long, founder member of The People Show, observes, 'You have to trust yourselves as artists, trust your art. Allow a situation where the sub-conscious of the group is enabled to emerge.'[1]

In the early stages of devising, it is important for a company to explore and experiment with a range of stimuli, to understand how the group operates in different situations. Group practical work and 'getting to know each other' exercises are vital to that exploration. Exercises in communication, concentration, trust, sensitivity, movement, voice and improvisation are all required for group development. In my experience, this preliminary but necessary work can be applied to all new groups coming together at any level, be they professional, amateur, young people, drama teachers in training or undergraduate students of theatre. Knowing, using and reflecting the strengths of people in the company are vital resources for the devising process and product.

Disagreement is a healthy way to select, clarify and simplify choice of materials and methods of procedure. The danger comes in everyone compromising to the lowest common denominator, which means starting from a mediocre position. Early work can be filled with problems, so that an enormous amount of time can be spent on material or ideas that are finally rejected. Every group has the right to fail and to learn from its mistakes, working positively from them until, as Long comments, 'you do finally find yourselves in the same track on the same train'. Devising is a craft, which is inevitably learnt on the job. Certain skills are acquired empirically, and it is difficult to imagine one system of working across the board.

Every project generates its own working process, so that the actual approach to devising is different every time. I adapt my approach to the demands of the particular task or assignment, considering the project itself, the audience to be addressed, the group or company one is working with, and the playing environment for the piece. It is vital to be fluid and instinctual at the start, whether improvising from initial research or constructing related practical exercises to explore the subject itself. The best work is done when everyone in the group

25

shares a common purpose, whether it is the desire to work with the homeless community of Canterbury, or to make a piece of site-specific outdoors theatre. A combination of instinct and learning is required to devise theatre. This can only be discovered through experience. In the early stages of work, it is important to be free and open, where anything that occurs to anybody in the group can be tried out in order to explore preliminary ideas further. I am keen to encourage students to 'workshop' ideas with the group, so that they gain practical experience of investigating content as well as group dynamics. At some point in the process, a director or 'outside eye' is needed to edit or discard material, make technical decisions and lead the group overall.

Choice is a key word when devising theatre. How to start working will be determined by the company; what the group wants to do is of primary importance. If the group is newly formed then it is crucial to include discussion in the early stages of work. Often the task of preliminarily researching a subject helps people to get to know each other through the process of sharing information, which in turn establishes individual ideas and opinions. For me, it has often been a fundamental need to have a strong personal association with the material or idea in order to express something about myself, as well as thinking of ways to bring ideas alive. My original starting point for devising a performance project with a group of Dutch students from the University of Utrecht in May 1992 was 'water'. I was interested in particular contradictions and ambiguities associated with the subject of water, and chose the bathroom as an initial location for preliminary investigation. The devising process needs to be searching, the work constantly sifted, re-examined, and criticised. Group analysis is required, which ultimately leads back to self-examination and self-criticism. The pertinent point must be that the strength of devised work is in its method of working, and of giving significance to the process itself. The group defines and controls its own conditions of progress, thus offering opportunities of working that no other theatre can provide.

WHY DEVISE?

What, then, are the central concerns for a group devising theatre from scratch? Are they considerations of form, content or audience, which must be decided in order of importance or relevance to the particular project? I am preoccupied with four areas of investigation, which individually assume greater or lesser significance with each project. The first is knowing what it is I want to devise, and why. Looking back over my own experience of devising theatre since 1977, it becomes clear that there are numerous reasons why I have wanted to pursue this particular kind of theatre. I think the primary appeal is to be able to make a personal statement within a group context, to feel that one is part of the making of a theatrical experience, not an interpreter of something already written. This desire to create an original piece of work brings an enormous freedom that is both terrifying and liberating at the same time. My first steps as a director/deviser were in my final undergraduate year at Exeter University in 1976-77, when 'practical essays' were every student's preoccupation and an important part of the overall degree. 'The Open Meeting' originated from a mixture of desires to explore personal experience, to investigate specifically the subject of women alcoholics in society, and to find a form that created an environment where the audience had a clearly defined role.

The structure for the piece was an Alcoholics Anonymous 'open meeting', which was set up with the serving of tea and biscuits by several characters to the audience, as though they were members or non-members arriving at the meeting. In my unpublished 'Practical Essay Diary 1977', I noted that:

> It was finally completed by being performed. It did not allow the audience to sit back as in a lecture theatre but made them unsure of what to expect. There was a general sense of uneasiness and tension from the beginning, further increased by the characters sitting next to members of the audience so that they were fully aware of being part of the structure. There seemed to be a 'heavy atmosphere' radiating from the audience and a feeling of close attentiveness.

I recorded the excitement of experimenting with form and

content in my production notebook, concluding that 'it achieved what it set out to do – inform people in an interesting and enlightening way about a problem that most people know little about.'

This devised theatre debut with a group of eight student actors was significant not because it was awarded a first-class mark, but for the sense of personal achievement I felt in making a unique piece of theatre with a group of people working towards the same goals. It was about freedom of choice of content and form, as well as sharing a creative, participatory method of working within a group situation. Other reasons for devising theatre have been: to give a voice to young people to express their interests and concerns through this medium; to explore the adaptation of text as a starting point for more creative, contemporary ideas; to research present-day situations related to women; and, more recently, to encourage students in higher education to explore and examine their ideas or opinions through this form of theatre.

DEVISE WHAT?

Second, I need to know what it is I want to say and share with others; what is the content, material or subject matter for a piece of theatre? In 1981 I took Arrabal's play, *Picnic on the Battlefield* as a starting point for devising a contemporary piece about the hunger strike of Bobby Sands in Northern Ireland – with sixth-form students from Mayflower School in Billericay, Essex. The final devised product was performed at the school, and attempted to explore the deeper issues of the Irish situation via a radical adaptation of the initial text, combining the use of humour, the style of the absurd, and present-day reality. The following year, I devised a Youth Theatre show with thirty young people, aged between fourteen and twenty-one years, which was based on the themes of communication, prejudice, and the outsider. This was an improvised piece which evolved from weekly evening sessions and was constructed over a working weekend to incorporate a range of selected ideas from the participants. The final product, performed by Mayflower Youth Theatre in 1982, included dance, mime, music, improvised scenes, and a more experimental section using movement, lighting, and sound.

FOR WHOM?

Third, I must establish who will be my audience for the work. In 1985 I worked as a member of the company Workshop Theatre Women to research, devise and perform a piece of touring theatre about the subject of women in prison, which was based on seven original taped interviews with ex-offenders and involved several of them in the devising process itself. There was much discussion within the company about playing to an all-women audience only, and a compromise was struck by giving selected 'women only' performances during the tour. A decision was made to play a range of seventeen venues in northern England during June and July, which included a probation centre in Lincoln, a community hall in Nottingham, and The Leadmill Theatre in Sheffield, as well as higher education colleges in Scarborough and Warrington. The show was also performed for the general public in the Mandela Theatre, at the Edinburgh Festival of August 1986.

'Women Imprisoned' played to ex-offenders, magistrates, criminology and drama students, and all those interested in theatre for, from, or by women. The nature of this devised performance changed with every venue, as the performer–spectator relationship altered in accordance with the expectations of both company and audience. A case in point was at the probation centre in Lincoln. The spectators vocalised their disdain for members of the prison service so vehemently that the performers had to adapt their playing style of performance, in order to promote a working rapport with this audience. Likewise, at those performances attended by ex-offenders or contributors to the devised product, the performers took on an extra awareness and sensitivity to the playing dynamics between actors and audience.

FORMATION

Last, I have to understand the kind of theatre I wish to create; I have to think about the form and structure of the theatrical experience. 'Not Tonight Shahriyar!' was a group devised performance project, which was performed at Portsmouth Polytechnic in 1986 with Bachelor of Education third-year students training to be primary 'Creative Arts' teachers. The aims of the project were: to examine how a piece of original theatre can grow from a literary text; to consider the role of director in performance; to experiment with techniques of improvising, writing, and interpreting script; and to use a range of theatre skills, and participate in the collaborative experience of making a piece of original group theatre. A range of material and ideas was considered by the group, which included *The Epic of Gilgamesh*,[2] *Beauty and the Beast* from the Opie fairy tale collection,[3] 'Sweeney Agonistes' by T.S. Eliot,[4] and a variety of song lyrics by Tom Waits.[5]

The final decision, however, was to use *Tales of the Arabian Nights*[6] as a source and stimulus for storytelling theatre, focusing on the resources of the actors within the group. The performance space was defined by a large white floor area, supported by a canopy or tent-like structure of folds of white gauze, muslin and silk. The performers wore a variety of coloured silk harem pants and matching tops, which highlighted the significance of the actors in the minimalist white space. The performance started in blackout with a group 'soundscape' of the stories, which were then told through visual images, sounds, movement and mime. The techniques of Mike Alfreds[7] and his work with Shared Experience were explored by the ensemble in their uses of narrative, group dynamics, and discovery of how an actor's resources can create or structure a theatrical experience.

These areas, in turn, become questions to the group or company, which are frequently addressed throughout the working process. This also leads to identification and examination of the company's aims and objectives, their roles for the project, the starting point for the work, and how to proceed. Methods and means are often discovered through the content or audience decisions made at the beginning, and this is where flexibility is needed within the preliminary four areas of investigation. For instance, theatre-in-education is probably going to place more emphasis at the outset on questioning the needs of the audience than experimental theatre; content may be a starting point for community theatre whilst for another company it will evolve out of experimentation with the initial decision to look at a physical, visual structure or form. Inevitably, wherever one begins or whatever kind of theatre is to be created, a group has to address these fundamental questions when starting to work together.

ORIGINS

What then are the starting points or stimuli for a group devising theatre? The decision of where to begin is linked to answering the key questions that focus and distinguish the initial areas of emphasis or investigation. Mark Long considers the possibilities of beginning a show:

> Sometimes the starting point for a People Show is a set, a book, a picture; sometimes it's just a sentence or a line. It has once been a poster. It varies enormously. The initial parameter can be very small or fairly large, and from there as a group you start.

A devised musical score may form the basis and starting point for a show, as in the case of 'Burning Horizon – People Show No. 97' (1990), where every group member was given a fifty-minute recorded tape of music composed by George Khan. Identifying the kind of theatre to be created often suggests whether to look at content, form or audience first, or in combination.

Targeting the audience

Age Exchange is a company, founded in 1983 by artistic director Pam Schweitzer, which produces reminiscence theatre for the elderly in the south London community. The company provides a particular form of community theatre for a specific audience, which involves its members from start to finish. Schweitzer works to a clearly defined, tried and tested model of practice. From process to product, Schweitzer works from, with, and for the audience. The elderly are the starting point, source material, and content of a show. Schweitzer defines devising as 'looking for a thread through the reminiscence material we have collected.'[8] In 'On the River' (1989), the show was virtually constructed from verbatim statements made by pensioners from the Dockland area. The musical show resulted from a series of reminiscence sessions that recorded their memories of growing up by the river Thames in the 1920s and

1930s, and of their working lives as lightermen, dockers, and stevedores. The product evolved out of those particular experiences, and was performed by freelance actors especially chosen for the project. Having watched an evening's performance aboard a boat on the river Thames full of elderly people, there is no doubt that the experience was appreciated by all concerned. The enjoyment came from the recognition and realisation of those memories in a theatrical form.

The starting point for most shows usually involves taking suggestions for themes from the old-age pensioners, discussing the selected theme, listening to stories or memories of the client group, and recording them on audio-cassette tapes. After transcribing numerous hours of tape-recorded text, all the source materials are read through, and discussed by Schweitzer and the actors for a possible structure and outline scenario. Themes are chosen for their significance and bearing on today, and have included unemployment, race, health, migration, housing, and retirement. Schweitzer describes a strong link with the audience through the source material, 'a shared experience with the audience as the actors tell the tales to the pensioners . . . often the words are those given by old people in interviews during the research period.' Schweitzer comments that a theme has been explored through detailed reminiscence and personal experience rather than generalised statements.

Age Exchange's 'Christmas at War' (1989) resulted from the elderly community's suggestion of devising a show about the theme of evacuation. The source materials for the show came from individuals or groups of old people in south London, who were interviewed in-depth by actors and members of the company during an initial research period of work. These included the story of 'the wire bomb' that was phoned in as a response to a radio programme, and the text of an advertisement from a wartime issue of *Good Housekeeping* (1940) for a lipstick called 'Tangee' that changed according to the colour of the lips. Schweitzer recalls:

> All the pensioners remember it – 'Lips are the potent weapon in love's delicious armory'. We liked the warrior flavour of the thing for wartime Christmas; these things give a very good sense of the period and little details like that tend to place things for people.[9]

Songs, music and radio entertainment from the period were also used. Schweitzer received extensive written reminiscences from some pensioners, such as the memories of one evacuee from September 1939 to May 1945, which were incorporated into the final show. In effect, the audience of this community theatre company decided the content through its choice of selected theme, which in turn contributed source materials that defined the form and playing style of the piece.

Choice of audience is often the first decision to be made by any theatre-in-education company. It is crucial to decide who the piece is being devised for before any other decisions can be made. It is from this starting point that content and form constantly interrelate. Theatre-in-education must speak to its audience and challenge it, which means understanding the educational and cultural needs of young people in the context of today's society and world situation. Any group concerned with devising theatre-in-education must consider how people learn and look at the relationship between teachers, pupils and company. The starting points for Greenwich Young People's Theatre fourth-year secondary programme, 'The Edge of Reason', included decisions about form, content, and concepts.

It was decided to devise a day-long, fully participatory programme around the French Revolution of 1789 that explored the concepts of freedom and justice. The order of priority was determined by the original aims and objectives of the programme, the material, and the team. Content and form were explored within broad educational aims related to the perceived needs of fourth-year pupils (observed from a number of visits into local schools and discussions with teachers or students), condensing those aims into several questions.

The central question – 'What would you sacrifice for liberty?' – expressed a contradiction that opened out the company's thinking into the principal concepts the team aimed to cover in the programme. Experiencing concepts of loyalty and betrayal, choice and decisions, or freedom and change via drama and theatre enabled young people to discriminate and judge their own set of values. Key moments or images from the French Revolution that expressed the central question were investigated through research, improvisation, and the exploration of different theatre and participation forms, from which a story and scenario were created that had artistic or theatrical possibilities as well as educational challenges.

Stimuli

A story or a starting text may provide the basis of a primary decision about the content of a proposed devised product. It is often the content that initiates a project, and is the first consideration for a company. Annie Griffin believes that a concrete starting point is essential, whether it is a Tammy Wynette song, as in the case of her one-woman show 'Almost Persuaded', or the Strauss opera 'Ariadne Auf Naxos' in Gloria's devised show 'Ariadne' (1989–90). Griffin recalls, 'I was thinking about this image of somebody clinging to a rock, waiting for death, instead of just letting go.'[10] Her collaboration with Laura Ford, a sculptor/painter, and Nicholas Bloomfield, a musical composer/director, comes from a belief that devising with people who think differently to herself changes the process of working together. Griffin states: 'it's very much experimental theatre. The idea of experimenting and not knowing where you're going is very important to the work process.'

Listening to music, reading and researching the Greek myth of Ariadne were stimuli for the process of creating and engaging with a starting text, before writing a scenario which was also based on knowing the performers and discussing preliminary ideas about the eight characters with them. There were two structural decisions in the early stages of devising, which were to have two acts and professional musicians (two trumpeters and a pianist) playing throughout the piece. As director/deviser of 'Ariadne', a multi-layered performance piece described by one critic as 'a cunning jigsaw of images, words, music and movement'[11],Griffin believes that it is very important to have something that is rich and interesting to start with.

Initial meetings and discussion between Griffin, Ford, and Bloomfield led to an outline written scenario, the beginnings of a sculptured world to work in, costume designs, and ideas for musical composition, arrangements and score. The company included an opera singer, dancers, actors, and musicians who were chosen specifically for the project and had not worked together previously as one group. Griffin describes how the

Gloria company read the scenario, and then basically dropped the words, but kept the scene structure. As rehearsals began, Griffin, Ford and Bloomfield collaborated together, each involved in every stage of the rehearsal process. Griffin would set tasks; the performers would go away singly or in groups and invent presentations in response to those tasks using their choreographic, acting or musical skills. Styles of play were improvised with some performers experimenting or trying out ideas throughout the rehearsal period. The performers' involvement in the creation of their roles varied with each individual artist, but was inspired and focussed by Griffin's ideas of characterisation. Each actor needed a different kind of direction, and Griffin's working relationship with each of the eight performers was unique.

Multi-vision

A visual concept can be an important starting point for a devising company. Considerations of form frequently determine initial devising decisions, such as the intention to create or construct a visual space at the beginning of the process for the actors. In direct contrast to a group of people specifically chosen to work together for one project only, Forced Entertainment Theatre Co-operative is a company whose starting points for a new show arise out of the previous one. Tim Etchells, a writer and director with the Sheffield-based company, suggests that devising is about *not* starting from a single thing. As Forced Entertainment is a collective of seven members, Etchells likes the possibility of input from anywhere or anyone within the company.

Forced Entertainment Theatre Co-operative began in November 1984, and aims to produce work that is larger than any one single intention or idea. There are few cooperatives living and working together in Britain as fully as this particular company, choosing to start from a vague and intangible set of references and working towards a product over a long period of time. Company member Terry O'Connor describes their practice:

> We're involved in a process built up by tradition, where we start a show with a more or less blank sheet of paper

with perhaps elements from the show before. It's exciting to be working on ideas that are at the edge, or pushing a theatre form so that you believe you're creating new things, which you're not seeing other people doing.[12]

Forced Entertainment Theatre Co-operative has worked for over nine years with more or less a permanent company, developing an awareness of personal dynamics at work within the group, and certain ground rules in dealing with people. Etchells elaborates further: 'a long set of shared work experiences inevitably builds some kind of collective shorthand. We've developed a set of terms, of reference points, and theoretical frameworks that underpin and give precision to our struggles in making work.' During a period of touring an old show, problems or high points may lead to suggestions of narrative, images, text, music, or the set design of the next piece.

'Some Confusions in the Law about Love' (1989–90) partly developed out of decisions to extend particular areas of interest from the previous show, '200% & Bloody Thirsty' (1988–89), which included the use of text and video on stage, as well as the interaction of live performers with those on video. Ideas arise, fragmentary moments are taken from television, life or other people's work, provoking discussion between different combinations of company personnel. Informal conversations lead to formal meetings of the group that attempt to clarify these ideas and thoughts. An exploratory period of devising follows, which involves working in crude mock-ups of potential spaces, improvising and working from texts and transcripts. Often fragments of text are amongst the first inputs on a project, which are sometimes intended for use but frequently serve to help define a tone or set of tones which can be used in making action or set. Etchells describes a typical pattern as one or two days of practical work, followed by four or five days' discussion, analysis, writing and model building. From four to six weeks of this, comes the basic set design, text ground rules and a performance 'feel', which are important starting points for this company's work. As a performer in 'Some Confusions in the Law about Love', O'Connor observes that it is difficult to pinpoint exactly where the move for a particular feel for a show or idea really comes from.

1 Richard Lowdon and Cathy Naden in '200% & Bloody Thirsty'.
Forced Entertainment Theatre Co-operative, 1988–89.
(Photo: Hugo Glendinning.)

Form is an important initial consideration for Forced Entertainment, underlining the company's approach to structure as having to satisfy a basic meaning in addition to developing a clear, articulate structural architecture made up of many removed and complicated ideas. Form is also a central preoccupation for any company devising a site-specific piece of theatre. Implicit in the choice of a performance space is an immediate, clear starting point with the location itself. The nature of a site-specific performance demands that thought is given to a varying combination of form, content, and audience from the beginning.

Environment

The Jubilee swimming pool on the cliffs at Penzance in Cornwall was the stimulus for Lumiere & Son's site-specific residential devised theatre project 'Fifty Five Years of the Swallow and the Butterfly' (1990), which included community involvement with students from Falmouth College of Art, Dartington College in Devon, and various non-professional performers from the Penzance area. Hilary Westlake, artistic director of Lumiere & Son, describes the setting as an extraordinary location for the company. An enormous, difficult space that posed technical problems for sound and lighting, the Jubilee pool offered endless possibilities and ideas for experimental performance from a requiem for the pool to ideas of hydrophobia, ritualistic enactments of the movement of birds, and love poems to the sea set to music, with large-scale choreography being a major feature. Westlake researched the history of Penzance, swimming, and the Jubilee pool to discover points of interest such as the death of Edward Mersthem in 1934, when he dived from a cliff in order to escape an overwhelming fear of water (never to be seen again), or the origins of the pool's design in 1936, with its celebratory rituals of helping any hydrophobic overcome their fears. From this, and an 'atmosphere' in her head, Westlake constructed an outline scenario to be worked on further by her collaborative team of David Gale, Jeremy Peyton-Jones, and Simon Corder to create the structural components of text, music, lighting projections, and choreography.

The initial idea of 'fear of water' came from the location, and

Westlake envisaged the content of the text as fiction with a 'feel' of reality, asking Gale to supply dialogue and song lyrics to support the theme of the curing of people who have a morbid fear of water. Gale is praised by Westlake for his ability to tell a tale through images in his writing, and has contributed text to previous Lumiere & Son site-specific shows, including 'Deadwood' (1986), which was performed in Kew Gardens. Westlake wanted the music in 'Fifty Five Years of the Swallow and the Butterfly' to be associated with a chorus who moved and chanted throughout the piece, commenting on the progress of those suffering from hydrophobia. Westlake's unpublished notes of April 1990 state her intentions for lighting: 'The creation of strange images relating to the pool is also a possibility as indeed is the use of projected birds (projectors or gobos).' The concept of the show was initiated and developed by the director; Westlake's specifications shaped the text, music, and technical input, as well as determining the performance structure.

Westlake is aware of a need for contingency plans when devising site-specific work, and comments in the same notes of April 1990 that, 'When you're envisaging your next piece of work, you're envisaging it done perfectly'. However, her past approach of starting on day one with an idea has changed with numerous experiences of working with a wide range of participants with unknown qualities. Her 'overwhelming anxiety is the people', she told me in April 1990, prior to meeting the group of strangers in mid-May, when she would have a fifteen-day devising period with them before the first performance over the Bank Holiday weekend. When Westlake is working well, she enjoys the development of ideas with performers in rehearsal. Westlake wishes to see an idea enlarged by performer input, providing the people are charismatic or particularly interesting performers, but no planning can project this to be the case. The appeal of devising is fading for Westlake as it is too unpredictable and so much depends on the imaginations or abilities of non-professional participants. However, Westlake observes that the pleasure of devising site-specific theatre comes from 'seeing it work in location'.[13]

For any group devising theatre from scratch, it is most important to identify how and where to begin the process of working together. This may be apparent right from the start,

2 Joanna Neary, Paul Finlay, Cindy Oswin, and Trevor Stuart in 'Fifty Five Years of the Swallow and the Butterfly'. Lumiere & Son, 1990. (Photo: Hilary Westlake.)

and indeed be the very reason why a group has congregated around a particular issue, interest, or kind of theatre. Even experienced professional companies may need to re-address their function and purpose in devising theatre at regular intervals. As a general theory, I want to conclude this chapter by highlighting the questions that can be asked by any group or company starting work together:

1 What is it you want to devise, and why? What kind of theatre do you want to create?
2 Who are you devising for, and why?
3 What are your initial aims and objectives as a company for this project?
4 Is your content or subject matter the starting point for the work? What are the source materials?
5 Is the form or structure an important preliminary area for exploration?

3

PROCESS
Ways and means of making theatre

If you have something you wish to say, it is not so difficult
to find out how to say it.
(Hilary Westlake, Artistic Director of Lumiere & Son)

The most fundamental requirement for devising theatre is a
passion or desire to say something, a need to question or make
sense of a starting point that encourages you to investigate
further through a variety of processes and close enquiry. It is
essential to identify the potential tools of devising that can be
used to search, shape and structure the investigative route to
be taken. It is also necessary to make early decisions with
regard to how the group will operate throughout the devising
process. This involves choices about how working structures
relate to recognised roles or responsibilities of individuals
within a company, as well as selecting the most appropriate
approach to the work or employing processes that seem
relevant to the particular situation.

Implicit in the organisation of every devising company's
operation, whether an artistically democratic collective or a
hierarchical structure of skill-sharing and specialisation, is a
unique set of working relationships between individual
specialist members that are different to the production hierarchy often associated with the literary theatre tradition. How
then are the conventional roles of director, writer, and designer
used in an alternative way by companies devising theatre?
What are the ways and means of making a theatrical performance out of a non-uniform arrangement of variable contributing areas of expertise? Which processes are most commonly
adopted as part of a devising methodology?

42

THE DIRECTOR/DEVISER
I want to address these questions by looking at how different companies define the particular roles that give rise to specific processes of devising and working practice. How does leadership determine the process of creating a performance? This depends on whether a group functions hierarchically or democratically; whether there is a director or not. I wish to describe two examples from the area of experimental theatre to illustrate differing roles of leadership in the devising process. The People Show is a group of visual artists who work without a director. Founder member Mark Long states the belief that 'At some point in the creative, collaborative process, you do arrive at a group certainty. That is not to say that you are all necessarily driving towards exactly the same objective, but there is a line of agreement.'[1]

The People Show has always had a strong underlying philosophy of everyone having a definite visual comprehension of costume and set construction, as well as an understanding of building and lighting. The work has always been very technical, involving use of props and effects. This is vital to the company's sense of a strong, creative, collaborative process, and important to every artist's understanding of how to devise a People Show. Long comments: 'Otherwise, you're denying yourself certain colours or certain paints. It's important for people to comment on other people's areas of work in terms of light, sound, or acting.'[2]

The devising company for 'Burning Horizon – People Show No. 97' (1990) included a designer, a painter/photographer, a sculptor, a visual artist who sculpts, two musicians, and Long, who describes himself as a Jack-of-all-trades. This show involved everyone in the group being responsible for something in the set, and included nearly all group members in physically building it. Long has described the show as very symbolic, a juxtaposition of images rather like a Magritte painting.

At the start of the 1980s, Long described a general pattern of working for The People Show thus:

we talk for a week and discuss a hundred things and just maybe one of them will happen. When you look at a People Show, you'll see half a percent of everything that was talked about – most of the time is spent in getting rid of things.[3]

Without a director, the process of communication and criticism becomes vital with the making of the work. Long believes that the artists themselves are the best critics, and that an inability to criticise each other is an unhealthy option. Artistic decisions are made out of a constant re-assessment by company members of the work, and a ruthless determination to preserve both individual interests and the development of the product.

Similarly, Forced Entertainment are keen to continually evaluate and debate the development of ongoing process and product. In contrast to The People Show, Forced Entertainment's practice is to have two directors, sharing responsibility for rehearsals, performance quality, steering meetings, and the eventual form of the show. Having worked together over a long period of time, company members have developed a full awareness of their strengths or weaknesses, and how they can contribute to each other. People know what each other's positions will be, as Tim Etchells observes:

> If you're pleased with an idea you'll take it to Robin [Arthur], because he'll generally pull it apart, which is good. You make sure you don't see Robin until you want that to happen to your idea. You make sure you do see him when it's vital that it happens.[4]

Terry O'Connor believes that the role of director is also about helping the performers keep in touch with what they were originally doing: 'Helping them find a new definition of the show they're touring, so the show retains an integrity and freshness.' This company does not assume collective responsibility for everything, and perhaps a weakness in company development has been to play to the strengths people have built up, which narrows opportunities for learning new skills. Roles are essentially defined for the company, but can vary according to the project.

Both these companies have a clear, established working practice in relation to how either no leadership or two directors can determine the devising process. This is often not the case when a freelance director/deviser is employed by a theatre-in-education company for a specific project. Coventry's Belgrade

Theatre-in-Education Company is a department of the Belgrade Theatre, but operates a policy of internal democratic management structure where every company member is expected to contribute fully to discussion and decision-making. Brian Bishop is a permanent member holding the position of head of department, and is responsible to the artistic director of the Belgrade and the Theatre Trust for all aspects of the company's work, which is planned collectively by all long-term members at weekly company meetings. Everything is regarded as everyone's responsibility, so that each company member is committed to and caring about all areas of work. The company provides a free service to all Coventry state schools, and creates 'original work designed to enable young people to question and change the world in which they live'.[5] Devising is defined by the company as a collective way of arriving at a finished product through discussion, improvisation, and writing.

Outside the company

In early 1990 the two sub-companies were both devising programmes with freelance director/devisers. The sub-company who devised the special schools programme 'Monkey' for primary-aged children of varied severe learning difficulties felt that they were all coming from different directions, and yet to a certain extent presumed they were all coming from the same. The sub-company included several freelance members with a range of theatre-in-education experiences, which meant finding a way of working together as a new group of both freelance and permanent members. Everyone involved with this programme acknowledged the difficulties of the devising period. Freelance actor Sarah Westaway points out:

> What's interesting about the problems we encountered during the devising process was that we started by looking at it as something different. That's when we started blocking ourselves. Also, we decided early on that we wanted to move away from celebratory or environmentally based stuff, and that we wanted to develop a different approach to special schools' work without really knowing what that meant in itself.[6]

It is evident from this example that constant clarification of original aims and objectives are vital in the early stages of any new group's work. They provide the basis for the process to unfold, grow, and change. Permanent company member Steve Nolan illustrates this point further:

> I think it has been a process of cutting back on what we've had, a developing and cutting process really, trying to get to the essence of things. This is my fifth consecutive freshly devised piece of theatre and no two have ever been the same; the process of devising has never been the same twice.

Westaway describes the role of the director in the project as a way of developing theories of process from experience within a context of understanding art, how the world functions, and how people learn. The devising process of 'Monkey' presented many problems for the company, which were increased when the director took sick leave and the group had to take on the role of director/deviser together. Thus, all company members had to look more closely at what they were doing. People felt freer to contribute ideas and take a more active part, which suggests an important need to clearly define what is required from both freelance director/deviser and each individual member of the group.

All sorts of expectations are tied up with the process of devising and should be clarified at the start. A company may employ a freelance director for a variety of reasons. One reason might be that a company is having problems with devising as a result of clashes between new and established group members, which confuses or muddles the company's perception of where it is heading. The director is brought in to help give the process a direction. Gail McIntyre, formerly a director of Leeds Theatre-in-Education Company, is now a freelance director. McIntyre has worked with several theatre-in-education companies in this capacity, and emphasises that the role is more than just the creator of a product. McIntyre stresses that as an outside director, 'you're not integral to the company development in its total sense'.[7]

Alternatively, a freelance director/deviser may be needed to initiate and lead a group through a devising process, which was part of McIntyre's brief when working with Red Ladder on a youth clubs piece in 1988. Another reason is simply that a company requires a different input or set of skills at a particular time; as McIntyre observes, 'they wish to draw on another skill that isn't present'. McIntyre believes that it is crucial for any freelance person to know the expectations of the company, and to be clear about everyone's roles within a project. McIntyre comments further that most companies expect a freelance director/deviser to lead and initiate the process: 'you have to keep checking the ground and negotiate. Have you done what they wanted and expected? Perhaps challenge it.' The excitement of freelance directing/devising for McIntyre is having control of the work, feeling inspired by the process, creating the product, being committed to the material, and working in an exploratory way with either form or content.

Clarification

Any group of people coming together with a wide variety of backgrounds and experiences needs to develop a new approach to a devised project in theatre-in-education. Aims and objectives must be identified in terms of children's needs, the company's needs, a learning area for the piece, and initial decisions related to form, content and methodology. If this is not established from the outset, difficulties may occur in terms of direction and knowing where to go next in the devising process. It is vital for any director to understand their role and functions within the particular set of devising circumstances, whether it is a collective process or not.

A theatre-in-education company with both a hierarchical structure and team approach to the devising process demands clearly defined roles and relationship between company director and theatre-in-education team leader. This is exemplified in the case of Greenwich Young People's Theatre, whose policy is to provide a professional theatre-in-education service for local schools, as well as offering 'a comprehensive programme of theatre/arts activities for young people in their own time'.[8] The director of the company, Chris Vine, describes the devising process as essentially eclectic with numerous possible starting points. Viv Harris is the theatre-in-education team leader, who leads a sub-company on a particular project and directs the final product. Harris recounts an example of a typical devising process within the company:

we would discuss, test out on the floor the educational
aims and holding form that we've chosen to explore those
aims with. People will then come up with ideas which you
test out on the floor. This can be done by breaking up into
groups of twos or threes, going off and coming back with
ideas that you share with the rest. It may be focused by
the director or the writer, having done some particular
research beforehand, but would still be very much there
for the company to take on, developing their ideas and
coming up with different proposals.[9]

Collaboration

Devising theatre is often a difficult, problem-solving process,
and creating a participatory theatre-in-education programme is
no exception. The team leader may liaise with the director
when devising the participatory section of the programme. Part
of the team leader's role is to focus ideas or research for the
team to take on, and develop and come up with different
proposals. In the case of 'The Edge of Reason' (1989–90), the
programme was devised with a group who knew where they
were heading through the clear leadership of both team leader
and director.

Vine led a series of sessions on participation with the team
related to key questions about the meaning of freedom. Harris
explains: 'Chris proposed a direct, interactive way of involving
the young people in the key concept of freedom and we agreed
on the two questions to be put at the beginning of the day as a
focus for the programme.' For Harris, however, this was a
frustrating process as lack of time prevented her involvement
with the participation because of more pressing production
problems, such as technical decisions or lighting design.

Harris observes that one of the most difficult aspects in
devising the whole programme was the link between play and
participation. The team set out to maintain a developing
relationship between play and participation throughout the
devising process, but as Harris states, 'the impact of the play,
the input it was to make became a priority and the participation
was set to one side until the programme was very close to
opening'. For both team leader and director, the problem arises
of how to integrate and develop both aspects of play and

participation within a limited time frame, whilst utilising the relationship and expertise of both directorial roles within the devising process of a theatre-in-education programme.

THE WRITER/DEVISER

In the same way that leadership or the role of a director varies in every devising company, so the role of a writer is significantly different from the conventional initiator and author of a script. The writer's role is often specifically located within a company's practice, and has a particular relationship to the devising process. The ongoing debate of authorship between writer and devisers often draws a fine line between writer's theatre and a devised product. If a freelance writer is employed specifically to research a subject in collaboration with the company to write a play, then clearly this is a different task to that of the playwright who works alone to fulfil a commission or charge to write a play on a determined subject. The former activity is dependent on others' ideas and research, the latter is a single activity requiring no interaction with people whatsoever.

One of the major areas of debate in the Theatre Writers Union is the writer's relationship to devising, which is discussed in the article 'Devising as writing', where Julie Wilkinson states:

Many companies generate their work simply by devising, but people (in the union) are very wary of it as a way of working. The union gets a lot of complaints about devising companies claiming to have done what they've done, and arguing about who the work belongs to – who has actually done the work. We get a lot of enquiries about how writers should approach companies who devise.[10]

With regard to issues of authorship or script control, the Theatre Writers Union supports the belief that whoever scripts the material within the group is the author, regardless of whether the play has been group devised or not. Problems of script control were experienced by Kathleen McCreery, a member of the mid-1970s Red Ladder Theatre Company who devised *Strike While the Iron is Hot*, which was published in 1980 as part of a collection of plays on 'Sexual politics in the theatre'. In the article 'The (Woman) Writer and T.I.E. Part II', McCreery comments, 'Four of us in the company actually wrote the play, yet I didn't even know that the play was being published. . . . I was not asked for permission, not paid. And then we had to **buy** our own play in print.'[11]

Some playwrights, however, are keen to use the devising process with a company as it provides the opportunity to collaborate with a group, sharing ideas and creative space. The 1970s saw many companies, notably in theatre-in-education, acknowledging the playwright but also describing the piece as being 'devised by the company'. Gay Sweatshop clearly outlined the relationship of writer to devising process when they invited Michelene Wandor to script their material of scenario, story and characters. Kate Crutchley and Nancy Diuguid describe Wandor's role of 'writing original material where necessary, editing and tightening and reorganising material we already had' in an introduction to the script of 'Care and Control' contained in the volume *Strike While the Iron is Hot*.[12] This was discussed with the company who had researched and improvised the material beforehand. The programme for the show included the individual acknowledgements of researcher, devisers and writer.

Caryl Churchill is also clear in her role as writer for Joint Stock in the introduction to 'Light Shining in Buckhamingshire':

> The play is not improvised: it is a written text and the actors did not make up its lines. But many of the characters and scenes were based on ideas that came from improvisation at the workshop and during rehearsal. I could give endless examples of how something said or done by one of the actors is directly connected to something in the text.[13]

This description of Churchill's role as writer in relation to the company represents a direct contrast to collective writing, where a group combines all their ideas and views, which often results in 'get-it-all-in-ism'. Steve Gooch describes this process as leading to 'some incredible rambling, shapeless shows, but from time to time the very rawness of the experience described, or the very originality of subject-matter and treatment, made the consequent productions real eye-openers'.[14]

Groups that write collectively have often been accused of producing poorly crafted plays that suffer from a lack of cohesive style and clear single vision. The difficulties of translating the whole experience of the group into a final script are expressed in Libby Mason's afterword to 'Double Vision', a piece she devised with the Women's Theatre Group. Mason states: 'There are virtually no stage directions in the script because the way the words were spoken and the physical pictures they created had already been invented and were familiar to all of us.'[15] A group devising and writing collectively needs to allow substantial time for this process, which I suspect is harder and longer than for the playwright employed by a company to come in and write a play from and with the group.

Role

It is vital that a group is clear about the writer's function and the extent to which, if any, performers may be involved in the writing process. This was the case in 'Ariadne' (1989–90). Annie Griffin comments that the best writing is often done in rehearsals, 'when someone takes an hour or so with pen and paper, and puts something together.'[16] A group must identify what it wants from a freelance writer before collaboration begins, agreeing the responsibilities and crediting specialised skills as needed. The writer's relationship with the group is crucial to an understanding of what the process aims to produce.

The role of a writer-in-residence varies with every company, but often involves them working together, going away for a period of time, and constantly negotiating the work as it develops. John Wood was writer-in-residence with Greenwich Young People's Theatre from 1985 to 1990, and wrote the play that was part of the theatre-in-education participatory programme, 'The Edge of Reason'. Wood worked in close collaboration with the team leader and company members, exploring many ideas around the material. He then came up with a scenario in consultation with others, where the material dictated a need for a three-act play. The company then split up into a number of groups for act one, discussed and improvised the material until there was an agreed shared understanding of how to get to act two, whilst, Wood comments, 'knowing all the time that we had an aiming point in act three that I had already devised anyway'. The group looked at what it thought should be the pivotal scenes of the first two acts, as well as exploring what the heart of each act should be, which then became the main part of Wood's brief, to weave the action around these scenes and to develop the main substance of act three. These scenes were directly related to the key learning areas of the programme, but as Harris observes, what was finally needed was 'one person's brain to riddle all those things through '. It was acknowledged that the play could not be written by committee, and that the writer's role was to produce a script out of the collaboration with others.

Wood needed to involve himself in the politics of the period, which inevitably threw up problems of how to resolve research with the characters that were being improvised 'on the floor'. It became a healthy clash between politics, people, the writer's personal stand, and the actor-teachers' creation of characters. This all contributed to pushing Wood to look again at whether he had characterised them correctly. It also raised the question of whether the writer was 'tightening the screw down too much, keeping them too much on my track?' The re-work and re-write process of 'The Edge of Reason' considered what needed clarification, including the participation work, and provided a clearer indication of character for both actor and audience. Changes were made in the light of discussion with the whole team on two re-work days following the first few performances of the programme. There was no substantial re-writing in terms of specifics, although there were changes in the number and nature of lines. Harris observes:

> That's an inevitable spin-off of the devising process, where you don't have the opportunity to re-draft before feedback. The first draft is your working draft until you have an opportunity to work it on the floor and usually to an audience.

WRITING A TEXT

A re-work or re-write process is also used by Forced Entertainment, and usually lasts about ten days. This allows group members to address problems arising out of the first performances, which means that chunks are re-written, changed, thrown out, or re-ordered. For this company, the idea of devising is linked to the notion of a permanent ensemble, which means mutual support and responsible criticism. It is important to create an environment where risks can be taken. Tim Etchells describes the devising process as work that has an in-built plurality and spaciousness, a breadth of ideas and inputs. Text ideas are explored through practical work, discussion, criticism and revision. Writing is sometimes based on improvisations, but more normally on ideas and discussions with the rest of the group. Etchells comments that the text is 'torn apart, re-written in the same way that action sections or set ideas are set up and then constantly revised'. As the writer, Etchells feels that he gets more time to work alone than anyone else in the company. The company structure tries to ensure that the writer gets the vital space, support and criticism in appropriate doses, just like everyone else. It is not uncommon for Etchells to turn up at rehearsals with a text that no one was expecting, 'or equally frequent', he adds, 'are the days I turn up with bland re-workings of yesterday's ideas, or nothing at all.'

Inside the company, the role of writer is one of writer of text within the devising process, rather than writer of a show. The company talks about shows, and creates between its members ideas for places where text might go or what it might be about, and then the writer fulfils his brief. The role has only changed with the more frequent use of text, shifting from taped text to video-text to live text, which has created a parallel shift in the kinds of things that are written. The last shows have been 'very open texts', which allow the audience to find their own way through a piece. There is no authorial message, but a certain freedom for the audience. An open reading of the work is encouraged, although the writer acknowledges the tendency for others to construct narratives out of shows. '200% & Bloody Thirsty' (1988–89) was described by critics in a number of ways, from being a show about new neighbours who went to a party and were desperate for accommodation (missing the fact that they were Mary, Joseph, and the Innkeeper), to being a seething attack on inner-city deprivation. Etchells believes that this says more about what people want to see experimental performance work about. For Etchells, trying to define the show often monopolises its meanings, although he accepts that people are entitled to do this, since it is an open piece. He is most interested in responses that talk about the ambiguity of moments, or the diversity of meanings, which are the nearest reactions to how the company sees the work.

The role of writer as contributor of text to the devising process, and as a participating member of the company making a performance,is common in experimental theatre practice. The change in status and significance of certain conventional roles linked to play production has created a new set of working relationships within many devising companies. I want to consider a particular collocation of roles and relationships in one company, which has produced a devising methodology and working practice for Lumiere & Son. I want to look at the roles of writer, technical director, and musical composer in relation to the director. Lumiere & Son's structure and methods of working are clearly identified through Hilary Westlake's role as initiator, creator, and director of the devised product. Westlake's understanding of the term 'devised theatre' applies to any show that is being prepared in ways other than the pre-written script. Westlake argues that devising implies a high degree of democracy in all areas of the work, so that all members of a group could potentially have equal input into the work. However, she no longer uses the term 'devising', which originally meant a process of working where she created a show in rehearsal with the performers, but now prefers the term 'creating' to describe her method of working with the company. Westlake suggests 'creating' implies, 'a single vision but with the creative imagination of others being given the opportunity of being involved'.[17]

One methodology

Westlake's role of artistic director of Lumiere & Son has developed and changed over the years. Since David Gale left the company in 1983, Lumiere & Son's shows have changed considerably in their style and structure, with a greater emphasis on music and projections. Westlake conceives a complete treatment of a show, before commissioning her collaborators to create contributions of written text, photographic projections, or musical score. Specific briefs are sent to the writer, musical composer, technical director or designer, who work independently of each other and in direct communication with the director. Westlake has a symbiotic relationship with the artists, resulting in a collaborative working process in which she is the final arbiter. Decisions are often influenced by those working closely with her, and may be based on individuals' specific areas of interest. Lumiere & Son's particular style and methodology have developed out of many years of experience, and are now distinguished by the lack of democracy in the creative process. The prospect of any company member being able to discuss every aspect of the process does not appeal to Westlake, although she acknowledges discussion as a vital ingredient in the devising process. Westlake believes that art is not necessarily best served by such democracy.

Composition

Gale was a full-time member of Lumiere & Son from 1973 to 1983, nominating themes for shows and realising them in the form of full scripts in his role as writer with the company. His writing was based on and derived from only themes that totally absorbed him. Gale's relationship with Westlake was as a writer devising a script in collaboration with a director devising the best means of realising it, rather than, as Gale comments, 'a rehearsal process that depends largely and centrally upon the mounting of speculative exercises with fully contributing actors'. This meant that the script determined rehearsals rather than being a process of discovery by performers through group improvisation and research. However, this method of working was certainly used in the early years of the company, characterised in shows that used physical mannerism and choreographic work that Gale describes as 'often prefaced by exercises in which the performers search for gestures which Hilary will later refine and recombine'.

Since 1983, Gale has become a freelance writer and continues to be commissioned by Westlake to furnish texts for projects devised and shaped by the director. Although these shows have been well received, Gale has not found the process particularly fulfilling. Gale describes it as 'curiously frustrating when the brief comes from a source so close to my history and development as a theatre scriptwriter'. He believes it is easier to write film or television scripts about subjects of passing interest than to write an external brief for Lumiere & Son. Gale observes that he has to be totally absorbed by research and preparation before he can write, expecting to spend 'about four times longer in preparation than in the process of actually writing what would eventually become the script'. He is aware of the contradiction of leaving Lumiere & Son in order to relinquish responsibility for the production of themes while complaining 'of the frustrations attached to supplying texts that have not been fully prepared, when I made a decision precisely to forsake the pleasures associated with devising my own texts'.

Gale's writing brief for 'Fifty Five Years of the Swallow and the Butterfly' in 1990 produced the notion of a 'commère' who introduced, counselled, and cured a variety of exotic hydrophobics. These sufferers were initiated into Penzance's Jubilee pool water gradually, climaxing in the total immersion of the last hydrophobic. Gale's dissatisfaction with this site-specific piece came from a variety of reasons. He acknowledges that site-specific work often creates difficulties of working with amateurs or local people, and believes that this particular show was severely compromised by a high drop-out rate amongst local people who had been willing to participate at the start of the project. Gale comments: 'The spectacle of amateur performers murdering my carefully crafted lines was not pleasant. I don't blame the amateurs – they are amateur.' Equally, the small budget for the show and limited resources handicapped the full expression of ideas related to the location itself.

The 1990s have seen the use of freelance directors or writers as useful to groups devising theatre in a range of chosen, clearly defined roles. However, the writer must be aware that a group devising process often involves the person functioning as someone who transcribes, interprets and assembles the ideas of a group. For writers like Gale, collective authorship, which is implicit as an objective of the devising process, means that 'the role of the writer is thereby diminished'. The writer's personal imaginative development is devalued and Gale argues that the process of devising is 'properly potentiated' without a writer, as group members may be skilled in editing and assembling material that 'will bring something of a textual aesthetic to the product'. Gale points out that the process may benefit from this

3 Naoko Kawase, Joanna Neary, Chris Newland, Trevor Stuart, and Cindy Oswin in 'Fifty Five Years of the Swallow and the Butterfly'. Lumiere & Son, 1990. (Photo: Simon Corder.)

but the product may suffer, which he sees reflected in the disappointing quality of some devised work. He feels that the world has changed so significantly since 1983 that he must re-think and re-evaluate his work as a writer related to 'performance theatre', without losing the unique experience of Lumiere & Son's work, which is both textual and visual theatre.

IMAGERY

Hilary Westlake's process of creating visual choreographic images for 'Fifty Five Years of the Swallow and the Butterfly' was to start with a physical warm-up incorporating exercises around bathing, diving, bird-like movements, or rippling actions that might go into the show. Some of the participants had done little movement work, so she concentrated on doing less, and polishing simple sequences of moves in conjunction with chants and musical backing. This process has been established through her wide experience of devising visual images for theatre; she often teaches a rhythm to performers so that they can move off or on the beat, which is followed by imaginative improvised movement (in the example above, swimming or bird dances), allowing ideas to be experimented with and tried out. In this way, Westlake goes into a rehearsal with ideas of movement that can be developed and shaped by the resident group or company of professionals.

The creation of technical images is a strong interest of Simon Corder, the technical director of Lumiere & Son. Corder is keen to create theatre with lighting or sound, exploring the design, shape and functions of a space or environment. His work is best illustrated by the photographic projections and lighting used in 'Panic' (1987) and 'Paradise' (1988–89). Site-specific projects appeal to him greatly, although there are real difficulties when working with low budgets and not enough technical equipment – 'we're always overstretched'. Corder enjoys the excitement of expressing and developing technical ideas, feelings or atmos-pheres from the site through sound and lighting. However, he argues that to be true environmental artists, time and money is needed to produce large-scale work. Previous experience of site-specific projects such as 'Deadwood' (1986) in Kew Gardens or 'Wardance' (1989) at Nottingham Castle has pre-pared him for the possible catastrophes of bad weather, rusting equipment, scheduling problems, or actors not turning up on site for rehearsals. This conflict of interests is reflected in the group dynamics and inter-disciplinary relationships of Lumiere & Son, which in turn makes for interesting devised theatre.

Vocal music

As with the relationship between technical director and director, so the role of musical composer also finds a place alongside Westlake. Jeremy Peyton-Jones has been commissioned to compose music for Lumiere & Son on numerous occasions. In the case of site-specific work or touring shows, there are practical questions to be asked, such as whether the music is for live musicians or recorded tape, the approximate structure of the show, the sort of material being used, whether a pulse is needed for choreography, or if music is to be used underneath speech. Peyton-Jones has experienced difficulties with site-specific work in terms of the reliability of local people; for instance, in 'Deadwood' he wanted a live choir, but because of changing numbers at every rehearsal he ended up taping twelve people for the choir. It is this experience that makes him want to use professional musicians or only to ask something simple of local participants.

Similiarly, with 'Fifty Five Years of the Swallow and the Butterfly', Peyton-Jones wanted a choir or brass band whose sound wavered on or off until he decided to make a tape with one singer only. His brief as composer was to provide music for choreography and songs to punctuate the show, but he would have liked more time to allow the music to have more structure. He was also concerned about the relationship of music and text, with the practical problems involved in hearing words above music. He sent Westlake tapes to work with, but missed the opportunity to work with her developing music and choreography together. In terms of site-specific work, he sees the main problems as not having enough time to work with people, to develop their ideas, and to use the location to its full potential.

Peyton-Jones favours a more collaborative process, such as previous working experiences with Impact Theatre, where there was a thrashing out of ideas within the company rather than a single idea that was pursued practically without group discussion of composer, writer or technical contributor during the devising process. As musical composer for many of Lumiere & Son's shows, he is requested by Westlake to use his skills to write music from ideas rather than from seeing the text: 'we speak the same language, I know what she means.' This will finally be drawn together by the director and is symptomatic of Westlake's approach to the devising process. However, in 'Panic' (1987) and 'Paradise' (1988–89), Peyton-Jones had a much clearer idea of an overall musical structure that made its own sense, which he wanted to incorporate into these shows. He likes the combination of music, image and text in live performance, and enjoys composing for the voice. His preference is for a physical, visual theatre with a strong musical score throughout.

Lumiere & Son's methodology and 'creating' (devising) practice can be compared to 'directors' theatre', where the director is ultimately in charge of the overall production. In this example, the basic difference between these two forms of theatre is in the opportunity provided by the devising process for the writer, technical director, or musical composer to make important contributions from the start that move the work in new directions away from the director's original intentions.

THE DESIGNER/DEVISER

Processes that explore visual structures, whether through building the set together or through defining and making a performance space, provide alternative approaches to writing text when devising theatre. Design and technical input are often determined by the kind of theatre being created and the extent of emphasis on the creation of visual images, constructed through the use of set, props, costumes or sculpture, as well as through choreographic movement or dance. The place of design in devised work varies enormously, from the more traditional role of designer as the visual interpreter of a director or writer's idea at the start, to the designer contributing a significant input from the beginning to a devising process that explores and develops visual ideas, used particularly by performance artists in their work.

Annie Griffin's collaboration with Laura Ford, sculptor and

painter, has been significant in using the visual arts to express and articulate her experience. Griffin comments: 'I didn't work with Laura because I was looking for a painter to make sets. I found that I could talk about work with her and was very stimulated by her ideas, by the way she saw and understood.' Their first collaboration, 'The Deadly Grove', was in 1988, which Griffin acknowledges as a very confusing work process, with little sense of what they wanted the show to be. Creating a visual, physical world from the start was important in 'Ariadne' (1989–90), allowing the performers to explore ideas of moving amongst the sculpted, geometric green wooden waves, and experiment with the possibilities of a large rock covered in seaweed. Two of the performers used their dance experience to invent choreographic images that were visually stimulating and pleasing. In Jim Hiley's article 'Nexus of Ariadne', performer Liz Ranken observes, 'I can push my talent where I like, instead of pushing my body through someone else's steps.'[18] The startling costumes – of Zerbinetta, in green sequin top with rubber ring, trumpeters in gold bolero jackets, black leggings, and gold cod-pieces, and Dog's vibrant red and green costume with long tail – all contributed towards devising a piece that evolved through the experimentation of visual ideas, images, and structures.

Frustrations

Being a freelance set designer with an eight-week contract, employed to work as a member of Belgrade Theatre-in-Education's sub-company devising a programme for special schools ('Monkey'), raised particular difficulties for Jackie Trousedale. Time was the biggest problem in terms of finding and making costumes or props at the last moment. Trousedale recounts, 'It's very difficult when you're devising to actually say we're definitely going to use that, in order to get things prepared.' The design came out of the devising period and Trousedale's role was to assess what was necessary for the programme, providing a strong visual link of jungle environment to the centrally devised image of an ape chained to a post. From the group's point of view, they wanted to leave design decisions and options as late as possible, which was problematic for the designer, who wished to construct the set properly.

4 Franck E. Loiret and Liz Ranken in 'Ariadne'. Gloria Production Company, 1989–90. (Photo: Stephen Sweet.)

A position of compromise was reached, actor-teacher Sarah Westaway comments, 'making do and botching up because demands are on them to come up with the goods and there's no time'. Trousedale believes that the visual side often suffers when devising a theatre-in-education programme, and that there should be a deadline for devising, so that proper preparation can be given to the creation of visual structures.

The set that was finally used included a background of several flats painted brightly with a jungle scene behind a defined performance area of circular green carpet. A cream wooden triangle was positioned in the centre to which the ape, played by permanent company member Lindsay Johnson, was tethered. One of the most exciting things about the set was that small boxes in the flats could be opened by the pupils. The aim was to encourage a sensory experience for the pupils when they felt and discovered a range of jungle-related objects in the boxes. This activity was a source of fascination to the special school pupils, who needed to relate directly to visual images throughout the programme. But this idea was never fully developed, and was perhaps partly a result of not working practically with the concept in the early stages of the devising process.

The set and costume designer for Greenwich Young People's Theatre programme 'The Edge of Reason', Sarah-Jane Ash, worked alongside other team members (including actor-teachers, writer, director, educational liaison officer, and musical director) in the early stages of discussion and exploration of material. The team leader, Viv Harris, states, 'but as the process developed all team members worked more specifically according to their role.' Ash initiated visual workshops with the team, some full-day or shorter sessions, which enabled a two-way process of the designer discovering the actor-teachers' growing perceptions of their characters. Harris describes the designer's role in the process, 'which she [Ash] then took into both costume and set design, *and* enabled the actor-teachers to experiment in a visual medium with the potential of their characters and situation'. The set and ideas for costume developed out of a period of experimenting and working on different levels during the devising and rehearsal process, in consultation with individual members of the company as well as team discussions on these particular areas.

5 Stuart McCartney in 'Monkey'. Belgrade Theatre-in-Education
Company, 1990. (Photo: Jackie Trousedale.)

THE PERFORMER/DEVISER

Whatever the specialist nature of an individual's role within a devising group, there has to be an overall flexibility, versatility, and integration between the often multi-talented members and their relationships or responsibilities within a company. The role of the performer/deviser usually requires involvement in several processes, which often include improvisation, research, and discussion. I want to suggest that these processes are commonly adopted as part of a company's devising methodology. Clearly, the working structure of the company, whether hierarchical or democratic, sets boundaries for the extent to which roles or responsibilities can integrate or overlap to the degree of allowing a performer to contribute fully to the devising process as well as to the product.

This is the case for performers devising shows with Trestle Theatre, where the work is generated by everybody. As a theatre cooperative, all company members are involved in policy decisions. Having worked together for three years at Middlesex Polytechnic, Trestle Theatre set out to popularise mask, mime, and visual theatre, creating its own unique style of mask theatre, for which it is renowned. The company determines decisions about the developing shape of the product, which are further defined as the work progresses by particular members with specific responsibilities for performing, dramaturgy, visual realisation of ideas, or direction.

John Wright, artistic director, compares the devising process to a planned improvisation. Wright believes that devising is a very charged and satisfying way of working, and stresses the importance of a spontaneous, imaginative process that enables individuals to constantly suggest ideas for exploration. For Wright, devising a show is about having an idea, image, or series of questions that follows a logic through to the creation of a product. The skills of physical theatre depend on the visual, and Wright believes that the work of mime artists such as Jacques Lecoq or Philippe Gaulier has a great deal in common with devised theatre. Wright describes the company's devised productions as theatre that works physically, visually, and that uses language.

Trestle Theatre works with masks using a style that recognises personas, which gives the performers plenty of freedom.

In the early shows, three or four performers played between fifteen and twenty parts. In 'Plastered' (1985), the group decided on two locations, a pub and a hospital, devising what happened in the pub that ended in the hospital. The performers needed to devise characters, so they built a pub set and made a collection of masks. The masks were then 'liberated', and out of 'auditioning' the various bunches of characters, a cast was assembled. The group tried out various improvisations with the masks from which a thread of action was established. Then with painstaking choreography, the group attempted to clarify the story, so that the audience could seize on the action immediately.

With 'Top Storey' (1990), Trestle Theatre needed to develop the style of the work, so started thinking about this whilst touring another show. They returned from the tour with a set of rough starting points, which were to be explored through an event. They hired the Shaw Theatre in London, and twelve actors, for a month, with the intention of getting away from the idea of frivolous comedies. Wright ran workshops that resulted in four group members each devising a piece that they wanted to do. There was a 'whodunnit', a piece of social realism with detailed observations, a romp about yuppies, and a tragedy about infanticide. One member of the group, Sally Cook, wrote down everything from the workshops, taking on the role of dramaturge and writing a structured scenario from the montage scenes. The idea of an attic provided a good starting point and setting for the show. The company then devised from a linear, narrative structure through montage and imagistic work.

The devising process changes with every show to meet the mood or new personnel of the company. Wright suggests that devising depends on relationships and chemistry between people, which means that the feeling of the group must be maintained, particularly when a show's title and publicity have been decided prior to the company knowing what the piece will be about. Wright believes that the performers, with their social or domestic situations, are central to a successful, balanced creative input being given to the group. When key people or roles change, it inevitably alters everything in the group. Wright observes, 'We're like an amoeba, never really in control if devising.'[19]

6   Thomasina Carlyle and Toby Wilsher in 'Top Storey'. Trestle
Theatre Company 1987–90. (Photo: Joff Chafer.)

Spontaneity and imagination

Improvisation is a crucial process for many companies, particularly where no writer is specifically involved in the work. Annie Griffin of Gloria relies on improvisation throughout the rehearsal period. Griffin describes the process as 'being in a room for four to six weeks, on my feet, working it out, either with myself or with a group of actors'. She defines the process of improvising as 'playing in rehearsal and letting oneself invent as part of the playing'. During the rehearsals for 'Ariadne', Griffin would set a task and the performers would go off, either singly or in groups, and invent a presentation in response to that task. In the early sessions, tasks were open-ended – for instance, improvising a 'burial at sea' – until the group progressed to more specific aspects of the piece. This process demands a continual, committed involvement from the performers, which means trying things out at every rehearsal.

One performer's role increased from her willingness to try everything in rehearsal, while another encountered problems with the style of the play, comic timing, and the direct relationship with the audience. The actor playing the character 'Dog' tried out numerous dog types in rehearsal, only to discover that he did not need to act like an animal, but just needed a precise kind of movement. Griffin states: 'He found the right note halfway through rehearsals, the right base from which to play, the strong, friendly, funny Dog.' Griffin attempted to give the performers as much as she could about how she saw their characters, what was working, and ideas for further development.

Devised theatre demands contributions of ideas from the performers in a group, causing both frustration and satisfaction much of the time. If a character is being improvised from nothing, then this can be creatively exciting or may encourage feelings of drowning in a sea of ideas and getting nowhere. Pam Schweitzer has clear expectations of performers devising reminiscence theatre for Age Exchange's elderly community. First and foremost, they must enjoy working with old people, be able to look the audience in the eye, and, as Schweitzer observes, 'be able to improvise because anything can happen'.[20] Actors must be versatile, good story-tellers, fast learners, and able to switch roles or leap from one mood to another very quickly. Age Exchange's first shows were often devised through improvisation, with each actor coming up with a different idea based on a thorough perusal of the transcripts of interviews. Schweitzer comments that each actor's ideas were 'worked through until the best format was found'. These performers are also expected to have strong musical skills, which include a good singing voice and the ability to play at least one musical instrument.

THE MUSICIAN/DEVISER

The specialist process of musical composition may be needed when devising theatre, from community documentary to theatre-in-education, and in experimental work. Musical composition is often an important contributing process to Age Exchange's devising of reminiscence shows for the elderly. Music increases the celebratory feel of the shows, functioning as a memory trigger for old people, and, as Schweitzer comments, 'a way back into a show for anyone who has lost the thread or lost concentration'. Schweitzer frequently uses music of the period when devising shows, which often comments ironically on the text.

In Gloria's 'Ariadne', the process of musical composition and the creation of Nicholas Bloomfield's musical score was an integral part of the developing devising process in rehearsals. As Griffin observes, 'music always lifts what is happening on stage, inspires, makes things move or appear to move'. In the case of Forced Entertainment's work, the music is composed out of the devising process and is used as a continuous soundtrack throughout the show. The music always accompanies what has developed from the work. The writer, Tim Etchells, states: 'Atmospherically we work off the music, but we don't start with it and ask what we could do with this.' Although not a member of the company, John Avery, the composer, works closely with the group from the early stages of Arts Council application onwards. His involvement includes attending meetings, seeing early runs of possible material, and creating musical sketches in response to what he sees and hears. At some point later in the process, the company tries to work out exactly the kinds and lengths of music needed for the show. Final versions of the sountrack usually reach them in the few days before the first performance.

ENQUIRY

There are certain fundamental processes to be used to a greater or lesser extent by any group devising theatre. The process of researching material can vary from group members reading individually over a prescribed period and then sharing information together to the delegation of specific research activities for small sub-groups to investigate and report back through practical demonstration. Pam Schweitzer of Age Exchange sees the research process as changing with every project, observing that 'it can take anything from two months to two years, depending on the funds available and the dedication of the interviewers'. Transcripts of tape-recorded interviews are the basis of verbatim scripts. Schweitzer comments on the way 'in which several people's stories are woven together to create a collage'.

The actors' involvement in research is encouraged, as is actively contributing to the dramatic shaping of material. It is usually Schweitzer who scripts material with the actors' help, as her prime concern is to find a structure to hold the material together. Schweitzer elaborates further: 'This requires a very thorough knowledge of all the research material available to the project, including documentary visuals and music, on behalf of everyone involved.' Additionally, to every devised product there is a publication of edited and illustrated reminiscences as well as related documentary material collected during the research period. Schweitzer comments that Age Exchange has published over twenty books, 'which sell nationally, and have a life independent of the shows which generated them'.

DEBATE

The use of discussion within the devising process is different for every group or company. From my own experience of working with student groups, it is clear that a balance is needed between discussion, analysis, and 'on the floor' work. These processes should be integrated when devising theatre, as the dangers of too much talking become apparent in the final product. It becomes a question of running out of time and rushing significant stages of examination or development of work. A common weakness for inexperienced student companies is to try and say immediately what the product will be, prior to any initial practical exploration of ideas, materials, or each other. The opposite is also true, where group members do not allow a space in the devising period for evaluation and assessment of ongoing practice.

Members of Forced Entertainment are clear about the role of discussion in their approach to work. Some discussions involve the whole group, many do not. Very early on, they discovered the whole group to be an unwieldy object, and that a sub-committee moves faster and more radically. The sub-committee of two or three tends to be the two directors, plus one performer. They follow up work sessions and group discussions, making practical, pragmatic decisions, whilst always returning to the whole group for criticism and help. Every group or company utilises the basic processes of improvisation, research, or discussion in some way or other. They are an implicit part of devising theatre. Processes of writing or visual experimentation are also integral to many companies creating a theatrical performance or product.

ADMINISTRATION

It is usual for a professional company devising theatre to have an administrator in its group, but it is rare that this role extends into the devising process itself. This is sometimes the case in theatre-in-education, where an administrator may become part of the devising team in the early stages of the work. A group must decide whether to maintain the more traditional responsibilities associated with an administrator's role, such as booking a tour, promoting the product and organising the budget, or to incorporate the administrator into creative decisions made by the company. These decisions also apply to other roles, such as educational liaison officer in a theatre-in-education company, where a balance is needed between devising with the company, communicating with local teachers, and being responsible for producing the 'teachers' pack'. Hilary Hodgson, educational liaison officer for Greenwich Young People's Theatre from 1987 to 1991, finds it difficult to integrate all aspects of her job at times, but believes that being fully involved means sacrifices and gains have to be made throughout the devising process. It is important for her to promote feedback from the teachers to the company, and to encourage a range of follow-up work that teachers can pursue back at school.

How a group operates is dependent on how the members wish to utilise the tools of devising: whether they want to employ a variety of processes available to them in their allocated roles within the company, or if their ways and means of working are determined by hierarchical or collective structures that suggest specific methodologies of practice. What is important to acknowledge is an awareness that there are many possibilities when devising theatre and that, in the end, it is a question of making choices or decisions that are considered relevant or appropriate by the company for the product in mind. This means returning to original objectives, and questioning whether the tools or processes fit the needs of the work. This evaluation relies on an acknowledgement at the same time of the spontaneous and instinctive development of the group. In chapters four and five, I give further consideration to the similarities and differences of particular devising methodologies, examining how the process of devising relates to a particular working practice, ideology, and product.

4

FROM PROCESS TO PRODUCT
Relationship and practice

It's a situation offering the chance to produce work with a group of people whose ideas I respect so much, and with whom the working process is so good that I know the result is going to be much greater than what I could do myself.

(Terry O'Connor, Forced Entertainment)

Company structure, roles or responsibilities within the group, and the use of a variety of processes all contribute to the making of the devised product. I want to now examine two selected examples of the relationship between practice, process and product from community theatre and experimental theatre. What kinds of product did the devising process create or construct in the case of Age Exchange or Forced Entertainment in 1989 and 1990? Both products used the processes of research, discussion, improvisation, design, writing text, and musical composition to varying degrees in relation to their original aims and objectives or initial decisions about form, content,or audience. It should also be noted that each company inevitably worked out of their last product; this often determines ideas or material for preliminary discussion and planning of their next project.

AGE EXCHANGE

This is a very stretching way of working when you have to see the material from a scattered set of fragments of memory to a shaped and coherent whole. The whole is greater than the sum of its parts.

(Pam Schweitzer, Artistic Director of Age Exchange)

Age Exchange claims to be the only full-time professional Reminiscence Theatre company in Great Britain.[1] This company aims to 'improve the quality of life of older people by emphasising the value of their reminiscences to old and young, through pioneering artistic, educational and welfare activities'.[2] The Reminiscence Centre opened in June 1987, and is a unique community centre providing a focus for a range of creative activities for older people. These include the production of books on community history, which put the memories in a permanent, lasting form, adding more significance to the event. Pam Schweitzer points out that those giving their memories for shows are usually thrilled to be in print as well as on stage. Schweitzer claims, 'We involve them in the editing process where possible and they have a say in what goes in to the book; many donate photos as well.'[3] Exhibitions of three-dimensional displays of photographs, objects, murals and memories concentrate on important reminiscence themes that are available before or after a show. The museum allows visitors to handle objects from its collection. Associated with the Centre is the Reminiscence Project, which trains residential workers and health service staff in reminiscence skills, as well as offering training opportunities to anyone wishing to broaden and augment ways of working with elderly people.

Theatre activities are equally varied, and include professional touring productions to the community that last between five and twelve weeks, theatre-in-education participatory projects for classes of primary school children in the Reminiscence Centre using professional actors as well as elderly volunteers, and Youth Theatre productions. Schweitzer believes that the Youth Theatre work brings young people and old-age pensioners together, using similar methods to the adult company, although devising more through improvisation than through transcription and verbatim theatre. Young people work on projects with professional directors and all design work, such as set and props, is supervised by professional staff from Age Exchange.

Personnel and funding

Such diverse pursuits mean that the permanent core staff must relate widely to all activities, resulting in the employment of

7 Milly Gardner and Irene Swanton (volunteers) with visiting schoolchildren in the Reminiscence Centre, 1990. (Photo: Age Exchange.)

freelance actors, musicians, writers, designers, and researchers for every particular theatre project. Company posts specifically linked to devising community theatre are those of artistic director, press and publicity officer, administrator, and production manager. Although the company's organisation and management is hierarchically structured, there is a collaborative feel to every project in light of the majority of theatre personnel being on short-term contracts to work together over a predetermined period. Funding for work comes from numerous sources and includes sponsors for particular projects or posts. The company relies heavily on funding from the two local boroughs of Greenwich and Lewisham, on the London Borough Grants Scheme, and on the Department of Health for its reminiscence work. Budgets for theatre projects vary tremendously and often income has to be earned from the performances.

Methodology

Age Exchange has established a particular pattern of working on community theatre projects. This involves close liaison with The Reminiscence Group, which gives feedback on Schweitzer's initial outline for a show, helps and advises on themes, including attendance at rehearsals, and writes material itself. Schweitzer describes the group's involvement:

> The old people enjoy it when we are devising a play because they are all creatively involved in it. They get to know the actors quite well and take an interest in the process. The actors take the work seriously because their sources are particularly close at hand.

This approach has developed out of the company's early experiences from its origins in April 1983, when shows were often devised through improvisation. The actors interviewed the elderly, incorporating the better stories around strongly devised characters and a clear plot line, Schweitzer elaborates further, 'improvising within a given shape once the actors have read the material and scripting from these improvisations'. Schweitzer has also collaborated with writers to help structure the verbatim material, such as Joyce Holliday in 1985 on 'Can We Afford the Doctor?' The writer has an editorial role and is bound by the verbatim approach. However, Schweitzer comments that more recent projects reveal a frequent use of the actual words of old people, returning to a 'verbatim format for the greater feel of authenticity it gives'. The research period for a show can vary considerably, but is usually longer than the devising period itself. Since 1983, at least twenty shows have been devised within a timescale of two to five weeks. Schweitzer argues that devising means planning structures to achieve objectives, thinking through the shape of a piece, discussing it with fellow artists and with people whose material is being processed. She has used the process of improvisation to discover ways through material in order to develop dialogue, character or motive. Schweitzer observes that 'sometimes it is a way of finding the meaning behind a story which is already scripted but lacks life for its interpreters – a way in to the script'. Schweitzer enjoys working in collaboration with others, devising and scripting a show out of an assemblage of edited material.

Illustrative of this method of working was 'Christmas at War' (1989), which was devised on a budget of about £1,000 over two weeks, followed by another two weeks rehearsing over thirty music cues, as well as producing a set and costumes appropriate to the Christmas-time period of 1940. The idea for this show developed out of research on the theme of evacuation for a previous project, which was the basis for a theatre-in-education programme, 'Goodnight Children Everywhere'. Andy Andrews, an actor with the company, researched the material by interviewing elderly people and recording their stories and memories of Christmas 1940. Andrews worked in collaboration with old-age pensioners at the Reminiscence Centre, as well as visiting two sheltered housing units in South London. Faced with a pile of material, which included stories, eye-witness accounts of bombings, and factual information about the war, both Andrews and Schweitzer were immediately faced with how to make the stories come alive and not simply just become a repetition of oral reminiscences.

An outline scenario was roughly shaped around the stories from the transcripts, which started with the idea of three characters and their relatives. Schweitzer suggests that 'it was about how to husband what we had, how to fashion it into something rather than nothing'. Stories were either listed and

77

classified as indirect, for instance, things that happened to people's relatives or children, or as direct, which involved them personally in the telling of things that they had encountered. Various stories were allocated to the three central characters. A list of spoofs was also noted, including how to keep the hair nice for the Christmas party, or how to make Christmas pudding based on a recipe using potatoes and carrots. This was followed by Andrews and Schweitzer working in unison on the process of scripting, assembling material, editing, and piecing it together, as well as writing from the resources themselves.

The research produced a great deal of information about a rest centre in the war years, which seemed a good setting for a variety of characters to come together. From the point where the scenario and overall idea were drawn up, the set designer was given a brief to create a portable, practical set for touring community venues. Andrews and Schweitzer also became aware that radio entertainment was an important part of people's lives. In view of the fact that the show would be toured and performed at several Christmas parties, combined with an objective not to make the show too gloomy or downbeat, it was decided to have lots of songs and references to specific radio comedy, reminding the audience about Tommy Hanley, Rob Wilton, and other big stars of the period. Two pensioners scripted a little sketch in the style of Gert and Daisy, which was included in the show. Serious, sad material about a bomb raid that killed two children the day before Christmas Eve was juxtaposed with humour and entertainment. One pensioner, Frank Ball, acted as musical adviser, collating songs and recording artists of the time, checking the musical material of the period. The musical director was invited to discuss the role of music in the show and to contribute to the script. This involved the creation of musical devices to overcome the difficulties of script, devising musical links within the show, as well as rehearsing all the songs and music. Schweitzer had worked in collaboration with both musical director Paula Gardiner and set designer Lisa Wilson over a period of five years prior to this production.

Andrews and Schweitzer devised the show knowing the target audience would be elderly people, many of whom would be at Christmas parties. They also knew that most of the audience would be women, which prompted the decision to have a cast of two women and one man. The two actresses in 'Christmas at War' were auditioned on November 1st, 1989 and were reading through the first draft of script on November 13th, knowing that the show would open and begin its tour on November 28th, 1989. Certain pensioners had become very involved in the devising process, using their stories to create characters for the piece. The cast was to play the three central characters of an Air Raid Warden, a Cook, and an Auxiliary Nurse who works for the Red Cross, along with fifteen to twenty other characters, who were directly or indirectly related to their families. The style of writing was dissimilar to 'On the River' (1989), where characters were always speaking as though from memory, but was now written as though they were performing in the present. Writing from the stories meant more work on characterisation for Andrews and Schweitzer, which was requested by the actors after the first read-through. Schweitzer explains:

The actors liked it but felt we needed more establishing shots of the three characters, so we went away and scripted in some more bits which were mostly based on material we had, although some of it was slightly freer scripting than we normally do.

Pensioners sitting in on rehearsals also suggested changes to the first draft based on their memories of particular scenes or stories. Script revisions were often made in rehearsal as actors, musical director, or pensioners had ideas or good suggestions.

Connections continued to be made with characters throughout the rehearsal process and sections were re-written accordingly. The piece had a naturalistic feel, incorporating details of the period that would place things for the audience. Devising this show in the year of the fiftieth anniversary of the outbreak of the Second World War meant that it was a frequent topic of conversation for many elderly people, encouraging fresh memories and reminiscences related to the theme of the show. Many pensioners wanted the stories of the war experience to be taken very seriously in the play, and according to Schweitzer these moments tended to be shown in a documentary format, so that they became more detached. Schweitzer believes that the 'lightest touch' can trigger the material, so that there is no need for graphic descriptions, or talking directly about death.

The crucial elements of the show were to be about the separation of families, the City falling down, people trying to keep cheerful, working mad hours, and the economics of making do in the situation. Themes of women in the forces, the home guard, evacuation and civilian bombings were integrated through the three characters, who swapped stories about themselves and their families in a brief respite over the Christmas period at the height of the Blitz. The subsequent devised play is described by Schweitzer as 'a humorous evocation of a war-time Christmas through the memories of Londoners.'

The product

The final devised play script evolved out of a process that starts and ends with the elderly community, integrating the reminiscences of individual pensioners together. These experiences and memories are realised for the audience through the live performance of the play, producing a particular form of reminiscence theatre. It is December 15th, 1989 and I am attending a 'Christmas at War' afternoon performance at Meeting Point, Swanley, in Kent. The atmosphere is one of anticipation and excitement as the production manager, Helen Gaynor, steps forward to introduce the show, telling the audience that all the stories are true and have been told by friends of Age Exchange. The show is to last one hour. It begins with the 'Blackout Stroll' and Andy Andrews, as Fred the Air Raid Patrol Warden, provides a background for us of Christmas 1940. Statistical information is given of thirty thousand dead and three million homes destroyed between September and Christmas 1940. Fred, Doreen, and Lil establish their characters and their relationship to the situation. A gasp goes up from the audience of pensioners at the first musical reference to listening to the radio; they remember it well!

The set is simple in design and construction, representing a room in a London Rest Centre. A variety of musical instruments, such as guitar, banjo, accordion and double bass, are placed at the side of the performance space within the rather rectangular room of this popular community venue. There is a coat-stand filled with numerous garments and hats, offering the actors a quick change from one character to another. Fred the Air Raid Patrol Warden speedily plays Frank, a child performing Joseph in the Christmas Nativity. An extract from an unpublished copy of the 1989 script records the humour between Doreen and Frank:

Doreen: Well it's all going well till they come to the bit where the three wise men offer the gifts. I bring you gold. . . frankinsence (*sic*). . . and myrrh. . . And little Frank's started crying. Well, the whole play stopped so I went up and said to him, 'What are you crying for?' And he says:

Frank· They keep making fun of me.

Doreen: What do you mean?

Frank: They keep saying Frank's got no sense.

Doreen: I explained it to him, and gave him a cuddle, but he's still crying, so I says, 'What is it now?' And he says:

Frank: They say I've got myrrh. I might have nits, but I haven't got myrrh.

This is representative of the style of playing where a change of costume, often a coat or a hat, denotes a new character, whether it is Lil's daughter Deidre, an evacuee in Cornwall playing a butterfly in the local village pantomime, or her eldest daughter, Margaret, who attempted to escape back to London by cycling in the snow late at night, only to be caught by a policeman and returned to her village. Actors move in and out of narratives, but always return to their last positions as the three central characters to continue the underlying thread of action.

The use of music and singing songs are integral to this show. The three performers sing 'Goodnight Children Everywhere', which immediately causes much talking in the audience. The song 'Home on Leave' is a good example of performers singing in harmony together, and illustrates the versatility, energy, and attack of the cast. References to advertisements or products of the period elicit a huge response from the audience. Doreen's story about making face cream from lard and glycerine to give as Christmas presents in Shippams fish paste jars is thoroughly enjoyed, which immediately results in the audience joining the cast in the singing of 'Keep Young and Beautiful if you want to be Loved'. More stories follow, including the one about Fred's dog called Sandy, who got drunk from licking all the alcoholic liquid pouring down the cellar walls from the upstairs shop, and the story about the unexploded bomb that turned out to be water from an overflowing pipe dripping into an old tin bath.

The storytelling works well, juxtaposing humour and pathos throughout the show. There is a strong sense of the period and the radio entertainment material seems particularly effective with the pensioners. The serious references to raids for seventy-six nights continuously, or living conditions inside an air-raid shelter, are balanced against cast and audience singing 'Roll out the Barrel' in a warm, responsive manner. The show ends and one of the actresses tells the audience that books about these reminiscences, such as *All Our Christmases*, are available at the other end of the room. The audience clap once more to a last chorus of 'Roll out the Barrel', which is followed by the Mayor of Swanley thanking the cast and recalling his memories of Christmas 1940 and 'the Blitz'. I observed an audience who laughed, cried and acknowledged their memories of this period, further substantiated in discussion with the pensioners after the show. The cast always talk to the audience after each performance. For the performers, it has been a 'physically gruelling' and stressful show, as there was so much in it and no possibility of fooling this particular audience.

Evaluation

'Christmas at War' was devised for, with, and from a specifically targeted elderly audience. This particular community initiated and participated in various ways towards the creation of a theatrical performance, which produced a unique experience between performers and spectators. Age Exchange's working practice raises a number of interesting questions with wider theoretical implications about the value and significance of devising theatre for a particular community (including reminiscence theatre for the elderly), and the importance of evaluating the process in relationship to the product. There is no common critical language in which devised theatre can be assessed or understood, which implies a need to differentiate and articulate ways of looking at community theatre. How is

8 Clare Summerskill, Andy Andrews, ard Rebecca Clow in 'Christmas at War'. Age Exchange Theatre Company, 1989. (Photo: Alex Schweitzer.)

excellence or success to be judged in light of accessibility for the audience to create the product?

I want to examine the relationship between the devising process of 'Christmas at War' and the touring theatrical performance to community centres, sheltered homes, clubs, and hospitals. The devising process of 'Christmas at War' involved the active participation of old-age pensioners in the creation of the product. The elderly local community contributed to the process through research, writing, and input into rehearsals. It is the pensioners' stories, reminiscences, and source material that formed the basis for developing work. The involvement of members of the Reminiscence Group in rehearsals constantly reminded the company of the purpose of the devised product and its intended audience. The product in performance is illustrative of where the process started and how it has been completed: from the early reminiscences of the local community with some members of the company to a wide-ranging discussion of the performance (and subsequent memories) between performers and spectators after the show.

Devising reminiscence theatre is a collaborative experience that brings pleasure to those it is intended for. The enjoyment is in the recognition of the content, the participation in the form, and being part of the whole experience. There is a sense of entertainment in the work, witnessed in the enjoyment gained by pensioners revising the script during rehearsals, or in the overall playing style and format of the performance. Age Exchange certainly fulfils the aim of wanting to entertain and inform through the company's exploration of living memory.

However, is there a therapeutic value in devising a piece of reminiscence theatre, or indeed in the spectating of the created product? What is the value of devising theatre for the elderly? The performance goes beyond that initial converstion between two pensioners recalling their memories of Christmas 1940, and provides a focus for communal sharing, communication, and interaction. (This is evident from the audience's sense of togetherness in the laughter at the comedy, or in the singing with the performers.) Indeed, this is the basis when devising theatre for any community, as are preliminary objectives or statements of intention specific to the nature of the project. Thus, the evaluation arises out of initial aims or goals in relation to the development of both process and product.

FORCED ENTERTAINMENT

The process for this show is different to the last one and the one before. It's about creating something that has a different engagement with its audience than the last piece had, which means pushing at developments in form all the time.

(Terry O'Connor, Forced Entertainment)

With these tools we're trying to make a theatre that's both emotionally and intellectually engaging, allowing audiences to create their own meanings in the spaces between its texts, a theatre that trusts in its audience to find its own ways through.

(Tim Etchells, Forced Entertainment)

Since 1984 Forced Entertainment Theatre Co-operative has devised nine innovative theatre pieces for touring in Britain and abroad. The company is regarded as one of the most inspiring new British permanent ensembles to be creating experimental work out of the 1980s and into the 1990s, 'at the sharp end of the nation's cultural self-expression.'[4] In April 1987, Claire MacDonald (co-founder of Impact Theatre) described Forced Entertainment as:

the most interesting and dynamic company on offer. Their work is highly expressionistic and is in a continual process of reinventing the languages of postmodern fiction and film for the space of theatre. It is also work which makes a serious attempt to confront the political and cultural reality of contemporary Britain through the fictional representation of urban life.[5]

Certainly, they are eclectic in their sources and original in their ideas, devising work that combines complex use of video, choreography, set, lighting, text, and specially commissioned soundtracks by Sheffield musician John Avery. As for every devised show, the company works collectively and collaboratively, with every group member in a particular role, or responsible for specific aspects of the work.

Personnel

'Some Confusions in the Law about Love' (1989-90) involved two new members for this piece, Claire Marshall and Fred McVittie, challenging the group to look anew at each member's contribution and relationship to the work. The company wanted to broaden their experience, communicate with new people from outside, clarify past methods of working, and benefit from a fresh input of ideas and a critical outside eye. There were five performers addressing a variety of aspects of the devising process, all of whom were in charge of other areas, such as contributing to stage management, costumes, video work, or daily administration. The two directors, Richard Lowdon and Tim Etchells, were also individually responsible for set and lighting, or text in the show.

Etchells explains the necessity of company members being committed to the development of the work: 'We don't hire in actors, the traditional theatre notion of hiring actors is an anathema to us.'[6] The company acknowledges that it is probably the hardest way to work with the least rules to fall back on, demanding most of an individual and costing a great deal in terms of relationships with others. Etchells concludes that if a company devises work to no fixed formula, then there is a big cost to each individual, and all group members get used to 'putting a lot on the line for the company.'

The company's work has progressed from using found atmospheres from television, film or fictional worlds as starting points to combining images from a range of sources, and then evolving a world around them. Their work presents the concerns of the time and their relationship with mass culture in a theatrical language that is constructed out of fragments from television, film, music, literature, advertisements and the company's own experiences. They are committed to a number of fundamental objectives in the development of their theatrical work. They aim to pursue non-naturalistic dramatic structures, which may contain hints of narrative, but are not obliged to tell a story. They wish to reveal a range of levels of performance within a show, so that performers may be viewed as being aware of the fictions they take on. The company wants pieces to contain contradiction and a multiplicity of meanings or interpretations, engaging its audience on a number of levels, emotionally, viscerally, or through ideas. They juxtapose meanings that are generated from different sources, such as a variety of texts on stage, taped voice, video, and music.

Finance

The company spent its first two years supported by some funding from Sheffield City Council and Yorkshire Arts (now Yorkshire and Humberside Arts), as well as small amounts of commissioning money from venues. 'Let the Water Run its Course (To the Sea that Made the Promise)' (1986) produced a significant change in the work as well as bringing their first Arts Council of Great Britain Project grant. Others have followed since then for '200% & Bloody Thirsty' (1988–89) and 'Some Confusions in the Law about Love' (1989–90), as well as sponsorship and support from Barclays Bank, as part of the New Stages Awards, for 'Marina & Lee' (1991) and 'Emanuelle Enchanted' (1992–93). The British Council has consistently supported the group in its touring abroad, and the company also receives income from workshops, residencies, lectures, and talks.

Approach

Forced Entertainment is interested in devising work that has an organic life of its own. The company gathers together an almost random pile of text, images, ideas and personal experiences, out of which comes the subject matter for a piece. The process of placing texts or images against each other happens in rehearsal, and it may be weeks or months before the meanings or resonances of the material are realised. Forced Entertainment makes work that is about the way people define themselves against and through the mass culture. It is the language by which the company addresses and defines everything else in a piece. The company uses a variety of processes to create a performance world with a clear structure, and its own rules and vocabulary of speech and movement. Members are keen to create work that enriches or enhances the audience's perception of their own situation, acknowledging the power and role of spectators in the completion of a piece. A company pamphlet of 1988 describes the work:

87

By making art, we shape and re-shape the world in the same way as we all must live our lives: struggling to orient ourselves in the midst of our past and presents, assembling and re-assembling our contradictory experiences of the world. Memories, aspirations, stories, ideologies and desires are combined in endless attempts to find new and better structures to make sense of ourselves and our world.[7]

'Some Confusions in the Law about Love' exemplifies a practice and process that is continually ongoing, changing with every performance and discussion of the work. The devising of this show is not particularly typical of the nine pieces created since 1984, but reflects a turning point in the company's work with the exploration of live text on stage spoken through microphones, integrated with video performers and a musical soundtrack. The beginnings of the devising process started in summer 1989; the first work-in-progress preview was at Nottingham Polytechnic on October 31st, 1989, and the show toured throughout Britain and Europe in 1990. Within the course of a year, I monitored both process and product, observing discussion, the use of early improvisations, experimentation with texts, and rehearsals, as well as seeing four different versions of the show in Nottingham, London, and Basildon, Essex.

Forced Entertainment wanted to extend their work out of '200% & Bloody Thirsty', where they had used text on stage for the first time, having previously worked with taped text or performers using a gibberish language comprising entirely of sound or vocal rhythm as in 'Let the Water Run its Course (To the Sea that Made the Promise)'. '200% & Bloody Thirsty' is described by Etchells in the article 'Forced Entertainment, You and The City' as follows:

In the show a trio of characters awoke on the bed centre stage and then dressed up in very bad costumes and wigs to enact a series of scenes and fragments that concerned them. Chief amongst these was the Nativity story, replayed several times at drunken manic speed, before finally being acted out by the performers dressed in cardboard angels wings, very sweetly, very quietly. The whole proceedings were watched over by two further angels on video.[8]

The company wanted to develop further the use of performers on video, as well as looking at the complex relationship or interaction between live performers on stage and those on video. Out of the set design and stage world of '200% & Bloody Thirsty' grew a preoccupation with skeletal theatricality. Etchells comments, 'the more we can re-use from old pieces in a slightly different way the better – that feels very comfortable.' In terms of material, the company wanted to include things that had been previously discussed, such as Elvis Presley, or develop themes from the characters in '200% & Bloody Thirsty'. The company was keen to continue an exploration of form, ideas (for instance, the concept of something beyond human experience, or developing themes of miraculous power), and style of performance where characters act out a number of different identities and roles.

Stimuli

The process for 'Some Confusions in the Law about Love' started with a variety of initial ideas, images and source materials, including ghosts, poltergeists, mediums, stand-up comics, romantic notions of love, and a small stage with red curtains, which related to a tacky style of nightclub present- ation, and was more overtly theatrical than previous work. As part of a rather shoddy nightclub feel, the company discussed strange sorts of spiritualist acts that incorporated hypnotism, seances and mind reading. They tried out and improvised various ideas to do with hypnotic regression, but these proved uninteresting for they produced a form that held few possibilities for surrealism or the unexpected. The company worked in a series of mocked-up models of the intended performance space, designed by Lowdon and constructed by the group. In the early stages of the devising process a wide range of texts was examined, including the love stories of Plato's *Symposium*, and the book *Elvis Presley Speaks* by Hans Holzer, reporting the case history of a New Jersey housewife called Dorothy Sherry, who claimed that she was visited by the spirit of Elvis Presley after his death.

The group explored the personal relationship between Dorothy and Elvis, imagined or otherwise, and were interested to look at the variety of claims that have been made about him, such as, Presley speaking beyond the grave and faking his own death. Forced Entertainment had been interested in Elvis Presley material for two years, but also wanted to pursue the notion of second-rate, supernatural acts and the way that they often focus on death. Their exploration of the differences between those who are dead, those who fake death, and people who become ghosts, prompted a number of questions for further examination. Questions about spirituality in an alienating world where the possibilities of belief have been reduced; enquiries into what it is to be human, whether it is possible to believe in anything, or what it takes to make people feel something: these have been present in every piece of work.

The idea of ghosts comes from a potent image and form that is still alive in contemporary culture, cartoons, and films. According to O'Connor, who co-directed '200% & Bloody Thirsty' and performs in 'Some Confusions in the Law about Love', it holds a meaning that has become very sophisticated and tongue-in-cheek, almost trashy. O'Connor considers it a serious theme in terms of exploring what lies outside the human existence, questioning how much of the ghost is a real person and how much is not. O'Connor states:

> there is a constant flux of images and symbols that are being used, recreated, or reappropriated all the time. It's something we do without much effort, you stick a sheet over you and you're a ghost. It has that instantaneous quality.

Time was given to exposing themselves to various materials, including watching films like *Topper* with Cary Grant, or *Poltergeist*, and reading Noel Coward's play *Blithe Spirit* together. They also decided that they needed an alternative literary source of input to counter these ideas, becoming interested in the acting out of great romantic texts and exploration of romantic ideals.

The visual tone of the piece was important at the start of the devising process, as envisaged in the original image of a shoddy stage with red curtains, peopled by men in maroon velvet suits, stand-up comics, and dancing girls with jackets over their shoulders. Linked to the design concept of a theatre within a theatre was the idea of the relationship between audience and performer. In the same way that the company experimented with texts, they considered different visual structures, building various mock-ups so that people could be seen against the set, and working within the proposed performance space. This company always devises within the designed performing area in order to feel a sense of the space, discovering more about a particular environment. For 'Some Confusions in the Law about Love' initial ideas of naturalistic locations for the action – especially a hotel bedroom and a nightclub stage – soon gave way to a design that referred to these locations without exactly depicting either of them. In a play between naturalism and abstraction, solid surfaces like walls were indicated with skeletal steel structures, the floor gained trapdoors and the night-time sky (beyond the window of the room, or perhaps backing the stage) was represented tackily with a curtain of electric stars. As with the set, there is a wide catchment area of ideas for about ten basic costumes, including exploration of made-up skeleton outfits, girls in mock Greek, white flowing robes with gold cord at the waist, and showgirls in sequinned swimming costumes, which will have been reduced to two or three by the time the show is performed.

Ways of working

The length of process varies with every show, and is described by O'Connor as 'serving the work, rather than the work coming out of the process that has been decided upon'. 'Some Confusions in the Law about Love' was envisaged to take five to six months' hard work, allowing for trying things out and throwing them away. Financially, the company can not afford this length of devising period (money from the Arts Council covers about twelve weeks' rehearsal), but believes that time is essential for finding its way towards an end. Etchells is clear that the final product will be nothing like that from which they are starting. Discussion is open to every company member and shared by everyone, although Etchells suggests that the danger is always not to interrogate ideas to everyone's satisfaction. Commitment to a set of specific ideas is essential in order to define what is to happen on stage, and plotting the progression of the material enables the discovery of what it does to the characters.

Central to the devising process is the creation of performance personas who will inhabit the stage world and give rise to its action. These personas (close to the hearts of the performers themselves, but not the same as them) feature in 'Some Confusions in the Law about Love' and much of the company's work, and they are used to present a number of contradictory layered performances. Thus, the crisis Robin Arthur presents on stage lies somewhere between that of a hopeless Birmingham Elvis impersonator and the drug-induced confusion of Presley himself. The personas that exist on stage are often only glimpsed through layers of other fictions and pretences – here 'characters', if they can be called such, exist only in the gaps between other texts. Etchells observes, 'that's a kind of paradigm for what will be happening behind the piece, that you're never really sure where the put-ons and acts begin or end.' A strong preoccupation is whether to have a core character or interlocutor, who stands between the audience and the acts, independent of decisions about what the video monitors will show, and how they will interact with the performers on stage. The character of 'Hans' was developed so that he had a series of monologues in the nightclub, becoming a kind of host or compère for the show. The group tried out many ideas with videos, which provided an alternative text for the performer playing Hans to interview a tawdry sex act (Mike and Dolores), via satellite from Hawaii. Elsewhere in the show, the same performers represent skeletons emerging from trapdoors in the stage floor to enact a Japanese romantic narrative. For Etchells, a key consideration became how to combine material they had basically found, vandalised or cobbled together from other sources, with material that they had written or made up entirely.

Linked to this is the problem of how to deal with action, when the decision has been made to use microphones, which limit opportunities for performers to move on stage. The company is keen to integrate text and movement whose actions are smaller and more detailed than in previous work, and is adopting a different approach and emphasis to the large, caricatured cartoon-like gestures of earlier shows. More often than not, the company works out of the narrative or fiction,

9 Claire Marshall, Fred McVittie, and Robin Arthur in 'Some Confusions in the Law about Love'. Forced Entertainment Theatre Co-operative, 1989-90. (Photo: Hugo Glendinning.)

using it as a kind of springboard to produce imagistic or textual material. Etchells observes that 'by the time we open the show, perhaps only two thirds of that narrative will be visible'. Starting with something quite fictional and 'blowing it to pieces' was a process also directed at the set, which began as a tiny, toy theatre stage, and ended up as a wide, deconstructed, metal structure that Etchells describes as looking, 'a little bit like a stage, but also a bit like a room'.

Forced Entertainment is interested in pushing a theatre form that creates new work that is not common to other companies. Devising is a way of rearranging the world for members themselves, confronting their audience with an emotionally, intellectually, complex experience that is indicative of their particular perceptions of the world. Although aware of a particular audience interest, the company wants the work to appeal to anybody and does not concentrate on devising for any one group of people. What is important to members is to find a form that is appropriate to the piece they are devising, as Etchells points out: 'we're working in a tradition that is established by twenty five years of theatre experimentation and devised theatre of a particular kind in this country.' However, it is also evident that the company has been inspired and influenced by devised experimental work outside of Britain. The Wooster Group from New York[9] has been influential on Forced Entertainment in developing an aesthetic about urban culture, film, and television, as well as creating a texture of confusion and technical chaos, whilst utilising collage or fast undercutting of found sources as a way of making work.

The product

The first performance of 'Some Confusions in the Law about Love' was given at a work-in-progress preview at Nottingham Polytechnic on October 30th, 1989. The opening mood of the piece is soft, full of love, and set against the background of a dark, starlit sky viewed between the steel girders of a platform stage, which is defined by velvet curtains and fairy lights that are wrapped around the metal structure, upright microphones, and a centrally positioned bed. There is a nightclub host, Hans, (played by Robin Arthur) working alongside a rather dowdy act of two badly wigged performers (played by Terry O'Connor and Cathy Naden), who both represent the New Jersey housewife Dorothy Sherry speaking as a medium, who in turn becomes Elvis Presley during the seance part of their act. This is clearly indicated when the two women place white muslin sheets over them, saying in false deep voices that 'heaven is inside all of us.'

In contrast to the relaxing, lilting soundtrack of late-night or tinpot hotel music throughout the piece, are two skeletons (played by Claire Marshall and Fred McVittie) who enter through trapdoors in the stage, acting out their Japanese narratives. They speak into Hans' hand-held microphone in a deliberately pretend playing style. There is a sharp contrast between these two groups of characters, particularly evident in the soft, quiet quality of non-acting that is revealed when the skeletons move around behind Hans and the two Dorothys. Hans now stands in his white underpants covering himself in talcum powder behind a sheet of muslin, held by the two skeletons. Powdered white, Hans makes a speech about love, in which he fancies Socrates, and later tells 'the dirty story about life in strange cities'. Three video monitors (covered in muslin) are employed on the set, revealing another nightclub routine entitled 'Mike and Dolores', beamed in from Hawaii; this is an inferior, second-rate love duo involved in violent, sexual acts that include shooting and poisoning each other.

The piece works on several levels. The pace is varied, and there is a certain energy at times from the two women playing Elvis. Humour is revealed in their continued love stories of Plato. The piece is all about quoted sexualities, with the Socrates story about homosexuality appearing as the character's revelation about his own sexuality. The show lasts one hour and twenty minutes.

Assessment

The work-in-progress preview of 'Some Confusions in the Law about Love' is too long, needs more integration between the visual and textual aspects, greater variety of pace, tone and rhythm, stronger contrast of atmospheres and playing styles, tighter choreography, and the ending could be clearer. The

10 Terry O'Connor, Fred McVittie, Robin Arthur, Claire Marshall, and Cathy Naden in 'Some Confusions in the Law about Love'. Forced Entertainment Theatre Co-operative, 1989–90. (Photo: Hugo Glendinning.)

general view of the company after this performance is that the material needs to become more private and selfish, with less direct relationship to the audience. Etchells suggests that the material needs to be fragmented: 'at the moment there are no oppositional dynamics, it has a collaborative feel.'

The central issue is what is happening to the skeletons when they are not speaking the text. The question arises as to whether they are performing a play, or whether they are 'real'. They are portrayed as childlike, needing someone to hold the microphone, as they do not quite understand the technology. Sometimes they know it is a play, but other times they seem to believe the events or stories they are enacting are real. Etchells believes that there is not enough savagery or bite, that the piece has not found its place, with one of the problems being that all the material is equally weighted. The company will review the show later in the week. A team of three members will work together, trying things out. The company are touring '200% & Bloody Thirsty' in Poland during the month of November, so the bulk of the work will be done in January 1990, which includes the re-filming of the videos before the tour proper commences in February 1990.

In fact, the re-work period looks at the role of the two women and their relationship to 'Hans'. They are unclear about why the women are acting out the 'Dorothy' material, and so attempt to find the motivation and fiction for the women being in the room or stage space. The question arises of 'Elvis' visiting two showgirls in a hotel room with the change that these characters are now seen as three people together at the start of the piece. The characters are united, but not at an equal level. The womens' speeches about sex, love or romance shape the show, and their characters seem much more involved or caring in their commitment to the onstage project. A new section is devised, known internally by the company as 'The Presley Play', which is a trashy, semi-pornographic text about a ghost 'Elvis' taking two showgirls on a magical trip to Graceland, to Memphis. 'The Presley Play' raises more questions about pretence, pretending, and play acting. Now, the audience knows that Arthur is not 'Elvis Presley', and that the three characters, with their false, plastic breasts and penis, are not in a hotel room, Memphis, or Birmingham. 'The Presley Play' works well in contrast to other sections of the piece. Forced

Entertainment is constantly preoccupied with what is real and what is fake throughout this period, as well as into the spring tour of 1990.

Changes

During its two-week run at the Institute of Contemporary Arts in London, the company works on the piece daily. Etchells acknowledges that the show needs re-writing, but they experiment with performance and playing style. Observing performances at the start and end of this run with various students convinces me that I have watched two almost entirely different versions of the same material. This appears to be linked to a re-ordering and altering of material – for example, the opening of the show, which makes the audience read the rest of the material in a different way. The first opening, of three characters watching the videos of Mike and Dolores, talking about love and the stars, suggests three people locked in their play world, seemingly situated in a powerless and equal relationship. Alternatively, the second opening, of the women asleep on the bed, waking and putting their wigs on, frames the material differently again, indicating the beginning of some sort of performance with the focus on who they are, rather than the fiction they are about to create.

There is also a subtle change of acting style pursued by the performers, who are in danger of performing in a manner so monotone and minimal that members of the audience may simply mistake it for poor acting skills. An original impression for some is also of numerous conversations using bad language about sex, love or drugs – for example, the comment, 'I'm pissed and fucked up, and worse than that, I'm dead.' Positive evidence of the re-work is seen in the fuller integration between video performers and live performers on stage. The ending is much improved too, with the characters thanking the audience for having them, and bidding all good night.

'Some Confusions in the Law about Love' was described in a review by one critic as 'theatre of the terminus'[10], raising the question of whether it is possible to still feel something when all has gone. The show is about failure, both in the literal sense of sex acts that fail, and in a group of performers being unable to reach a crescendo of performance. Etchells describes the process as taking the engine out of the car, with the product being all the bits of that engine laid out on the ground. O'Connor describes it as 'a kind of half-inhabited fiction', where nothing real happens.

Further work

At the end of March, the company re-works the piece for a final time during a period of six weeks, when it is also considering ideas for the next show, 'Marina and Lee'. The devising process has changed during the project, becoming more unwieldy with a greater use of text in the piece. The company acknowledges that it will change the process or way of working for the next show by concentrating on more areas of work before rehearsals begin. The use of microphones in the show is viewed as hugely alienating, and prevents certain emotional areas being articulated. Vocally, the microphones give the voice an authoritative, professional quality to such an extent that the audience is never able to forget that characters are always performing.

During six weeks in April and May, the company decides to return to the notion of people explicitly presenting some sort of actual performance at the start of the show, rather than getting involved in their own narrative. They review Arthur's central role of 'Hans', so that he becomes a rather bad Presley impersonator, which links better with the second half of the play when he becomes the ghost of Elvis Presley. Second, they get rid of the seance material to support a clearer and firmer structure to the piece. Last, they decide to cut one video and make the remaining four all interviews, which suggest a constant interaction between video performers and live performers on stage. O'Connor points out that the final re-work process was about simplifying the work as 'there were all sorts of different kinds of theatre battling against one another', and that the relationship between the first and second half made little sense theatrically, intellectually or emotionally: 'this last stage of working on the show was about being quite clearheaded about what we already had that worked, and trying to apply that to the earlier part of the show so that there was a clear, formal development.' The opening section becomes a group of people telling a story quite ironically, described by Etchells as though 'they're winking at you probably whilst they're telling the story.'

The most important consideration of this period was to clarify an articulate, structural architecture for the piece. This was one reason for losing the seance material, which could only provide a short-lived resonance rather than give any depth to the show. It was clear that there were two shows in the material being used, which did not fit together, underlining an important point about how Forced Entertainment approaches structure. O'Connor suggests that structure has 'to mean something and be satisfying on a very basic level, rather than just a kind of architecture that is made up of very removed and complicated ideas'. In grappling with the problems of bringing several strands of text on to the stage, the emotional crises clearly articulated in the company's earlier shows, 'Let the Water Run its Course (To the Sea that Made the Promise)' and '200% & Bloody Thirsty', have become mislaid amongst the debris of structure and form in 'Some Confusions in the Law about Love'.

Performance

After the last re-work of 'Some Confusions in the Law about Love', I saw an early version of the new product at the Mirren Studio, Towngate Theatre, Basildon, on May 11th, 1990. I was slightly confused by the opening of the show, which now suggested that Arthur was performing some kind of poor-quality Elvis Presley act. I felt rather alienated and less involved as the women, a shabby sex act, reported on events surrounding 'Elvis', the 'crap' hotel, and so on. As spirits, the women were still covered in white muslin sheets, but were now in heaven looking down at earth with its cities and towns. The videos were more effective because they were all interviews, consistent in their presentational form, and integrated well with the text. The general playing style lacked bold definition. However, it must be said that I viewed the show in light of the three other versions I had seen, which did not enable me, as a spectator, to completely look afresh at the final, re-worked product.

Evaluation

The devising process for 'Some Confusions in the Law about Love' was relatively unusual for Forced Entertainment in the way the product changed so much. Within a five- to six-month working period, the company certainly generates and discards a vast amount of material, but normally only has one substantial re-work after the opening preview performances. This show had three or four fairly substantial re-workings, and it was still felt by the company that the show lacked the finished quality of their previous two products. It was felt to be a long, drawn out process, an uphill struggle, that did not fall inevitably into place after the first re-work, which was usually the experience with earlier shows. The company accepts that there is too much emphasis on the text in this piece, but believes that the devising process and product of 1989 to 1990 have brought a development of what Etchells describes as a 'whole system of strategies and approaches to text that we'll probably be exploiting again and again'.

This particular process has also been their first experience of working with people outside the core group of the company, which Etchells suggests has proved useful and interesting in terms of future inter-personal relationships, what that has done for the work, and the company's perception of it. Likewise, every show reveals deficiencies or weaknesses in the working structure of the company, or in group dynamics, as Etchells points out:

> I think it's been quite revelatory in that respect, probably because it's been incredibly pressurised, it didn't come right after one go, so it put more stress on all the people, on all the relationships, and on all the mechanics of the group's working.

The company discuss these issues informally, as Etchells recounts 'what you got out of the project, what you hated about it, where you felt let down, where you felt supported, wanted support or didn't get any'. This provokes a gut feeling of what to do, or not to do, next time. It is an instinctual reaction.

With regard to the next project, 'Marina and Lee' (1991), the company thought about action and finding a way of moving on stage before tackling the text. O'Connor indicates a desire not to let the text consume the whole experience of the show. 'Some Confusions in the Law about Love' became so text-based that the performers' role in the devising process changed considerably, because they were always waiting for the re-written text to arrive in the rehearsal room. O'Connor describes this role as 'applying what they could to it, making suggestions for the next re-write, talking about any ideas they'd had for the text', to the extent that the whole process became one that was based much more on discussion, rather than practical exploration or experimentation of ideas.

This was a different kind of generative process to the one used in 'Let the Water Run its Course (To the Sea that Made the Promise)', where all the structural or physical sections of the show came out of ideas that were then turned into improvisations, which were then tightened up and rehearsed as little set pieces. The energy of the whole piece evolved from bouncing off any physical energy that came out of improvis-ation or in rehearsal. By working primarily on action in 'Marina and Lee', the company hoped to arrive at a style of movement and a source of areas of possibly repeated action, described by O'Connor as 'giving us some clues as to the world of the people, what their interests are, what their kind of language is like'. The hope was that from this starting point, the company could make connections with text. This decision about the next process came out of their most recent experience of devising 'Some Confusions in the Law about Love', as O'Connor observes, 'starting with the action first in order to remedy the shortfall of action in the last show.'

SOME CONCLUSIONS

Forced Entertainment's working practice reveals the import-ance of a developmental process over time, as well as a sharp critical awareness and analysis of the relationship of process to product. The company's most recent show, 'Emanuelle Enchanted' (1992–93), demonstrates clearly the progression of work since 'Some Confusions in the Law about Love' in 1990. Since 1990, Forced Entertainment has moved in a new direc-tion, growing out of the problems and difficulties encountered with 'Some Confusions in the Law about Love', whilst building on the foundations of previous shows to produce an extraordinarily exciting piece of work in 'Emanuelle Enchanted'. This latest show displays a balanced integration of action, text, video, and visual and choreographic imagery. There is a maturity in 'Emanuelle Enchanted', which has both clarity and precision, combined with a rich performance playing style. The engine of 'Some Confusions in the Law about Love' has not just been put back together, but has been re-constituted to create highly innovative work.

The significance of these examples of Forced Entertainment's practice is to illustrate that devising is an ever-changing process. How this group works together making art raises questions about how to document such a process or product, the form of language or critical vocabulary to analyse work that integrates different kinds of 'text' (physical, visual, verbal), and the appropriate criteria to evaluate this area of devised experimental performance. I wish to discuss the theoretical implications of these issues later in this book, and here simply want to identify some areas for criticism and analysis within the wider context of the devising theatre debate.

Reflecting on the two selected examples of working practice from both ends of the devising spectrum, it is apparent that a theatrical performance can be created in a very short time on a limited budget, or over a much longer period with different decisions being made about the use of finance and resources in relation to the company's lifestyle. There are choices to be made regarding how much time is available to the process in relationship to the product, the ways that money is allocated or distributed within the project, and what is important about the making of the work. The value of the devising experience is not only for the company, but also for the audience participating in the theatrical communion. The elderly empathise with memories from the past that are represented in a linear, narrative storytelling framework, whilst those watching a Forced Entertainment performance construct their own narratives out of the present fragmentary moments or fractured images of culture and society. The space is there to take or make a personal picture of the world, and that is the magic of theatre.

What then are the similarities and differences of Age Exchange and Forced Entertainment's devising methodologies? A central difference between the companies is that Age

Exchange has a clearly targeted audience in the elderly, and a specific community interest in devising theatre. The company's intentions are narrowly defined to focus on a form of theatre that can be created in a number of ways, but is always working towards the goal of reminiscence theatre for the elderly. Pam Schweitzer has constructed a devising methodology that can be applied to any theme, although no two shows will ever be the same. In the case of Forced Entertainment, there is no devising methodology as such, only the previous experience of devising that enriches the next process or piece of work to be created. This is not to say that there are no thoughtful processes of working, or recognised patterns by the company of various ways to make a performance text, but rather to reiterate that every devising process is unique and integral to the creation of a particular, original theatrical experience.

In considering two very different kinds of theatre companies, working practices, processes, and subsequent shows, it is easy to see the breadth and nature of the devising experience from process to product. Perhaps it is a question of how much risk a company is prepared to take in its work, or simply of being clear on a starting point that still allows the freedom to change direction within the devising process. It is certainly about trusting a process that provides enough opportunity and space all the way through, which is often frightening, but is also at the core of being an artist and making art. This is not to suggest that a safety net of early knowledge of subject matter (be it theme, legend, or oral history) or form is disreputable, but rather to illustrate the point that a balance is needed of both security and risk.

5

FROM PROCESS TO PRODUCT

The participatory theatre-in-education programme

What's emerged from the programme is slightly different
for every group because they bring something different to
it, but the questions of freedom, rights and justice are very
centrally there, as well as loyalty and betrayal which are at
the heart of the programme.
(Viv Harris, Theatre-in-Education Team Leader,
Greenwich Young People's Theatre)

When considering a range of devised theatre products, it is
clear that they are the result of how a company combines a
variety of processes from its particular structure of operation.
The input and interest of a group of individuals determines
how the work will proceed. This interaction between company
members can inspire, engage or promote conflict about the
work, which is part of the devising process and creation of the
product. Leadership is essential in order to focus direction,
establish the way forward, and maintain an overall eye on the
developing work. Devising a theatre-in-education programme
utilises the many processes involved in creating community or
experimental theatre, but, in focussing on the needs and
interests of young people, also demands other ways of working
that are specific to this particular product.

The conscious decision to make a participatory programme
implies a desire to look at concepts, ideas, or source materials in
a number of different ways, as well as in relation to a particular
group of young people. A 'programme' suggests various
viewpoints, approaches, or ways of looking at the subject. The
theatre-in-education company wants its intended audience to
participate in the making of the programme, and in the
realisation of the product. It is the specific interaction between

actor-teachers and audience during the programme that makes a unique learning experience every time, with the possibility of always moving in a new, and ever-changing direction. Participation indicates a willingness between both actor-teachers and audience to cooperate, to share, to join in, and to have a say in the matter.

The audience is the focus for early decisions that relate to educational aims or objectives, learning areas, content, and form. The age range, type of children, and school environment all contribute to determining the kind of devised product or programme required. Assessing how to meet the needs of young people requires essential communication and interaction with pupils and teachers. Pre-visits to schools and potential audiences are vital to discover these interests so that the devising company may work from its audience at the start. During the devising process, it may prove important to 'workshop' potential ideas and material with an intended audience in order to keep sight of the reason for creating the theatre-in-education product. Using questions as a structural means of investigating concepts, subjects or issues is a popular tool employed in this area, as is investigation through exploring images to discover attitudes, ideas, or content. The extent to which a programme is participatory will also determine how the audience will experience the product, which clearly relates to decisions of structure and form.

STARTING POINTS

The decision to devise a theatre-in-education programme for upper secondary pupils by Greenwich Young People's Theatre was made a year prior to the theatre-in-education company determining the needs and interests of pupils and teachers against their own obsessions. An initial full, free-ranging company discussion in 1989 considered possible content, themes, issues, and concepts, which isolated the areas of Aids and the French Revolution for further discussion. The Revolution's Bicentenary celebrations, the Tiananmen Square atrocities in China, and events in Poland and Eastern Europe were all influential in contributing to discussions about perceptions in 1989, how people perceive the status quo as unchangeable, and what happens in terms of change when the hegemony of ideas is challenged. A third area of interest, homelessness, arose out of another debate on relevant material for young people. Although there were no formal meetings with teachers from local secondary schools, the education liaison officer talked with a selection of contact teachers for their initial responses to the proposed material.

Half a term later, a three-day workshop was held involving those company members who were to become the devising and performing team. Time was given to practically exploring material, discussing its contemporary relevance, and identifying the artistic and educational potential of each area. Workshops were led by three company members who had undertaken initial research. A decision was made to focus on events arising from the French Revolution as having the most educational and artistic potential of the three interests. At this stage, the prime concern was with the involvement of the French in the United Irishmen's Rebellion in 1798. A core team of theatre-in-education team leader, writer, musical director, and education liaison officer researched the material, keeping in close contact with the rest of the team by sharing research and keeping them in touch with changes in thinking. The potential use of music was also being discussed by the team, and it was during this period that the United Irishmen Rebellion disappeared in favour of a French setting.

Theatre-in-education team leader Viv Harris observes: 'At the beginning of each programme everyone within the team will identify the particular areas they may want to concentrate on, whether they be strengths or weaknesses.'[1] The dynamics of Greenwich Young People's Theatre is such that the four actor-teachers involved in 'The Edge of Reason' were unable to be active from the starting point of the process and came back later to the work via the specialist core team. Although the Greenwich company is hierarchically structured, the theatre-in-education team work cooperatively with the actor-teachers, who contribute significantly to the devising process in addition to performing, and this takes account of both individual and objective needs of the work. Whatever the starting point, the team must constantly return to addressing the original aims and objectives of the company. An unpublished company policy statement of July 1987 asserts that 'Our thoughts and our attitudes, as well as our material lives, are dominated by the ideology and values of the white patriarchal, capitalist society in which we live.' As a company, Greenwich Young People's Theatre is committed to using drama and theatre in an educational context to raise awareness and consciousness of that situation. This is affirmed in the same 1987 policy statement:

> As educationalists, our task is not to give pupils the right answers but to find the right, the most useful, questions and empower the pupils to develop their own understandings, raise their own questions and find their own answers. As artists we acknowledge our responsibility to use and develop our skills to create high quality theatre. However, if it is to be an effective tool for liberation of thought and action, our theatre must reflect our educational aims in both content and form.

Greenwich Young People's Theatre is also committed to developing participatory forms 'that empower young people to take control of their creativity and their own learning' (1987 policy statement). In this same document the director of the company, Chris Vine, stresses the need to challenge dialectically, to 'recognise the contradictions of experience and seek to sharpen these (emotionally and intellectually) employing the full range of forms available'. Vine argues that 'The task is not to endorse the last answer, but to pose the next question.' Participation is part of the company's policy, and at some point the theatre-in-education team must decide whether the programme will be fully participatory or not. Other early decisions include the degree of theatricality in the piece, whether it is to be a touring show or an in-house programme, the budget allocated to the 'Teachers' Notes' or 'Follow-up Work', as well as issues relating to the company's overall activities, such as the external constraints of scheduling youth shows, special needs projects and the timetabling commitment of technical staff.

Preparation

'The Edge of Reason' will be freely available to approximately thirty secondary schools in the Greenwich and Lewisham areas of south London. A resource pack of 'Teachers' Notes' that offers preparatory materials with specified aims and objectives is sent to all those involved. There will be a pre-programme teachers' session after school hours about two weeks prior to the opening of the programme, when an extract of the play or participatory section may be shown, and teachers are briefed on what pupils should have done before their visit. Vine suggests that there is good Drama practice in local schools with a very supportive Drama Inspector and Drama Teachers' Support Group. However, all may change from April 1990, when the Inner London Education Authority is disbanded and the company works in collaboration with the Boroughs of Greenwich and Lewisham,[2] who will provide funding alonside the London Borough Grants Scheme, and via The Arts Council of Great Britain's grant to the parent company, The Greenwich Theatre.[3]

At the end of the summer term 1989, a structural framework for a day's participatory programme has been established, and includes an introductory section, a play, and some form of 'role play' situation. The relationship of individual and collective freedom is examined over a period of four days, when the team 'workshop' and improvise both form and content. This leads to an agreed outline scenario of a 'Holding scene' (proposed by the writer), and educational aims leading from it. Later to become the play's ending, this scene of a father's betrayal of a loyal daughter contains all the concepts of the programme, providing a focus for a way forward to developing the work. The scenario refers to the play part of the programme, and establishes four central characters, a setting in a village bakery outside Paris, as well as ideas for using music, mime, and movement. The team also agrees the brief that a play be at the heart of the programme, preceded by an introduction to the historical and social context of the play, which will be explored non-naturalistically through dance/drama. Possible areas for active involvement of the pupils are also earmarked at this stage, which may examine the legacy of revolution through other contemporary revolutionary situations and how people take control. Individuals take responsibility for specific and general research over the vacation, such as examining revolutions in the nineteenth and twentieth centuries, or considering possible images for the introduction. This will be the working situation when the whole team comes together in September 1989.

Objectives

One of the aims of the programme is not to engage young people in a historical exposition of the French Revolution, but in agreed concepts of what people would sacrifice for liberty, or where values come from. 1789 is a vehicle to explore these concepts. It is through experiencing the concepts and issues via theatre or drama that young people make choices and decisions, drawing on their own experiences, and relating to their world. However, the actor-teachers must improvise and discuss a range of research materials linked to the French Revolution in order to create the reality of a village, Crèvecœur, in northern France.

In the first week of the new academic year 1989–90, markers are laid down for the form and content of the introductory 'dance/drama'. The group makes a sound picture of images arising from the material so far, and participates in a visual exercise that creates two-dimensional representations of the Revolution in 1789 and 1794 from the point of view of each of the four characters. A scenario/script discussion examines whether the material inevitably leads to naturalism, and questions the overall objectives of the play including the functional objectives of the characters. Possible titles for the programme are 'brainstormed' by the company, and a draft copy of the leaflet for the schools' handout is agreed.

Methodology

The company reviews its work weekly, keeping a log-book or diary of its activities, looking ahead and planning next week's objectives. The following week sees individual discussions with the team leader and musical director, identifying that everyone wants to develop his or her voice and use harmony, and is keen to include musical anachronism and an integrated musical form. The unpublished company diary for September 12th, 1989 records, 'N.B.:– For your voices sake don't smoke, don't eat cheese, do eat apricots.'

Practical exercises are set up to consider the different ways that individual freedom is restricted, with particular reference to the Baker's daughter. This is done through company members 'brainstorming' ideas, creating and discussing pictorial, static, group images or tableaux. Character histories are built-up for the Baker, Cézar Cachelin, his sister Charlotte, his daughter Rhea, and the Jacobin, Lefer. The studio space becomes covered in wall posters that note these developments, and a blackboard is used to chart specific areas of research.

On entering Studio One (one of Greenwich Young People's Theatre's two theatre spaces), I am confronted with a wealth of materials that includes a section of floor covered with musical instruments, a presentation of visual images that display the characters in 1789 and 1794, and numerous 'sheets' of hanging wallpaper that indicate individual qualities of characters and how they are perceived by others. A further exercise to develop characterisation is for each character to list their feelings, actions, and mental and physical attitudes. (See Appendix II for example of Baker's daughter.) The characteristics of each character as perceived by the others are explored through improvisation as if they were animal, element, sound, meal, material, or colour. Each actor-teacher visits and investigates the three others' special or secret spaces, noting how it makes them feel physically as an animal in that particular area of the studio. (See Appendix II for illustration of Baker's daughter's perceptions of others.)

The story and accessibility of material so far is discussed in terms of points to be developed, form and style. There is a brief reference to casting, including the possibility of cross-casting in the introductory section. The education liasion officer takes the company through two possible exercises for the 'Teachers' Notes' pack. There is also a read-through of monologues which the writer has prepared prior to a pre-visit to two local secondary schools. (See Appendix II for specimen monologues.)

PRELIMINARY AUDIENCE FEEDBACK

Visiting local schools before and during the process is common to many companies devising a theatre-in-education pro-gramme. The aims of such visits will vary, but they are often concerned with discovering more information about the pupils' interests in the classroom. The pre-visit by the Greenwich team to a fourth-year English group at Kidbrooke School on September 14th, 1989 aimed to find out what pupils knew about the French Revolution via the material, and where to pitch the show. A small group planned the visit to include a research exercise using the 'brainstorming' technique, and work that tested the concepts of freedom, individual rights, and liberty beyond the personal level. Three monologues were written by John Wood with the purpose of gaining initial feedback from the young people, through which the team hoped to establish and identify which chararacters provoked more sympathy, and why.

After a brief introduction that describes the company's work, one team member questions the class on what they think about the French Revolution. This is verbal 'brainstorming', and the answers are immediately written on the blackboard. Feelings, views and attitudes are encouraged through a series of further questions. The team leader asks the reasons why people were involved in the French Revolution, suggesting that this is discussed in pairs for one minute. Viv Harris summarises points from this, which leads to the question 'What is liberty?' The young people talk in groups for two minutes about what freedom means to them in 1989, establishing whether they are free today. In my group of three boys of mixed race, they decide that being free is not to be dominated by the adult world, which means not being oppressed by parents, teachers, or policemen. Following this, the scene is set in 1794 with the revolutionary government in power, and an event that might have happened involving three characters at the time.

An actor-teacher gives a preamble about fighting as a group and there being no freedom for the enemies of liberty. The team lines up to represent a queue as the first character's monologue is from a woman fed up with queuing for bread every day. The second offers the Baker's perspective on the situation from behind the counter, and the third establishes the character of the prosecutor, who reveals that the woman has stolen bread and is therefore an enemy of the revolution. The prosecutor presents the case to the class:

> Citizens. You have heard the testimonies. France is at war. There have to be sacrifices. This woman puts herself above everything. *She* is hungry. *She* is impatient. *She* is the enemy of the revolution! Leading a mob against the interests of the revolution makes her a counter revolu-

tionary. You shake your heads. No, you say, she did not intend to be that, she only wanted bread.[4]

Groups of pupils are allowed two minutes to discuss at least two questions that can be asked characters to find out more information. One group 'hot seats' the actor-teacher, playing the member of government 'in role', as to why the woman should be guillotined, and is told that this is one individual versus the freedom of the nation. The Baker is questioned about whether he would have felt the same way if a man had broken into his shop, and the Woman is asked to consider other women who did not receive bread the next day. In answer to why she is against the revolution, the woman replies that the revolution is not all equal.

The team leader brings the visit to a conclusion by asking questions that lead to the area of how easy it is to decide who is guilty and who is innocent. The vote to establish which character is right indicates that nearly all the class support the Woman, no-one is in favour of the Prosecutor, and most are suspicious of the Baker. The feedback from this visit suggests that the notion of collective government is alien to the pupils, with the language of the Jacobin's speech being difficult to follow, suggesting that this character will need to be totally engaging if the pupils are to relate to him. Both schools brought an immediate response to the Woman's plight and disliked the chauvinism of the Baker. These areas must be addressed through the theatre of the programme, which uses the vehicle of the French Revolution to set an agenda that addresses the issue of individualism against the group. This must also be explored through the participation section of the programme, which could use images to investigate how pupils make judgements further.

CLARIFYING GOALS

The devising process of theatre-in-education involves a constant re-evaluation of the work in light of educational and artistic objectives; for example, how can the characters in the scenario be used to explore the educational aims of the piece? It is a period of continued research through reading, visits to Museums, or personal resources, which contributes to 'on the floor' work and discussion. Creating a story about what might have been is based on this research, and includes theatrical possibilities as well as educational challenges. The play will be set in a village outside Paris in January 1794. The Baker, a self-made man and an opportunist, is against the Revolution. He is a widower and has a sixteen-year-old daughter. His sister lives in Paris, is a secret revolutionary, and helps politicise her brother's daughter. The Jacobin is an ambitious man, sent to purge the village of anti-revolutionary forces, but who falls in love with the Baker's daughter. Family loyalties and politics are at the heart of the drama, with the Baker denouncing his sister to cover himself, the daughter denouncing her father to protect her aunt, and the Jacobin challenged by the daughter to make the right decision. The participatory part of the programme is focussed and shaped, making the work more concrete and highlighting the fact that the pupils must be able to relate emotionally to the work. The programme has to address the conceptual level and language of fourth-year secondary pupils.

In the remaining weeks of the devising period, the team discusses scenario developments, such as the Introduction, which needs a concise input that covers oppression or injustice pre-1789, and considers the start of the play through the fragmentary presentation of the four characters, whether by staging or use of music. The group refocuses its educational aims by asking questions: 'Why do a programme on the French Revolution at this time?'; 'What are the educational or social needs of the young people at this time?'; or 'Does the material speak truthfully to the young people?' Working from a key scene at the heart of act two, the team speculates further on content, and improvisations are videoed around particular ideas. The writer then sets to work on the script. There are updates from the musical director on the development of music and song, from the education liaison officer on the 'Teachers' Notes', and a character costume workshop is led by the designer. The non-naturalistic visual opening planned to give a background to the French Revolution is abandonned as the transition to the play is difficult and unclear for the audience.

The original intentions behind the participation work were to involve the pupils in a strong, emotional way in the issues of freedom, change, loyalty and betrayal, as well as engaging them sensually in the conflicts of the period through a piece of physical theatre. These were modified in light of lack of devising time available, and the length of the play in relation to the programme. Chris Vine, the company's director, led various sessions on participation, and was responsible for this area of work. Three contrasting images of people who were not free were selected by Vine as part of the image forum work at the start of the programme. Pupils would be asked if they could see anyone unfree in each image, and to try to change the situation. The idea was to move from the familiar and close to home to considering different views of freedom in a wider world context. Later in the programme, after seeing the play, the young people would be confronted with the same challenges to individual and collective freedom as the characters faced in the play. A 'role play' section would explore the conflict between the rights of the individual and the need for collective action.

Devising a participatory programme that involves the audience in choices and decision-making means finding a subtle balance and relationship between constructed historical material and the present, socio-political, economic, and cultural climate or reality. This is not easy. It is not just a question of how much 'play' and how much 'participation', but concerns the kind of learning actively taking place through the chosen form of theatrical experience. In order to give space to both artistic and educational needs of the day-long programme, there is inevitably compromise in some areas of the work. This programme has chosen to focus on the devised play, written by the writer-in-residence, and performed as a piece of devised theatre. However, it is within the context of the pupils' immediate situation, and addressed through an examination of particular concepts and questions.

THE PRODUCT

The first performance of the full-day participatory programme 'The Edge of Reason' was given on November 2nd, 1989 to fourth- and fifth-year pupils from Eltham Green Comprehensive school. We wait in the lobby area to be collected and taken into the drama studio. An actor-teacher welcomes us into the space, followed by introductions by the team and an explanation of the day's programme. A sign is held up with a statement and question, 'For people to be happy, they need to be free', 'What does it mean to be free?', and the audience are asked for a response. An actor-teacher proposes that we get into groups to discuss what freedom means to us. I listen in to a discussion about less freedom at school, Margaret Thatcher taking away people's freedom, living on a desert island, only being free if totally alone, and 'there's no such thing as total freedom'. Back together again, another actor-teacher leads a general discussion, which moves to three actor-teachers making a still picture of a man on his knees with hands tied behind his back in between two others standing with sticks by his side. The audience are questioned about how they could change this picture, and after several interventions by the pupils, they are asked again about the altered image of freedom.

In the second constructed image, a pupil is dressed in an apron, holding a saucepan, ladle and baby, and the actor-teacher asks the young people to 'make the woman freer'. Different ideas are tried out, including the removal of the baby, placing the apron on a male pupil next to her, and the final image of two women bending down and pointing at the baby. The final picture also employs a pupil, sitting in a long black coat with a sign round his neck saying, 'Nowhere to live – Please help'. The discussion here centres on the issue of happiness, money, and freedom of choice. An actor-teacher questions the audience about all three pictures in terms of different kinds or types of freedom. The first image is considered the worst, as the man was tied up and could not simply walk away. One team member points out that the imprisoned man did have the freedom to think, which is met with the retort, 'That's not going to help him!' It is concluded that we cannot ever be totally free and that laws or rules are necessary to society. We are asked to refocus on the statement and question at the start during a five-minute break. The actor-teachers have facilitated an enquiry through questions, discussion, and forum image work. On our return, we will watch the play.

The seeds have been sown in terms of acknowledging the participatory framework for the programme. A form of enquiry has been initiated to encourage the pupils to think about the concept of freedom via group discussion and visual imagery. The images or still tableaux are effective in promoting an active dialogue between the young people and actor-teachers. The pictures have provoked an emotional reaction in the audience, which has then been explored further in the visual/verbal deconstruction and re-construction of the original images. The pupils' involvement in the participation has demonstrated the importance of both visual and verbal consensus, as well as emotional and intellectual understanding. This first section of the programme has introduced certain concepts and questions about the nature of freedom, challenging and exploring initial reactions to the subject.

The actors are dressed in period French Revolution costumes. The setting reminds me of a rural barn dotted with bales of straw, bags of grain and wooden farm implements. In front of a central wooden platform is an area of sand covered in feathers and pebbles. We are sitting on three sides of the studio space. It is an hour later, and the musical director explains that they are now going to perform a play called 'The Edge of Reason' set in France five years after the revolution. We focus on four characters from the village of Crèvecœur, who briefly introduce themselves before the lighting changes and the first scene commences. The Jacobin has a letter from the Committee and is ordered to collect the grain. Modern electric guitar music begins and the actor sings his first song as the Jacobin. The pupils show signs of embarassment at the contemporary music and direct singing approach to the audience. We then witness the Baker putting the flour into sacks, 'One for the revolution and one for me'. He then grates chalk into the revolution flour sack. The set is certainly impressive and includes a slide for the sacks to go down, a ladder, a pulley, and a hook. We learn that the Baker's sister, Charlotte, has arrived from Paris, and that the Jacobin is here to see the Baker.

The pace is a little slow in the first few scenes. The playing style is established with the use of musical sounds and song integrated into the text. Using the synthesiser to create an atmosphere on a dark night, we see two people wrapped in shawls stealing the flour. This raises the issue of whether stealing is acceptable when a woman is starving and eating grass. Rhea, the Baker's daughter, disputes this with the Jacobin, who argues the case for thinking of France first and foremost. On discovering a villager has one stolen bag of flour, the Jacobin has her hanged. Meanwhile, Charlotte has discovered the hidden bags of grain and suggests that her brother

11 Anthony Burbage, Lloyd Notice, Anne Clifford (Aine Clubhan), and Carole Lythgoe in 'The Edge of Reason'. Greenwich Young People's Theatre, 1989–90. (Photo: John Daniell.)

gives every villager an extra loaf free to get rid of the flour and to save face with the villagers after the Jacobin has left. It is at this point that we break for lunch, returning in the afternoon to watch the final act of the play.

Act three opens with the musical director on electric guitar in steel blue light playing an instrumental number. Issues and conflicts are already in place as the characters continue to argue about the needs of the individual against the needs of the village or of France. The Jacobin jumps to a hasty conclusion when he discovers Rhea with one of his letters open; he accuses her of being a spy. All the characters turn on each other with the Jacobin accusing Charlotte of 'counter-revolutionary activities', and Rhea telling her father that he is the enemy. The play ends and we are given five minutes to reflect on which of these characters we would trust most.

After a brief break, the audience discuss which characters believed in freedom, what choices they had, and whether any of them were happy in their situation. The pupils are then asked which of the four characters they would trust most to do the best for everyone. The characters are lined up according to the pupils' wishes, and Rhea is an ever-popular choice. This later alternates with Charlotte, and all are agreed that the Baker would be the last choice. From this, the team set up a participatory drama where the young people will play the villagers in a role-play situation. We are told that it is thirty minutes after the villager has been hanged by the Jacobin, and Charlotte has called a secret meeting with the villagers at the bakery. The musical director is to play the villager's husband, Jean, to help further potential action. The pupils are asked to consider what is justice, their needs and their rights. After several suggestions are given, they form into small groups to decide on three or four things they want to change in the village or in France. I listen in to a group discussing the issue of food, ownership of the mill, and how far they are prepared to go if the Baker will not give up his mill.

Each group reports back and the pupils discuss a plan of action. We are then told that Charlotte has been taken prisoner and she is chained up in front of us. The Jacobin addresses the villagers and says that all secret meetings must stop, the villagers must think of France, and all grain is to be collected for the soldiers, who are fighting for the good of France. It is the villagers' decision as to what should be done with the bags of grain. The actor-teachers initiate some seeds of discussion, such as the freeing of Charlotte in exchange for grain, the need to listen to each other's ideas, the problems of too many individual decisions and not enough collective agreement. The group decides to set Charlotte free before the Jacobin returns. He demands to know who untied her, and two pupils are arrested and sent to Paris. The villagers talk of killing the Jacobin and the alternatives available to them. At this point the role play ceases and we return to our seats.

The musical director reminds us of the sign with the statement and question, commenting that the villagers did not feel free, and that the Jacobin had the power of government behind him. One pupil suggests that they were weaker when everyone had different ideas and did not stick together. However, despite a majority decision, there were two young people who did not abide by the agreement. The team leads a more general discussion about freedom in terms of choices and life today, which relates back to the French Revolution and what happened after the people had taken action. A last question is posed: 'Is it worth making sacrifices if you want something badly?'

The play forms a long part of the day's programme, which means that the participatory work can only scratch the surface rather than grapple with the depths of the issue. The role play is too discursive, and pupils are sitting for a long time. Somehow there needs to be more action, rather than talking the consequences through. The forum image work allows the young people to try ideas out, but this occurs earlier in the programme. The team agrees that more concrete information is needed about Charlotte and the Jacobin if the role play is to progress further. All observations and comments will be fed back into two re-work days which will change material or shape the programme differently. I look forward to visiting again in light of these sessions.

THE RE-WORKED VERSION

On November 24th, 1989 I make my second visit to Greenwich Young People's Theatre, with fourth- and fifth-year pupils from Abbey Wood School. There are now two opening questions: 'What do people mean when they say they want to be free?' and 'Why does freedom mean different things to different people?' In discussing freedom, the young people decide that the most important freedom is to be able to do what you want. The still picture work has been developed to look at more alternative ways of improving the situation. The first image, of a man with his hands tied guarded by two others, is now contextualised as South Africa. The actor-teachers probe whether violence is the only means of settling the problem, and a role-play situation that includes new characters is acted out. A constant problem for the actor-teacher who facilitates the participation is to avoid asking the pupils closed questions or promoting a predetermined structure. The danger becomes imminent when there are no responses or answers forthcoming from the group. The main time is dedicated to the first image, with some discussion of the second picture about the woman, baby and saucepan. Freedom in this instance is paid help!

The difference at the start of the play is in the monologues by the four characters, which are clearer and more informative for the audience. We are able to identify with them more easily. The Jacobin now brings grain to be milled into flour from Paris, and informs the villagers that someone is storing grain that should be sent to Paris. There are minor changes in the script and slow gaps between scenes. Charlotte suggests that the mill should be communal, that 'everyone would have an equal share', with villagers helping to improve it. We are more aware that the Jacobin's job is in conflict with his personal feelings and relationships. The script seems more detailed in clarifying both characters and situation.

The questioning by the actor-teacher in the afternoon is more specific to the characters. What were their ambitions, desires, or objectives in the play? Charlotte is the character they would trust most, and yet the Jacobin is the person they would want to lead them in the revolution. Before the role-play drama begins, the audience are shown a short scene with the husband of the hanged villager. In the secret meeting at the Bakery, the group agrees rules, which include taking over the mill and providing equal food for everyone, and trying people that steal grain in the People's Court. Decisions are structured into the meeting through voting, and writing them on a blackboard. Joint leadership of Charlotte and one pupil is

12 Schoolchildren and Carole Lythgoe, Anthony Burbage, Lloyd Notice, Robbie McGovan, and Vivien Harris in 'The Edge of Reason'. Greenwich Young People's Theatre, 1989–90. (Photo: John Daniell.)

agreed, as well as a series of demands to present to the Jacobin. When requested to give all the grain back to the soldiers, the pupils discuss the possibilities in four groups. On knowing that Charlotte has been arrested for the counter-revolutionary activity of calling a secret meeting, the immediate response is to hide the grain and capture Charlotte. A kind of 'Forum Theatre' results where pupils try out their suggestions; for example, a villager attempts a reasoned argument with the Jacobin, in order to examine the central, underlying question of whether it is better to obey the leadership (and save France), or whether to think first of the villagers themselves. The Jacobin asks the young people if the English were invading, would they keep the grain as villagers or give it to the soldiers fighting for them? The participation is clearer and more concrete, yet the villagers are still faced with complex decisions related to themselves as a group, the grain, and Charlotte's position or predicament.

FUNCTION

Devising a participatory theatre-in-education programme for young people raises a general question about the purpose of making or creating a theatrical experience for any specified group or targeted audience. How and why does devising a participatory programme about the French Revolution make a different educational impact on secondary pupils than merely staging a play about it for schools? The simplest answer has to be that the programme has been devised for young people, and asks them to participate in a sharing, learning process of discovery with the actor-teachers. The programme enables the pupils to question what they see, to challenge what they are told, to look at the contradictions of a concept, and to creatively 'role play' a situation.

The audience is empowered to make decisions, to choose a course of action, to listen to various points of view, and to elect a way forward for themselves. Watching the single vision of a playwright's play about the French Revolution in isolation does not provide the learning experience gained from the participatory theatre-in-education programme. The pupils engage with the actor-teachers in a different way to being passive spectators of a play, or to their everyday pupil–teacher relationship in a classroom. The participatory nature of the programme provides an alternative educational and artistic experience, which encourages active learning, questions beliefs, and offers many possibilities of changing pre-conceived ideas or thinking. Such is the value and power of this particular form of devised theatre, as opposed to the performed play script where the audience watches, is told, and then goes away.

The devised participatory theatre-in-education programme allows young people the opportunity to explore and experience concepts, to socially rehearse their ideas, thoughts, or beliefs within an open-ended structure of learning. Each group of participants contributes and receives a unique knowledge from the programme, which is different for every visiting school. The targeted audience (the fourth-year secondary school pupils), have been part of both process and product, in the sense that the theatre-in-education team has devised for, from, and with them. It is vital to 'workshop' ideas with pupils in order to gain feedback from the intended audience while devising; it is integral to the learning process that young people 'hot seat' characters, 'role play' a difficult situation, or actively join in during the programme.

The team has constantly refered to agreed artistic and educational objectives throughout the devising process, addressing and re-assessing the purpose and function of making such a programme. Devising a participatory theatre-in-education programme is a decision to give young people time and space to express, exchange, and change their views or opinions generally. The power and value of this form of devised theatre cannot be overstated; it is yet another way of understanding the world we live in, and ourselves. Theatre-in-education has always been marginalised in terms of the dominant British literary theatre tradition, yet it offers young people the chance to enrich their social and cultural experience of contemporary life in Britain. In the 1990s it is needed even more now that Drama is not included in the National Curriculum, and there is even less potential for this kind of educational and artistic work. There is much uncertainty, change, and confusion as we move towards the twenty-first century, highlighting the need to continue opportunities to devise participatory theatre-in-education programmes for young people.

6

SPACE
Site-specific theatre

A devised show sets sail without quite knowing where it
will land. For this reason it feels quite risky but it can
produce surprises and respond to possibilities unrestricted
by fixed narrative.

(Collective statement of IOU Theatre)

I have argued that devised theatre may start from any number
of possible sources or stimuli, be they oral reminiscences, text,
image, music, concept, or an audience. In the case of site-
specific devised theatre, it is the location itself that provides the
potential structure, form, content, and participants for the
piece. A residency is defined by a company being resident in a
particular place, and creating a show specifically for that site.
For some professional companies this is only one aspect of their
overall work, whilst for others it is integral to their continuous
development in exploring and experimenting with alternative
ways of making theatre.

What is common to all companies involved in devising
theatre from a specific site, is the desire to make or create a
product from a particular environment, using their particular
skills or work practices as appropriate. There are often strong
elements of the visual, the physical, and the performance.
There may also be the notion of an event, a celebration, or a
spectacular occasion, which will vary and be determined by
every individual company, the special circumstances of the
residency, and available funding. Site-specific devised theatre
can include local involvement from a range of participants, and
be classed as community theatre in one sense, or, in contrast,
may consist of company members only working towards an
installation or piece of performance art.

125

In order to illustrate the spectrum of site-specific work, I want to take IOU Theatre as one example of the detailed, performance art area of devised theatre, and compare it to the large-scale events with communities created by Major Road Theatre Company. Both companies have a visual and musical emphasis, working collaboratively towards indoor or outdoor shows. Somewhere in between are examples from Fork-beard Fantasy and Lumiere & Son, as illustrated in the comic art of visual, sculptural constructions outdoors, or in the performance pieces devised in or out of the locations of Kew Gardens, Nottingham Castle, or the Penzance swimming pool.

THE NON-THEATRICAL SPACE

The current policy of IOU is:

> To invent and develop a rich form of theatre where music, imagery and words can combine with equal status. To present the work in a wide range of venues, indoor and outdoor touring shows being balanced with site specific productions. IOU's work is characterised by vivid images, distinctive sets and original music with an emphasis on atmosphere rather than plot.[1]

Since 1976 this company has prioritised devising work for landscapes and buildings not normally used as theatre venues, with the aim of reaching a wider cross-section of the public rather than a conventional theatre-going audience. Some of IOU's most memorable productions grew out of residencies in specially chosen locations, where the building or landscape influenced and shaped the show. It is the environment that inspires and stimulates the company's creative process, which is of prime importance when devising for a specific site. The company suggests that, 'the physical characteristics of the space condition the narrative, structurally and in content.'[2] It is the setting that generates and determines ideas for a show, which in IOU terms means building in to the place that they will be performing in. This company has devised shows in a variety of places, including disused houses, beaches, cathedrals, woods, castles, rooftops, mills, and others.

Residencies have enabled the company to create performances for a specific location, either indoor or outdoor, over a period of weeks on a site. Sometimes ambitious in scale, pieces have exploited particular environmental characteristics, producing a unique kind of devised theatre. One such example was 'The House', which was originally commissioned by Chapter Arts Centre in Cardiff; a second version was produced and performed in June 1982 for the Almeida Festival in London. An undertaker's derelict three-storey house and garden provided the setting for the London production. The company landscaped the garden, built outhouses and rooftop platforms, and constructed rooms inside the house to produce a show which used both indoor and outdoor space at the same time. The occupants of the house were observed in detail through the windows, with their everyday lives being interrupted by extraordinary visitations, including an angel descending from the rooftop down a sixty-foot ladder, giant bees crashing a stolen car into the bushes, and an aviator, who circled the rooftops and climbed out on to the wing of his aircraft to deliver a parcel of fire.

In an article, 'Back to the Garden', Meira Eilash described this piece as

a structure of collage or assemblage, in which an overall framework is given to a collection of elements, not necessarily connected to each other in a logical, informative manner, but creating in total an effect of perceptible, visual information; always rich and stimulating on the imagery level, sometimes one of conceptual accumulation, as well.[3]

'The House' demanded weeks of preparation and intensive work from a strong, artistic team. The diversity of work (administrative, technical, artistic, and practical construction) required a large amount of organisation at all stages of the devising process. Performance ideas were developed through discussions, from individuals' own work, from music, and from made objects for the site. Examples of objects or props were: the conversion of a lawnmower into a police motorcycle;the adaptation of a scrap car for the 'Bees' sequence; and the building of a twenty-five-foot aircraft and mounting it on to a revolving hydraulic access crane. The final shaping and editing of the show occured as late as possible. Once an order of main scenes was decided, linking or bridging scenes were devised and rehearsed. The fine tuning of all the performance elements did not happen until the dress rehearsal stage and run of performances.

When devising a show, the creativity of the performers is given as much scope as is physically and practically possible. A structure is needed in order to proceed, so core members of the company invent an initial framework that allows exploration of images and themes. Members of the company believe that it is important to get an overall shape, albeit perceived through a fog: 'images, themes, action, music and words have to keep being knitted, unpicked, and re-knitted.' It is necessary to be open-ended at every stage so that detail may surprise and contradict rather than be imposed in advance. It is this balance between improvisation and structure that is absolutely crucial for IOU, so that individual performers have the opportunity and freedom for exploring possibilities, as well as the chance to develop the various elements of the created world into a final product. This way of working demands space for spontaneity in the process, and also relies on particular individuals in the core group pursuing their own artistic preoccupations. Originally, IOU's work was motivated by a desire to develop alternatives to the gallery system, wanting to explore different ways of looking at paintings or sculpture, and how these could be combined with music. Theatre was the most appropriate medium for this group of artists, who were from a fine art or classical music background rather than performance.

Company structure

From 1976 to 1987, there was no overall director and it was the contradiction of individuals' ideas, pooled and shaped by each other, that created an energy that made IOU's work so particular. As a collective of six artists or so, and two administrators, they worked in collaboration as a tightly-knit group, seeing the work through all stages with no one person in charge. Core members tended to have roles that took account of their skills in relation to devising or making, such as songs, costumes, machines, poems, technical, music, and lighting design. Now, in the 1990s, the company has a more hierarchical structure. A director is often appointed for a show, with individual members taking responsibility for specific aspects of the project. For IOU, devising is about the combining of different people's ideas and talents into a complete show. It is during the process that these ideas define themselves against each other and 'a pattern emerges'.

Music is a foundation of any IOU created world, composed and performed live by musicians in the company, forming an equal strand with the action rather than simply having an illustrative function. The way that music, artefacts, props, costumes, and images are pieced together, as well as the way scenes move from one to another, is very particular to this company's work:

> IOU shows are pieced together in a very filmic way. Scenes are edited together, cut together abruptly or slid one into another. The music holds this non-narrative sequence together, the juxtaposition of familiar and unfamiliar instruments and styles is an integral part of the shifting atmospheres.

Likewise words are only one thread in the weave or pattern of work, and stories or meanings are never conveyed through speech or dialogue. In site-specific products the relationship of people to the material world observed is vital, with shows dipping in and referring to a wide range of ideas that have informed our culture. Meaning accumulates and surfaces through significant moments, images, insights, or the unusual and surprising connections that are one of the features of IOU's work.

Within the context of devising site-specific shows, IOU is excited by making theatre that explores the possibilities of varying combinations of art forms, including poetry, music, dance, puppetry, painting, and sculpture or mechanical devices, working out of the site and with the interests of the individual artists. Inevitably, this means experimenting with ideas, images, construction and painting, with the knowledge that the making and doing will be constantly replaced by new attempts to find the most appropriate means of expression. More recently, the company has been open to influences outside the core, working with other performers, which has brought a broader range of possibilities to the form of its pieces.

Products

Two such examples are 'Just Add Water' (1989) and 'Full Tilt' (1990–91). The former was a large-scale outdoor touring piece that explored the beaches of Britain. The performance suggests a traditional beach-type show at the outset, and includes: a magician, dressed in a long, blue gown and matching hat that looks like a whipped ice-cream, performing conjuring tricks; a female trapeze artist costumed in a pale blue silky leotard with rosettes on the knees, who swings high above; and a Punch and Judy show played from inside a red and white, horizontally striped tower that rises from the circular platform supported by scaffolding and a ladder. Having gathered around the troupe with particular expectations, the audience's attention is then diverted to the arrival of a team of scientists in a curious, white vehicle that is exploring the beach. The front section is similar to a space capsule with round windows on wheels, the middle part is reminiscent of a fork-lift truck, and the last section resembles a cylinder below a balcony with a plastic, transparent tent at one end, white railings, and a ladder to the sand. The show's interest is in the collision of these two worlds (the interaction of the familiar with the unreal) in a mixture of humour, music, images, and contradictory meanings.

This was also the case with 'Full Tilt', which was devised as an outdoor summer touring show for parks, city centres, fêtes, and festivals. It is a visual spectacle, full of colourful costumes, lively music, objects, and extraordinary machines. There is no narrative or single meaning to this show, but the spectators receive an experience of changing images, moods, perceptions, and portrayals. Exciting, rhythmic music plays as an elaborate machine is driven around the space; two acrobats in skin-tight, yellow flecked outfits tumble across a centrally positioned white performance mat; a woman in a red farthingale skirt opens either side of her constructed costume to store various objects; and someone on a tricycle horse (wearing a corrugated iron neck-piece collar and yellow armour) wields a weapon in pursuit of a black bin.

13   Deborah Pope in 'Just Add Water'. IOU Theatre, 1989. (Photo: Sheila Burnett.)

14   Chris Squire in 'Full Tilt'. IOU Theatre, 1990–91. (Photo: *Evening Courier*, Halifax.)

COMMUNITY EVENTS

In direct contrast to the detailed performance work of IOU's site-specific products is the approach taken by Major Road Theatre Company when devising large-scale, site-specific spectacles or events with local communities. Major Road Theatre Company was formed in London in 1973 by Graham Devlin, and in 1978 moved to Bradford, West Yorkshire, where it is based now. There are four full-time staff, and the company operates as an employing management, so that individuals are taken on for specific pieces of work. Major Road concentrates on touring new or little-performed work at small or middle-scale venues, and on devising performances with community casts in a variety of informal settings. Over the last ten years, this company has developed a particular approach to devising and creating theatre events with and for local communities. A residency involves a team of Major Road artists devising a performance event with a community of local people. The team acts as facilitators for a group of participants for between two to six weeks in a selected, suitable venue (indoor or outdoor), with the ownership of the final product being determined by everyone involved.

Residency shows are usually site-specific and often ambitious in scale. There is a strong emphasis on collaboration between art forms, such as dance, music, or visual, enabling the team or participants to explore and experiment via the devising process. The starting point for a residency is often theme- or issue-based, and is relevant to the particular community involved, providing them with a focus and a voice. Themes for previous residencies have included the politics of disability, adolescent sexuality, global environmental issues, and adaptations of existing texts – for example, Coleridge's 'The Ancient Mariner'.

Devising is used as a technique in residency work, according to Devlin. If it is a large-scale event (that is, upwards of one hundred people), then a thematic or scenario framework is needed, particularly for the design and technical team. Major Road's devised work has changed in style over the years from being more issue-based and political in the 1970s to more visually and physically based work in the 1990s. Devlin suggests that the shift away from being a permanent ensemble, where a group shares an ideology and is much more involved in

133

the process or development of the work, is for artistic rather than economic reasons. Devlin admits that in today's climate 'the economics of keeping an ensemble company all year round would scare me rigid'.[4] Now, artists or performers are involved for thirteen weeks from start to finish.

The key characteristics of Major Road's site-specific work must be the breadth of scale, the physical and musical expression, and the involvement with the community. This is significantly different to the smaller, finely observed performance work of IOU, and marks out another approach which differs from the recent visual, celebratory, site-specific work of Welfare State International with the people of Barrow-in-Furness.[5] What is interesting is that both Major Road, a theatre company that has developed the visual side, and Welfare State International, a group of artists who use theatre, often employ the same freelance personnel on a regular basis for these projects.

Process

The starting point for a Major Road site-specific project or residency is to identify a space to use and a community to work with. On the basis of these initial decisions, the company decides on a team for the project. Sometimes a writer is used, but more frequently a member of the team acts as dramaturge, mixing the scenario and improvisation together, says Devlin, 'in a freewheeling way as a response to the working process'. There are usually representatives from dance, music and design on the team, who will meet and determine a specific way of working together. This is the result of amalgamating and collaborating on a variety of approaches to devising site-specific work. Major Road has identified a pool of approximately thirty-five artists to choose from, and the intention is never to have more than two new people in a potential team of seven or eight members, as it is such an intense process of working.

Examples of residencies using specific communities have included: 'A Drop in the Ocean', a highly visual performance piece devised with profoundly disabled students from Thomas Delarue School in Kent; 'Faces of Repression', devised with a local youth theatre and performed in a museum gallery; and

'The Lake Lake Lake Show', which was a large-scale outdoor spectacular that took place in, on, and over a lake in Basildon, Essex. In the case of 'The Lake Lake Lake Show', there was a team of eight from the company working with young people aged from fifteen to twenty-five (students and unemployed) for three weeks in the summer of 1986. The audience were asked to participate in the spectacle at Basildon's Gloucester Park, where, according to Victoria Neumark's review in *The Times Educational Supplement*, they enjoyed 'waterside processions, strongly executed dance routines on an elevated walk-way above the lake, and a stunning finale featuring fibre optics, daring dives into the lake and air, destruction of the set, and spectacular rockets.'[6]

Apart from the obvious necessity of good working relationships within the team, Devlin argues that there is a kind of known language within the group, which serves as a working reference to past pieces of work, offering a form of shorthand for describing a situation. This is not simply a verbal language, where the semi-visual term 'installation' has the Major Road implication or meaning of physical or sculptural objects that have a performance element to them, but an unspoken shared understanding of two people improvising 'on the floor' and then moving in a new direction without discussion. This means of communication offers huge flexibility to the team.

Preparation and planning are vital to any devised residency. In addition to working from a budget, and the practical or technical considerations of the site, it is important to look at how to motivate the participants in a comparatively short period of time. The average residency is three weeks, which necessitates knowing how to structure the time carefully. In the same way, evaluating and assessing the project is an important part of Major Road's policy for site-specific work. Every residency has de-briefing sessions with the participants, either in the form of an open forum or a questionnaire, with the professionals, and with the host or organisation. Out of these discussions, reports are written and submitted to the company.

Devlin believes that this particular area of devised theatre gives a voice to people, empowering them, and enables opportunities for creativity. Within Major Road's vision and structure for a piece, there is the flexibility for participants to

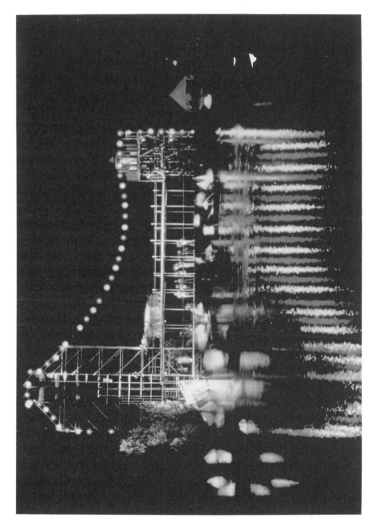

15 'The Lake Lake Lake Show'. Major Road, Basildon, 1986. (Photo: Steve Whitson.)

become part of an arts process and product. Major Road is attempting to blend or use language and performance disciplines to create extraordinary events that are non-naturalistic. The appeal and importance of this strand of work for Devlin is the opportunity it provides for interaction with other artists, so that music or design may lead the devising process, which contrasts with the alternative strand of working from a script in a more structured way.

Collaborative exploration

Devlin suggests that devising site-specific pieces or residencies provides a freedom to explore ideas or forms of theatre, where collaboration is the focus for that discovery. The residency work informs the touring work through ideas and personnel. The project director for a residency is usually a musician or visual artist, and experimentation with the set or design is strongly encouraged, as a scripted touring show will have far less room for manœuvre. The residency enables design and performance to work together, so that a major idea can be tried out and then abandoned. There is no doubt that devising site-specific work and residencies has developed Major Road visually. The freedom for a variety of artists and makers to work collaboratively, particularly in the development of set design, has fed into their touring work, as evidenced by the inventive, visually exciting touring sets of 'Ideal Homes' by Alan Dix, or 'Divided Kingdoms' by Garry Lyons.

A visual emphasis is an important aspect of any site-specific piece, and this is particularly relevant in the case of Forkbeard Fantasy, a company from Devon that works from a strong visual base, devising comic theatre and film. Since 1974, Forkbeard's activities have included small-scale touring theatre shows, Forkbeard films, street and outdoor performance, walk-through installations, animated sculptures, gallery events, and festival commissions. Company member Tim Britton points out, 'SETS: sets PERFORM in our shows. They are as important as the performers as performers!'[7] The three members of the company are all visually orientated, love making things, and are excited by the invention or trickery of props, set, and sculptural objects. None of them is drama trained, two having studied English literature at college, and the third coming from an art background. They are all involved in the devising process, from original ideas or images through design and construction, to lighting, sound, and the day-to-day running of the company. They have a 'filmic' attitude to their shows, always interested in the potential of integrating film and live performance. Britton recounts this process:

> We piece it together bit by bit – from already firm ideas or images, to new stuff that emerges through the process. The overall show is seen in musical terms really, although we are not musicians. It's a combination of the way music might be put together and the way a film script is put together.

Integrating film and live performance

Forkbeard Fantasy is the only British company devising theatre that works with film in the particular way described by Britton:

> directly interacting with it, climbing in and out of it, passing things back and forward, using it not as a back-drop or effect but as an extension of the *place*, of the set. The interactive approach is a fairly unique trademark.

This company is certainly unique in its whole style and approach to devised theatre, usually working with film or visual, sculptural construction in which the participants are as extensions of, or operators of the construction. The company wants to encourage people to discover ways of interacting with working, moving, sculptures. Within a residency, a group works together with Forkbeard Fantasy on an equal footing, with members of the company acting as catalysts to participants, nudging them in directions or discouraging them when their own experience indicates a particular line of enquiry will not work. The company is not afraid of wanting to entertain people, and frequently works with schools, colleges, and the disabled outside of their own devised shows. It is important for them to involve their audience as part of the show, whether as visitors from an institution, film-types, archaeologists, or in other roles.

16 'Headquarters'. Forkbeard Fantasy, 1983. (Photo: Penny Saunders.)

Approach to residencies

The form of theatre varies enormously from residency to residency, ranging from a two-day workshop that puts on an exhibition to a longer one that starts with an environment concept and results in a show. Clearly there are restrictions of scale, but there is always a theme, for example, 'industrial nightmares', 'insect struggles', or 'slaves to the machine', and certain types of materials are always provided. The company loves invention, as well as using cheap or junk materials. One example of a site-specific residency piece was 'The Corridor of Doors', where a whole Arts Centre (The Hornpipe in Portsmouth, 1986) was 'animated' by Forkbeard Fantasy, turning it into a corridor of doors. The participants were made up of art college students studying environment or architectural design, fourth-year secondary school pupils, and disabled groups, all working together. From the pupils' designs, the art students built and constructed an environment full of animated insects, objects, gadgets, and devices that all worked, whether by pulley system or by pressing knobs. Each individual or group was in a room with a door, and the audience watched as voyeurs by peeping through keyholes or opening doors on the events or actions within each room.

An alternative residency at The Albany Centre in Bristol used interactive film, involving live, facial, physical animation. The participants, young people aged between fifteen and sixteen years, were pushed into a machine that incorporated the screen, which Britton describes in the same interview: 'their (created) transmogrification, or metamorphosis that might take place (using stop-frame animation), and then they are spat out again.' Ten days' hard work only produced several minutes of film, which was sent off and processed during the week, so that it could be publicly shown as part of the resulting performance.

Forkbeard Fantasy believes that film can extend theatre in remarkable ways. The company loves using and exploring the possibilities of film, as in its residencies based on the theme of 'ghosts'. In the 1980s, the company devised a show called 'Ghosts', which opened with the Ghost Hunter narrating on tape, 'I approached the house from an uphill direction. . .', whilst the audience watched him on film approaching, through a cobwebbed window on the set. On film, he came to the window, peered through, tapped on the glass, and then burst through the set door in person. In this show the set and props were animated, and it was the start of live interaction between film and theatre. This is the most exciting aspect of Forkbeard Fantasy's devised products in recent years, and is illustrated well in one of Britton's own descriptions:

> Once we used the film so that seven brothers went into the film one by one; they were all going over the edge of a cliff in search of someone. There was a rope that came through the centre of the screen which the character on the stage would hold and then pass on to the next, until we ran out of brothers. Someone in the front row of the audience was given the rope holding all these men's lives at the other end! We made it *feel* quite heavy. A character on the film comes back and asks the person holding the rope to let go as they have run out of rope over the cliff. He or she does, and all the men fall screaming over the cliff. It had an extraordinary and mind-numbing effect on people; that you had this umbilical chord into a screen that you could feel pressure on at the other end, and people on the screen talked to YOU as an audience from a wild, windy, country location.

OUTDOORS

Location has always been crucial for any site-specific work of Lumiere & Son. One of the company's most successful site-specific devised pieces was 'Deadwood' in 1986, which was created out of Kew Gardens in London. This spectacle was a culmination of a range of individual talents working from the environment under the artistic direction of Hilary Westlake, who used the company's skills to devise and create visual images, music, text, choreography, and inventive illuminations. The performance started at dusk with the audience sipping wine and listening to music before being invited to journey through the gardens, which took on the appearance and atmosphere of a tropical rain forest. Through swirling mists, different images were perceived against a background of sounds of forest habitation. Various parts of the woody environment were illuminated, with clumps of bushes swathed in green or yellow light.

As a group of Victorian dressed performers walked through the grounds with the audience, an actor (Trevor Stuart) told them, 'At the centre of the earth is a piece of everything'. As they listened to the continuing text, creatures emerged out of the vegetation or were spotted amongst the trees. A family group in fur costumes with painted faces huddled close together, chattering to each other, seeming aware of being observed. Two leopards or similar wild cats were asleep, fully stretched out along the branches, as two exotic birds in another tree moved their heads from side to side. A group of grasshoppers, dressed in all-in-one green jodphur-like outfits with yellow sleeves, belts and matching caps, jumped along in unison, bounced off a trampoline and continued on their way with precisely choreographed movements. Large numbers of ants moved rhythmically through the forest, waving their arms up and down, whilst creatures in white turbans danced or leapt through the air, revealing a breadth of wings speckled with holes.

The audience arrived at the Temperate House, which was impressively lit against the evening sky in purple, blue and yellow, as a small conducted choir sang outside to a soundtrack composed by Jeremy Peyton-Jones, and a variety of live musicians played from a gallery structure inside, at the top of the magnificent glass building. The performers, in cream Victorian costumes, moved in repetitive patterns on the terrace amongst the cane chairs, watched by the audience from the grass as they listened to the continuing narrative poem and music. Dancers in tightly bodiced tunic dresses and harem pants, with elaborate plumes of feathers on their heads, moved up the steps towards the building, as the central speaking actor delivered a description of exotic butterflies above a pool into the microphone.

Back in the rain forest, a man in a white outfit hung from a rope, dropped to the ground and remained face to the earth. Black creatures hung upside down from branches, as the text now talked of the different woods being felled despite the destruction of wild life. Gradually all the animals, who were represented rather than played naturalistically, congregated in a clearing (line by line), adopting their own particular movement sequence. A visually exciting insect creature, constructed

17 Graham Newton and Paul Treacy in 'Deadwood'. Lumiere & Sor, 1986. (Photo: Simon Corder.)

of numerous tubes speckled and spangled in yellow and black, twirled a baton around as it moved to its position amongst the others. Together, they danced a simple routine of steps to the mounting musical chorus and final spoken words of the poem. The performance ended with each line of creatures disappearing off into the forest as the sounds or babble of forest life echoed on.

Participants

In Westlake's experience, site-specific devised products have their own particular set of problems. For her, the greatest difficulty has always been local involvement and working with non-professionals.[8] Lumiere & Son is not a community company, nor does it hold a community philosophy, which is clearly indicated in Westlake's attitude to the Penzance site-specific product. Westlake comments, 'If you have an ideological interest in community theatre then I am sure that such a project can be viewed with a degree of success; if, however, you want to produce exciting art it is hopeless.'[9] For Westlake, the overwhelming problem of devising 'Fifty Five years of the Swallow and the Butterfly' was 'the total unpredictability, unreliability and incompetence of local involvement'. For the chorus, Westlake expected forty available, fit eighteen- to thirty-year-olds, eager and keen, as well as equal numbers of men and women. She recalls, 'I got nothing like that. I was assured that there would be no problem finding them. So my chorus dropped from forty to twelve with most of those twelve able to attend only a small number of rehearsals.' Westlake suggests that the time commitment of amateur participants is always a problem in these projects, sometimes combined with them being relentlessly critical and conservative. The devising process for site-specific work involves delicate relationships with people, although some will drop out without communicating reasons and simply not turn up at the next rehearsal. A daily change in numbers means that group or ensemble work cannot be developed with the performers over the prescribed period.

The recruitment question has also been a problem for Major Road, with nobody turning up on the first day of a project as their worst example, which now means that they actively involve themselves in the recruiting process of local people. In direct contrast, Forkbeard Fantasy's initial problems were with too many participants; for instance, over one hundred seven- to eight-year-olds arrived at one Arts Centre for the day, making them feel used as a crèche whilst parents went shopping. Britton experienced 'terrible times helping Art Centres look strong on community commitment and hardly getting any results from the actual process', with the result that:

> Now we are very firm. Maybe up to thirty people is our maximum. We're strict on the place we're given to work in, the hours, and who! We don't let schools just dump their difficult problems on us. We say the kids must be picked for what they'll get out of it.

The extent to which participants are involved in site-specific residential work is dependent on each company's approach to every particular situation and its unique circumstances.

Difficulties

Practical problems arise throughout the devising process and preparation for any site-specific product. The practicalities of preparing the site for an audience are helped by advance planning, incorporating issues of car parking, disability access, power supply, and technical requirements. For IOU, the administrative work may begin a year prior to the planned site-specific event, and includes site visits with the promoters, obtaining necessary permits or licences for the show site, producing and distributing publicity, arranging insurance as necessary, accomodation, contacting extra artists or workers, and fundraising, sponsorship, and grant applications. Perhaps the hardest task is to communicate with all those involved in the process, being aware of instant needs, keeping abreast of all changes, as well as liaising with the host or organisation. Site-specific work also requires diplomacy, good management, and keeping a cool head in the event of a crisis. Artistically, it is vital to hold on to the central idea without getting sidetracked by interesting alternatives that are not relevant to the main objective of the piece. It is often necessary to edit or throw out exciting ideas that do not relate to the structure as a whole.

Working within a limited budget is always an underlying problem for this kind of devised theatre, because of the unknown elements that may arise in the particular situation. Environmental devised work requires planning in advance, time, and money. According to Devlin of Major Road, projects are always five times more expensive than the money available. The essential question is how to translate ambitious ideas into practical possibilities that are also cheap. Companies like Major Road, Lumiere & Son, or IOU need security for their equipment on site, which is often expensive with costs being covered out of box office takings. Any outdoor situation is dependent on the weather, which can mean rusting or damage to equipment, such as lanterns being ruined by salt and spray. The practical difficulties of lighting an outdoor space are sometimes costly, requiring the use of generators or extra equipment to achieve specific effects. Technical work for IOU usually includes making the site safe and secure, laying in electricity and water supplies, hiring and erecting scaffolding or raked seating, installing safety lighting, steps, ramps and toilets for the site, rigging special effects and sound amplification, as well as liaising with fire and safety officers.

It is quite clear from the professional practice of these four companies based in Halifax, Bradford, Tiverton, and London that devising residencies or site-specific products requires a reasonable budget, time, planning, and preparation. Good organisation, communication skills, flexibility, and inventiveness are essential if a show is to succeed. Where local participants or a community are involved, then it is important to encourage enthusiasm and goodwill from the outset. Much of this is dependent on individual personalities and previous experience of this kind of theatre. A company may simply perform, or members may facilitate others in the devising process, leading them towards a product. Ultimately, the success of every project will be judged in terms of its original objectives and particular focus or emphasis, whether it be a performance piece or a show devised with over a hundred local people for a specific location.

FURTHER INVESTIGATION

From this observation, it becomes even more apparent that any group that contemplates devising a site-specific piece of theatre or working in residency must address key additional questions to those outlined at the end of chapter two:

1 Who is the piece for? Is it company based only, or does it include other participants? Is there local involvement, or is the piece partly or wholly a community project?
2 Where will the devising take place? Is it an outdoor or indoor situation? Will it require permission, licences, extra facilities, or alteration to an existing location?
3 How much funding is available for the project?
  How much planning and preparation is needed prior to the performance?
  How much time will be scheduled in the location itself or for the residency?
  How will the piece be organised, administered or co-ordinated in relation to the site or residency?
4 What are the artistic, technical and practical considerations when devising a residential site-specific project?

7

THEORY AND PRACTICE

> People make work in such different ways for such differ-
> ent reasons, but often reading about someone, who may be
> working in a very different field, opens up something for
> me in my own work.
>
> (Annie Griffin, formerly of Gloria,
> now with Pirate Productions)

Researching and observing contemporary British professional
devised theatre practice in recent years confirms my own
experience of sixteen years: that devising is dependent on
people, their life experiences and motivation, why and what
they want to devise, and the pathfinder process chosen by them
to explore their particular set of circumstances. In the wider
context of the early 1990s, the implication is that time, money,
and space determine the parameters of the devising experience,
suggesting an initial structure within which to work. Perhaps
this explains the more recent trend of solo artists collaborating
with others on an individual project, but still working as an
ensemble.[1] Time, money, and space are fundamental pre-
requisites of every new devising equation created.

For me, the richness of devising theatre comes in the
sharing of experiences with others, from the risk factor
implicit in its production, from the efforts, enthusiasm, and
energy of those particular people, and from the sheer excitement of trying to express something through a collaborative
process that continually opens up a multitude of possibilities,
discoveries, or questions in an attempt to articulate yet
another new creative way of making theatre. The observation
and discussion of the work of professional companies, and
reading around the subject (often indirectly), are useful

148

stimuli for ideas of content, form, and audience. Something has to inspire the need or desire to artistically construct a piece of theatre, whether it is from an initial idea, feeling, image, concept, story, theme, written text, picture, music, location, group of people, or a specific community interest. The choices are infinite, the potential is enormous, and the thrill comes with every group's decision.

It is in the practical experience of devising theatre that much is to be learnt. There is no single theory that can embrace this amorphous subject; no formula or prescribed methodology can be applied that guarantees a particular product every time. It is questionable whether the skills of devising can be taught as such. I am constantly learning how to devise theatre with every new group of drama students that I encounter in their eager curiosity to discover the mysteries and magic of the subject in their fourth year of study at the University of Kent.[2] I do not wish to teach them in a prescriptive way (nor do I suggest that there is an agreed body of knowledge to be digested), but rather I want to encourage them to think, try out ideas, explore group dynamics, and develop their imaginative ability; I want to engage them in analysis, criticism or evaluation, inspire their enjoyment and enthusiasm with devised theatre, and somehow to facilitate that passion to want to make a unique theatrical experience with others. It is in the doing and making of theatre that mistakes are made, that failure occurs, and that is how one learns. Nobody wants to fail, but sometimes it is necessary in order to really understand a process, group dynamics, company administration, or the basic requirements of a specific form of theatre.

GUIDELINES

Reflecting on my observations of contemporary professional practice in tandem with my own devising philosophy and experience, I suggest some general points for consideration by any group devising theatre:

1 Do not be afraid to clearly establish roles and responsibilities within a particular project. Allocate specific functions or duties if appropriate, or decide how to structure the process of democratic decision-making.

2 Is there a need to write a 'Code of Practice' document incorporating company policy, objectives, procedure, and planning of meetings, evaluation, and assessment guidelines? (See Appendix III for an example of a professional theatre-in-education company's 'Code of Practice').

3 Establish leadership of project (if applicable), and how this will operate in terms of company decision-making. Delegate or form hierarchies according to skills and interests.

4 Have something that the group passionately wants to do, and is committed to exploring theatrically. Have an initial sense of what the group would like to achieve, aim for, or create.

5 Trust to feelings, instinct, and intuition about the development of the work.

6 Allow members of the group space to work on their own for part of the time. Consider dividing into smaller groups with specific tasks to report back on.

7 Ask questions throughout the process, and do not be afraid to return to original aims or objectives in order to clarify direction.

8 Consider space, setting or location that work will be devised from; for instance, if the set, visual stimulus, or location are the initial reasons for devising (notably in the case of site-specific pieces), then it is essential (if not always possible or practical) to work in that space from the start. Try and rehearse in that space as much as possible.

9 Analyse, criticise, assess, and evaluate the work as it progresses, in one form or other. Decide on the most appropriate methods or criteria to achieve this.

10 Try to maintain a critical 'outside eye' on the process and product, both as an observer at an objective level, and at a more subjective level of involvement. Avoid introspection and always be individually truthful, and to the group.

The above ten points are a guiding reference only, as the ideas, feeling, or vision have to come from the group! It is the participants who have to find their own dynamic as a group and be responsible to themselves. This means a commitment to the group, to the time period allocated for the project, and to the end product (the show), which ultimately involves a commitment to a relationship with an audience. If the product is the focus, then the group has to work together in a way that is practical and structured by agreed limits.

By offering a model of an open-ended structure of a devising process, groups can practically experiment with the possibilities that any one starting point may throw up. Examining the different routes that may be taken via practical discovery, in conjunction with parallel analysis and evaluation of the journey's progress, present opportunities to compare, contrast and broaden the devising experience. Therefore, in order to learn more about devising theatre, one way forward is to practically experiment with an outline model of process that allows for flexible decisions and spontaneity within the group. Never be afraid to abandon ideas or to start again, however hard that prospect appears at first! Devising is reliant on the motivation, interest and energy of a group that is willing to try out ideas that may fail, and yet may constantly surprise individuals in their further exploration or experimentation.

The construction and consideration of various models of practice are valuable in widening the devising debate of how a group works together. In this sense, a model serves as a springboard for creative exploration and discussion. Clearly, it is easier to suggest a model of practice based on the process of devising reminiscence theatre (as observed in the practice of Age Exchange Theatre Company) than to formulate a model from the work of Forced Entertainment Theatre Co-operative. However, this is not to imply that to follow the former example produces a replica of an Age Exchange product, but rather produces a specific form of reminiscence theatre. The latter example provides a model that is intuitive, largely based on aesthetics rather than on any ideological or pedagogical system, which is ultimately about what one thinks is beautiful, or what one believes is worth doing as art. Intuition, instinct, and aesthetic choice are vital elements in any devising process, which can never be directly taught or learnt.

MEANS OF ENQUIRY

I want now to consider a theoretical model of process, which addresses different stages of progression in an attempt to define and further question how a group devises theatre:

MODEL OF PROCESS

Stage one: PRE-PRODUCTION PLANNING
Questions: What do I want to devise and why?
              What kind of theatre do I want to create?
              Is there a starting stimulus for the show?
              Is there a combination of ideas, materials, and
              resources?
              Are there initial ideas for content, form, or
              audience?

Draw and define the preliminary boundaries at the start of the
project.

Stage two: QUESTIONING/EXPLORING/DISCUSSING
              THE PRELIMINARY DECISION
Questions: What are your initial aims and objectives as a
              company for this project?
              Who are you devising for and why?
              Is content or subject matter the starting point for
              the work? What are the source materials?
              Is the form or structure an important preliminary
              area for exploration?
              How to proceed – organisation, roles, respons-
              ibilities, method(s) of working?

Select appropriate ways and means to examine these questions,
for example, via research, practical work, or discussion.

Research: Audience – visits to; interviews with; discussion
              Content – range of reading materials; allocation
              and organisation of; visits to museums, site
              Members of the group – individual interests

Practical: Creation of an outline scenario or story
              Design for set, environment, masks
              'On the floor' work – trying out of ideas via
              improvisation, workshops on particular theme,
              topic
              Exploration of images, attitudes

Discussion: Form – skeletal outline, rough structure for pro-
              duct or programme, style of show

Further questions – Is the potential of the group being utilised? Does the work feel exciting, interesting, or dangerous?

Stage three: EXAMINING THE SPECIFICS OF THE DECISION

Working in constructed visual, physical space or environment if of primary importance

Writing a detailed scenario, pilot scenes, or opening scene for practical exploration and discussion

Building and developing characters through research, improvisation, 'hot seating' techniques, role play, and workshops

Further questions and discussion of central concept or starting point in order to ask further questions

Sharing research as a group in order to make new decisions about content or form of show

Practical considerations of form, structure, and performance

Is a 'WORK-IN-PROGRESS' useful or relevant at some stage?

Stage four: SOMEWHERE IN THE PROCESS
– DIFFICULTIES

Questions: What is this piece of theatre about, and why?

What is happening at this precise moment in the show?

Does this section or scene work? Why not?

How does the problem reveal itself in light of the whole structure?

Have we veered away from our original intentions, aims, or objectives? Consciously?

Is there a unity of style within the piece?

Does the material need to be re-written, reworked, or discarded?

Do we have to abandon completely and start again?

Within this model of process, it is immediately apparent that stages can be swopped, re-ordered, or re-arranged in light of the specific circumstances of the devising situation. It is also true that areas to be discussed in stage two may have already happened in stage one, as is the case for any of the stages. The suggested structure is skeletal, flexible, and designed to encourage greater group awareness, confidence in decision-making, and clarification of intention. A process develops with every decision taken by the group in its search for a particular direction. The impetus comes from numerous sources, which include the material itself, whether it is the development of characters through improvisation, an agreed theme, or the idea for a performance structure in a park.

It is possible to define models of practice based on the work of established companies, but even then a change of personnel or project can entirely alter the way a group devises its next product. All the elements or factors are flexible, changing positions of significance or importance as needed. What is important is the place and relationship of the key component parts of form, content or audience at the start of the devising process and their subsequent development. In a learning situation, it is useful to look at the different approaches that can be taken when each part is the central focus for the work. Again it is a question of identifying and clarifying the group's intention throughout the devising process.

The need to question how we see the world underlies any devising process, consciously or not. Devising is a means of re-arranging that world for a group; assembling and structuring an experience into a concrete form for others to see, which is often complex, both intellectually and emotionally. The drive or motivation comes from a desire to make sense of something, a need to speak, a will to investigate, as well as the passion to explore this through the means of theatre. However, a group can only work at its own level and pace. No amount of reading or theorising ultimately affects that starting decision of how to proceed. Once in the making, it may or may not be appropriate to look at live or video performances, books or other resource materials, but the pivotal or key decisions remain with the process adopted by the group. What concerns us is directly experiencing that process, defining and questioning what is happening, and engaging with the material in a personal and objective relationship at one and the same time.

'OUTSIDE EYE'

Watching the different devising processes of professional companies has enabled me to clarify how a lack of communication creates confusion between people to the extent that a group can complicate subject matter into six areas instead of clearly focussing on one, which, in turn, emphasises the importance of an outside commentator on the work. This might mean a director, co-ordinator, team leader, or a member of the company with that specific responsibility during a workshop session or rehearsal. Working 'on the floor' is a direct way forward for some companies, when feeling trapped by the material itself, or blocked in the development of the piece. 'Thinking on your feet' allows the individual to respond to new ideas or thoughts spontaneously, to sense and react to others so that the interaction or combined operation often produces unknown or unseen fresh material. This is not to underestimate the value or importance of group discussion, but to point out the danger of becoming preoccupied with talking and words. Companies vary the balance of emphasis placed on practical exploration and discussion, so that the input of theory and critical analysis may be of greater or lesser interest to them. In an ideal world, I would like to integrate theory and practice wherever possible, but original objectives often define a process that relies more heavily either on one or the other.

RESOURCES

Reading about the work of professional companies and their approaches to devising theatre provides a useful comparison of working methods, not to be replicated but rather to provoke or stimulate further thinking about the ways and means of devising theatre. It is interesting to note that research clearly showed that professional companies could not name any books that were of direct use to them in terms of how to devise theatre, but that a wide range of reading materials had been indirectly influential in a general sense, or of direct use within the context of a specific project. Individual practitioners felt that the most beneficial books were either extremely theoretical or analytical texts, including Keir Elam's *The Semiotics of Theatre and Drama* or Martin Esslin's *Field of Drama*, offering what

155

is in use when a group starts devising theatre, or books that described particular ways of approaching performance and art, about particular passions or attitudes to work, which can both clarify a group's position and become a source of inspiration. (See Appendix IV for 'Further selected reading list', based on the various suggestions of individual members of professional companies.)

It seems to me that much more is needed to promote a greater dialogue and understanding between practising members of the theatre profession and those training or studying drama and theatre in higher education. In this I include degree courses, teacher training programmes, vocational studies, and the drama school curriculum. There is no substitute for seeing live performance, practically engaging in workshops with visiting theatre practitioners, or being involved in thought-provoking debate with members of a professional company. It is the accumulation of these experiences that widens students' perspectives of the real world of professional theatre.

It is also vital to relate the learning situation to the professional world, and initiatives such as Enterprise in Higher Education[3] allow for the professionalisation of staff and student projects through the development of training skills that come from working with professional theatre companies in residency or workshop situations. In 1990–91 Kent University fourth-year drama students benefitted from working with professional practitioners and others from Lumiere & Son, Pirate Productions, Forced Entertainment Theatre Co-operative, the Royal Court Theatre, the Independent Theatre Council, and Wimbledon College of Art and Design. This provided their last year of study with a real working context and experience for the future, bringing together the areas of professional theatre, business, and education. This is a positive move towards an improved dialogue between the professional practitioner, those involved in education or training of drama students, and the general public.

DOCUMENTING WORK

Apart from wanting to increase liaison between professional and educational workers, more materials must be made available and accessible to those involved in theatre education. The issue of devising and documentation raises a number of questions about the purpose, functions, and role of documentation in relation to contemporary devised theatre. Does the dominant literary theatre tradition necessitate that devised theatre is documented? Documentation brings credibility and respectability. Perhaps the significance of devised theatre is in the ephemerality of the event, and in the importance of transience. The motives for documentation include popularising the work of particular companies, and promoting the alternative form of devised theatre – for posterity or inspiration, as a report, history or memory, as a work in itself to exhibit, and as a working method to bring a group together, in order to keep track of ideas and internal dialogue.

The documentation of devised theatre serves different functions for drama teachers or students in higher education, professional theatre practitioners, and those generally interested in the subject. Different forms of documentation, including video recordings of performances, written reviews, books about a specific company's work, or photographs, enable others to re-live another version of a performance, to sell or market a product, and to gain insight into a particular process of creativity. Who documents the work – for example, the company, the video maker, the outsider, the academic, or the theatre critic – and how it is documented are significant in the representation, interpretation, value and meanings attributed to devised theatre.

The intention and context for documentation is fundamental in that the 'document' is the work itself. It has a life of its own. Whatever form the document takes – for instance, an analytical article, a critical review, or a video – it is always a shadow of the original document (the live devised performance). This is where the importance of memory and imagination cannot be overstated: that immortal moment shared between the performer and spectator never to be recaptured again. Perhaps I do not want to see everything? Memory and imagination suffice.

I feel like this when I recall watching a performance of Impact Theatre Co-operative's 'The Carrier Frequency' at The Ralph Thoresby School in Leeds in the autumn of 1984. At the end of the performance, I just sat in my seat silently for ten minutes. I had no desire to speak to the friend sitting next to me, I simply wanted to be alone with my feelings, emotions, and the power of the theatrical experience. I had no need whatsoever to articulate verbally what I felt about this stunning performance. I shall never forget it, and words cannot describe how emotionally 'gutted' I felt. That moment of exchange between performers and spectator cannot be documented.

When I tell second-year performance students that 'The Carrier Frequency' was the most significant theatre performance I watched in the 1980s, they are confused. What they observe from the documented video extracts or written articles[4] about this performance did not contain the proximity of the spectator to the powerful set (a pool of water two feet deep, out of which rose scaffolding towers), the extraordinary soundtrack, and the desperate images that occured and re-occured throughout the piece. The video does not reveal how dangerous it was for the spectator, or the sheer physical energy emanating from the performers as they enacted a series of rituals in an attempt to continue their existence, those repeated actions of carrying each other through the water, that confusion about what was happening, and what was not. Of course, the live engagement between performer and spectator does not exist on video or in the written text.

What does the specialist and non-specialist reader want from documentation? To discover various ways of devising theatre, materials for research and teaching in education, inspiration for making original work, a system of effective networking, or new ways of 'reading' theatre? There is a difference between being documented and doing the documentation. How work is documented is never neutral; it has a language of its own. The document never signifies in isolation. The documenter and the 'reader' of the document give it new meanings and significance within the cultural context of both the time and place that it is 'read'. In this book, I have described various devised theatre performances that I watched between 1989 and 1993, in an attempt to provide the reader with a sense of what each performance conveyed at that particular moment. I am unable to capture the liveness or authenticity of the event, as this is in the physical bodies of both performer and spectator.

What then is the value of documenting the process of devising or the devised product? It depends on what the documentation is for – artistic, educational, political, or cultural

18   Steve Shill, Heather Ackroyd, and Niki Johnson in 'The Carrier
Frequency'. Impact Theatre Co-operative, 1984–86.
(Photo: Matthew Davison.)

reasons. When it is linked to politics, the pressures of press reviews, funding bodies and decisions, there is an uneasiness about the relationship of devising and documentation. In the 1990s, the marketing and selling of the product often mean promoting or publicising the event well before it is fully devised. The promotional video plays a significant part in determining how a group's work is presented, viewed, and critically received. There is a greater demand for high-quality publicity materials with devised products that have a strong, visual emphasis so that an audience has some indication of the intended work.

For those studying the subject of devising theatre, it can be inspiring to look at a company's working process, or useful to read about a company's problems or difficulties with the work. For some companies, the daily recording of the work's progress is an integral part and development of the process, particularly important in experimental performance. IOU has developed a method of documentation for the company, which is unique to them and would not work for anyone else. The act of notation cannot begin to reproduce the various elements that make up live performance. The notation, the text of the performance, is never made complete. Even video, which has become a prime medium of documentation, can never describe all the action. It can record the physicality of the performer, but the notations are full of gaps. Gestures, movements, whole sections of performed actions are lost. The limitations are with the 'eye' of the camera person, who chooses what to focus on for the audience. The live theatre performance moves the spectator through a process, the sense of engagement and dynamics between performer and spectator, which video can never capture. The video is a separate art form and performance product in itself.

Devised theatre demands different ways of writing about and recording performance. It needs various approaches to be taken, which mix disciplines and share a performance vocabulary. A multi-vision is required, which incorporates sketches, slides, reviews, memories, photographs, objects or props, videos, and traces of performance. Some of the more established companies do have archive collections, such as The People Show and Belgrade Theatre-in-Education Company, which are invaluable research resources, but demand time and money to be maintained efficiently.

It is my experience that the range of contemporary British devised theatre is such that it is vital to find ways to communicate this diverse wealth of material to others without losing the uniqueness of every created product. Within the context of my own research, the simplest way forward has been to compile three lists of information that relate to the professional companies devising theatre included in this book. (See Appendix V for 'Contact list', Appendix VI for 'Video availability list', and Appendix VII for 'Publications featuring the work of companies'.)

ASSESSMENT

How then to evaluate contemporary devised experimental performance? How does one notate the complex interaction of physical, visual, and verbal languages into the written word? There is certainly a strong argument for looking at alternative ways of assessing the current full range of devised theatre practice, so that a wider vocabulary of performance is developed, which is not solely reliant on the words and wisdom of London theatre critics writing their reviews in the daily national papers, or academics theorising about the mechanics or dynamics of performance! John McGrath makes this point in relation to the language of the complex social theatrical event:

> To complicate matters further, each occasion of theatre is different, evanescent and impossible to record. . . . But what it does do all too often is to reduce the language of theatre that is studied academically to the most easily obtainable – the words. . . . But words are not the 'language' of theatre, and by exclusively attending to them we reduce, impoverish the event for academic convenience.[5]

The acknowledged London group of theatre critics are responsible for analysing theatre performance across the board, which means that the same set of criteria is being applied to the work of the Royal National Theatre or the Royal Shakespeare Company (who are concerned with productions of written plays, whether classic texts, works by Shakespeare, or new writing) as to the devised work of IOU, Lumiere & Son, Forced

Entertainment, Station House Opera, or Forkbeard Fantasy. In this context, devised experimental performance is clearly inhibited by the great traditions of established theatre, which focus centrally on the written text, making any performance work without spoken words apparently elitist or irrelevant to the general public. Likewise, directors' theatre, which presents a single vision or interpretation of a play written by a playwright, sets the norm and criteria for judging work that is group-orientated, collaboratively devised, and that often incorporates various art forms or multi-media approaches in an attempt to integrate the complexity of that vision.

This reiterates a point made in the opening chapter about theatre criticism in conventional theatre being concerned with the relationship of writing and performance. Inevitably, there are problems for the critic writing about devised experimental performance in a culture of text-based theatre tradition reliant on interpretation, the primacy and the privileging of the word. Equally, there appears to be a desire to mythologise one person, that is, the director or the playwright. Theatre criticism is delivered out of a socio-political and cultural context too. The critic has to please the paper, the sub-editor, the readers (the general public), and the artists. The critic offers a subjective response to the work in a particular place and time, which is made objective within the written text of a newspaper, journal, or book. What is needed then, is a multiple subjectivity and a multiplicity of discourses.

LANGUAGE

In devised experimental theatre where the body is the primary signification of text, the gestural language (through the combination of narrative, text, and physical movement) is the performance vocabulary for the work. It is made up of visual images, movement, music, and use of objects or props in new ways. It is a different means of using a performance language, which in turn requires a critical language that relates to the work's vision and frames of reference. The body and the use of physical, visual imagery are the focus of the performance. Thus, a form of critical language or vocabulary is needed to analyse work that integrates different kinds of 'text', whether physical, visual, or verbal. Devised theatre also necessitates a new relationship between writing and the making of performance.

The framework and critical vocabulary that exists is for a British culture that ignores looking at a piece of theatrical art in aesthetic terms. This lack of analysis of how work is created both artistically and aesthetically reveals the necessity to examine the processes and aesthetic concerns of making theatre within our drama training programmes or education system. From early schooling through to higher education, there is a constant confirmation of a two-tier division of the 'Royals' on top, and alternative theatre below. Within education, there is little critical discourse of the 'second division' that is witnessed publicly in the media and national newspapers. Devised theatre is hampered by living in a specialised society that demands a specialisation of art forms, resulting in a lack of cross-disciplinary work, as well as leading to a series of separate cultural messages being created and transmitted to particular sections of society only.

WHO BENEFITS?

The nature of the devised performance suggests a value in the process as related to the end product. The significance is in the group's creativity and the intended audience's involvement with the performance. Fundamentally, it is what the elderly south London community, the fourth-year secondary pupils, or the local general public discover from the experience. The devising process becomes important in providing the opportunity and availability for others (including the non-specialists) to make or create a theatre performance. Within these parameters, judging or assessing success or excellence can only be determined by those participating in both process and product. Hilary Westlake of Lumiere & Son argues a mutual incompatibility between art and local involvement, based on the limitations of amateurs' commitment and performance ability. However, if the dominant literary theatre tradition and the restrictions of text-based work prevent non-specialist individuals from participating in the process of making art, then surely the alternative form of devised theatre embraces the struggle for artistic democracy in this country?

I am faced with the intrinsic question of who and what is art for? Therefore, what is the function of devised theatre in relation to traditional, text-based theatre? It is to offer accessibility and opportunity to groups of people to make, create, participate in and spectate theatre. Community-devised theatre is for a particular group of people; street theatre is for anyone passing by; performance art installations in public places are for everyone. The essential difference between the audiences of Welfare State's spectacles, or passers-by who stop to watch an IOU site-specific outside event, and those visiting a theatre production at an acknowledged venue is obvious; it involves a concrete decision of choosing to pay money to see art.

Devised theatre encourages and supports the notion of a group of people having the opportunity to be artists in their own right, to discover their own creativity in form and content. The importance of the devising process is to enable a number of individuals collaboratively to express, share, and articulate their views, beliefs, or opinions about British culture and society. The evaluation or assessment of such work is ultimately dependent on those making or participating in the theatrical event. Access can mean excellence. Devised theatre has a place alongside our literary theatre heritage. Both are necessary; they are neither in opposition nor in conflict.

DISCUSSION

Within the context of education and training, it is important for teachers to address the issues of how to bring greater accessibility of work to students, how to examine or judge art, and how to criticise or review contemporary devised theatre. Training programmes for intending artists must encourage them to discuss their work more frequently with artists from other disciplines, or to honestly share their true feelings about, or criticisms of, performance art. Similarly, in order to promote a greater dialogue between performers and audience, there must be more articles, books, and conferences to digest and discuss the subject of devised theatre within a public forum. The attendance of both professional devising theatre companies, theatre critics, academics, and graduate students at the Centre for Performance Research's conference in Cardiff on 'Devising and Documentation' in February 1993 was a great success.[6] It reflected a strong desire for artistic, intellectual, and educational debate on the subject of devised theatre.

Such debate illustrates the strength of appeal for companies devising theatre in the early 1990s. The attraction is in the devising process, in the alternative uses of time, money, and space to create a theatrical performance. The excitation is in the role of the performer/deviser, the relationship of the company to the audience in the non-theatrical space, and the visual and physical use of the playing environment. Every time a group devises a piece of theatre, it builds on previous experiences, but the uniqueness of the occasion demands a fresh approach to working together, an open mind, and a willingness to trust to the process rather than deciding too firmly in advance how the product will be created. The appeal of devising theatre lies in balancing and blending the various components together, in order to take control of the production of theatre.

8

LEARNING TO DEVISE
Practical ideas and suggestions

> . . . And so each venture
> Is a new beginning, a raid on the inarticulate
> With shabby equipment always deteriorating
> . . .
> For us, there is only the trying. The rest is not our
> business.
> ('East Coker', *Four Quartets*, T.S. Eliot)

This final chapter is for any new group devising theatre. It is intended for those people looking for signposts and directions in the form of practical ideas or suggestions. These can be taken either randomly or not on one of the many possible journeys of devising theatre. Having devised theatre with a number of groups in a variety of situations, taught and worked with students or young people in a range of educational institutions, and observed, researched and discussed contemporary British devised theatre practice with many professional practitioners, I wish to share what I have found useful from that discovery, learning and acquired knowledge. I offer a guide that is neither definitive nor presented as a recipe book for making theatre, but is just one approach to working together that is based on cumulative personal experiences over some years. Any ideas, suggestions or help that are proffered can be taken, tried out, adapted, or rejected, wherever it seems appropriate to the particular devising situation. They may be of value as learning models, for exploration and experimentation, or may simply serve to stimulate discussion about the processes and products of devised theatre.

What I have found most useful when devising theatre are a number of resources that are accessible and readily available.

The devising experience is often contradictory, unclear, and confusing. I need a structure that allows me to clarify, verify, and understand where I am going within the process. At the simplest level this might mean a pen and notebook to jot down observations and thoughts during initial sessions, or it could include detailed discussion time being purposefully planned by the group. It is important to acknowledge the contradictions in a positive way, and not attempt to solve early problems with a quick, compromising, mediocre answer.

There are books that are helpful to identify the practice of professional companies devising theatre, as well as those written by individual practitioners outlining practical ideas, games or exercises that can be used by any group working together. Selected examples of books that I would always recommend students to read in the former context are Rob Ritchie's *The Joint Stock Book*, Tony Coult and Baz Kershaw's *Engineers of the Imagination – The Welfare State Handbook*, David Savran's *Breaking the Rules: The Wooster Group*, and Elizabeth MacLennan's *The Moon Belongs to Everyone, Making Theatre with 7:84*.[1] However, it must be said that I have never picked up a book for practical working reference when 'on the floor' and immersed in the creative process of making theatre. Reading as widely as possible to increase daily awareness of the world, or to challenge new ideas or thinking, encourages further questioning, investigation, and exploration.

Going to see as much live devised theatre as possible is an obvious suggestion, but one that needs continual reiteration. Watching work that is exciting – or poor – stimulates ideas, inspiration, and material for discussion. Financing theatre visits or accessibility to performances in certain parts of the country can be problematic, but if all else fails, most companies video their productions as an ongoing record of their work. Festivals often provide a focus for a range of performances to be seen, such as the 'Showcase' season at the Brighton Festival, or the London International Festival of Theatre that brings wonderful work from abroad to Britain every two years.[2] Participation in workshops led by professional practitioners not only gives an insight into a company's approach or working method, but provides a practical learning experience of working with others.

When I started devising theatre as an undergraduate student in the 1970s, what most inspired and excited me was seeing such a tremendous range of professional work, which included, Shared Experience's early shows, Monstrous Regiment, Ken Campbell, Belt and Braces, Foco Novo, Incubus, and Footsbarn – the list is endless.[3] Trying out ideas, however, was the most important part of wanting to devise theatre with a group of people also interested in working together. There is no substitute for exploration and experimentation of ideas, knowing that all can be abandoned, and that the possibility to start again is always there. The making and examination of work 'on the floor' is the most important aspect of devising theatre for any group, because it moves the process forward practically towards the creation of the product.

Much of my teaching work is about facilitating ideas, discussing process or product, as well as advising on the possibilities of a devising situation. I want to consider how a group begins to work together, and ways of starting to devise theatre, to suggest ideas or stimuli for experimenting with form, content or audience, and to examine some problems or difficulties that may occur within the devising or rehearsal process. The written format of what follows is intended to be selectively used in the way that is most appropriate to the group's manner of making theatre. Individual personalities and reasons for motivation are fundamental to how a group decides to devise, which is why my suggestions or ideas can only be one way to investigate, build, and develop a working practice that is right for a group.

GROUP BEGINNINGS (1)

Decide how often to meet regularly as a group; for example, agree a weekly time or session to discuss company business or administrative matters, as well as time for advance planning of work, a weekly review, or evaluation of progress so far. It is important to establish how the group is going to assess progress, and this will very much depend on the nature of the participants and the project. One suggestion is to keep a company log-book or written record of progress, which will enable the group to look back at how devising decisions were arrived at, building on and consolidating the work further. This may take the form of diary entries, and can be a shared responsibility, for instance, a rota basis of weekly recording that includes all members of the group. Sometimes it is also appropriate for individuals to keep personal notebooks of jottings, notes, or observations during a workshop session that can be reflected on at a later stage of group discussion.

'Brainstorming'

Initial aims and objectives for the group, company, or project provide the boundaries at the start. How this is organised and determined will depend on the individuals' interests, experiences, and ideas for the project. What I have often found particularly useful at this early stage is to identify key questions for the group, and to 'brainstorm' answers over a specified period of time. This involves writing the questions on 'sheets' of wallpaper and asking members of the group to write their immediate responses to the questions (and to the answers of others) in silence over an agreed time limit. This provides a core of personal material as a basis for discussion, a stimulus for further questions and 'brainstorming', which eventually results in a shared written statement of intention, or agreement of principles, aims or objectives. If the group is devising in a permanent space, these 'sheets' can be displayed as a reminder of original decisions, or as a resource to return to as necessary.

I have also used this method of working when group discussion is blocked, negative, or dominated by the same people, as the disciplined conditions of the exercise ensure fairness to everyone to individually respond to the questions. Questioning techniques are vital in a devising process, but look out for the obvious danger of asking closed questions that direct or narrow the focus of discussion too soon. If motivation, interest, and intention are unanimous, then consider the opening parameters of the product to be devised. Never lose sight of the product or end performance. Work towards a goal of completion, which is identified through a series of deadlines or 'work-in-progress' stages. The group is devising a piece of theatre for an audience to watch at a particular time or place, which begs the question of how to devise the product, and what tools or means are available within the process.

Discussion is an early essential means of communication for the group. Explore different ways of structuring a discussion as a group, such as appointing a chairperson to lead, intervene as necessary, and summarise points of agreement. Try a system of everyone having the opportunity to speak in turn, rather than random ideas being offered by the same members, or those people with the loudest voice or the strongest personality. Adapt the 'conch' idea from William Golding's novel *Lord of the Flies*, so that a member may only speak when holding the selected object within the circle of discussion. Consider the suggestion of each individual's idea being given to the 'group pot of ideas', so that ownership of a personal contribution is surrendered in further debate. Sometimes a discussion needs to be as free-ranging as possible, whilst other occasions demand a clear focus and a more structured form of debate.

GROUP BEGINNINGS (2)

In order to get to know the group better, it may be useful to take a preliminary idea for content as a means to discovering more about individuals' interests, attitudes, beliefs, feelings, or views about a particular subject. Imagine that a group has expressed an early interest in the theme of crime as a possible starting point for devising a show. The first stage might involve using 'sheets' to 'brainstorm' personal responses to four key questions about crime, for example:

What is crime?
What is a criminal?
Is it a crime only when you are caught?
Is stealing always a crime?

The answers to these questions are discussed and immediately establish a difference (or not) in attitudes towards the subject. This may open up further questions and 'brainstorming', or it may suggest a particular line of enquiry to be pursued through a specific practical activity rather than through discussion. Alternatively, there may be one 'issue' that produces strong disagreement or conflict of opinion to the extent that it is adopted as the next area for practical examination. Examples of relevant practical exercises might include:

1 Individually: Present a physical image that reflects a personal view of crime.

2 Look at each image in turn, and discuss together what the image says to the group.
3 Try to make an agreed physical collective image of crime. Experiment with ideas using one member of the group as an 'outside eye' to comment on the work.
4 Create a physical and verbal collage of crime as a group, using movement, sounds, music, and any other appropriate resources available. (Work on the mood or atmosphere of the presentation.)
5 Individually: Tell a personal story of crime to the group.
6 Discuss these stories, choosing one that seems most appropriate to everyone, or that holds the most exciting material for theatrical exploration, or that combines ideas from all the stories to create a new narrative.
7 Agree an outline scenario for the story (written or improvised).
8 Decide on a number of characters in the story, based on people from the original material, or invented from discussion or improvisation.
9 Improvise a central scene from the story, or allocate members of the group to work together on different sections, in order to find out more information about characters, or to look at the development of a specific scene.
10 'Hot seat' each character as a group to establish a background knowledge or base line for further development.

Exploring a theme in this way brings people together and also identifies the needs of the group with regard to ways of working, material to be researched, ideas for the form or content of a show, and group dynamics. This might be one of several preliminary exercises of working together, or it might be the beginnings of a route to be taken towards devising a piece of theatre for ex-offenders about women in prison.

GROUP BEGINNINGS (3)

A group coming together for the first time may find introductory practical work an instrumental way of getting to know each other, using games, concentration, and trust exercises to develop a sense of discipline, fun, and spontaneity at the same time. Activities that promote skills of communication, confidence, trust and sensitivity all contribute to the training of a group in terms of establishing its identity, discovering its own dynamics, and improving basic skills of performance. Work to be covered includes movement and vocal training (with an emphasis on physical fitness, suppleness, and competence in various physical skills), games that encourage group creativity, concentration and trust, improvisation, and relaxation, as well as ways of focussing discussion, decision-making, and leadership.

It is important to point out that every group needs to select the most beneficial exercises or games that are pertinent to the growth and progression of individual members relating to, and interacting with, each other. For this reason, there is no definitive list of practical group exercises, because it is dependent on the nature of the project, the people involved, the theatre being created, and how the group chooses to incorporate initial practical activities into the overall working structure agreed at the start. In other words, out of one set of exercises come ideas for others, or alternatively, a decision to change direction completely through a written activity or discussion. Examples of books that provide valuable resources for a group in terms of reading about personal experiences, specific improvisatory techniques, or finding something that stimulates imagination and creativity are: Albert Hunt's *Hopes for Great Happenings*, in which he lists some examples of games that he has found useful in Appendix I;[4] Keith Johnstone's *IMPRO Improvisation and the Theatre*, which offers the reader a range of practical techniques, exercises, and ideas for spontaneous creativity;[5] Clive Barker's *Theatre Games*, which is a handbook about 'the work and art of the actor';[6] and *BODY SPACE IMAGE Notes Towards Improvisation and Performance* by Miranda Tufnell and Chris Crickmay, which is 'intended as a manual, an aid to action, but . . . is not in any sense a complete guide'.[7]

Whichever way you choose to start working practically as a group, it is important to establish a shared feeling of participation at the beginning of a session. This is most easily achieved through an introductory physical warm-up, which is important in terms of focussing concentration and creating a healthy working atmosphere. Appropriate loose clothing should be worn so that members are not restricted in their movements, for example of falling, being caught, or travelling in unison.

The warm-up might take the form of playing games, following a strict routine of aerobic exercises, the yogic 'Salute to the Sun', stretching and breathing exercises, or instituting 'the grid' as a way to start a session.

'The grid' involves skills of group awareness and discipline, concentration, and trust. An area is marked out for the group to move in, in as simple and neutral a way as possible (eyes front, head up, no arms swinging), walking in straight lines and turning at right angles (ninety degrees), changing direction whenever they encounter another person travelling towards them. Someone outside the group claps to indicate that everyone should stop. This is developed so that the group can stop and start without help, producing a performance style of neutrality. Once this has been achieved, the group can learn to stop and start in varying combinations, such as only a certain number of people moving at once, or all but one person moving together, building a base for more elaborate group performance work.

Influences

I have used and taught a number of warm-up exercises over the years, developing a personalised vocabulary based on the influences and ideas of others. I include Iyengar and Hatha Yoga (particularly breathing and relaxation), contemporary dance techniques, t'ai chi, and aerobics, as well as other adapted forms of warming-up suggested by theatre teachers or practitioners, such as Jerzy Grotowski and Augusto Boal, in an attempt to bring people together in an atmosphere of relaxed trust and cooperation. I will always remember a workshop run by members of Triple Action in the early 1980s for my students, where an actor asked the group to start 'warming-up'. Immediately, everyone (anxious to please) started to limber up using a series of stretching exercises that included Yoga's 'The Cat' and 'Salute to the Sun', contemporary dance back stretches, and other collectively learnt sections of aerobic workouts. After a period of observation, the actor stopped the students and asked them to define what they were doing in terms of his request. He suggested that they were warming-up for *his* benefit, that they were creating an image or picture of warming-up through these exercises or routines, rather than physically exerting themselves so that they felt pushed to the point of exhaustion.

He then led them through a Grotowski-based exercise in which they were to imagine themselves as horses in a meadow running and playing together, moving in bursts of energetic activity, or rolling gently on the grass in preparation for the next concentrated spurt of exercise. This was a long, continuous physical warm-up, which pushed the students to breaking point, but more importantly, focussed their attention, concentration, and energy on a specific objective or intention in preparation for the work that followed. I find the 'yogic' quality of some of Grotowski's preparatory exercises beneficial in tandem with specific practise of yoga poses, for example, the shoulderstand, dog pose, and squat. There is an emphasis on breathing correctly before, during, and after each exercise, encouraging a disciplined approach to the work. Here are two illustrations of this work:

1 Play the 'follow my leader' exercise, moving in squat jumps or alternative ways; run around the space and find the energy to include a jump and a scream that do not interrupt the flow of running; jump from a squat position, releasing the energy from the stomach, whilst screaming aloud and travelling through the space.
2 Imagine the arms are paralysed; there is a fly on the right shoulder, and the desire is to shake it off. In the same situation, there is a piece of silk placed on the head, which is to be thrown off using all of the body to do this.

A warm-up that I have used (inspired by the ideas of Grotowski) looks at body awareness and group concentration, contradicting the approach of practising a routine of exercises in order to make the body more supple and strong. Lying on the floor with the eyes closed, imagine the body shape or self-image against the ground. Become aware of the parts of the body that are heavy, warm, or tingling, or any other sensations associated with them. Think of the distance between parts of the body and hold up the fingers to indicate the distance between them – for instance, be aware of the distance between the ears or the equivalent length of one foot in relation to another part of the body. Draw a spontaneous map of the body, using colours to indicate the various areas of feeling, and illustrate other aspects of body awareness as appropriate. Test awareness further by stroking the left leg from thigh to foot. Concentrate all attention and love on to that leg until ready to move around the room. How does the leg compare with the right leg? Is it heavier, warmer, or stronger? Now, standing still with eyes closed, imagine the process of stroking the right leg. Remember how it felt, focussing on the earlier process and sensations. Walk around the room and become aware if the right leg feels any different.

Now find a place to stand in the room, marking the position or stance adopted in relation to others. Establish who is where, and how they are standing. On an agreed command, all move to someone else's position, trying to remember where everyone in the group started. Continue this process, correcting each other until everybody knows all the positions. Then without further commands, spontaneously move to new positions as a group, arriving at the same time. Each time, help anyone who is wrong or without a position. Continue the exercise until everyone can confidently change all positions within the group. This exercise warms up the participants in terms of concentration, memory, and group dynamics.

Group dynamics

It must be said, however, that it is the South American theatre practitioner Augusto Boal who has inspired, challenged, and influenced me most in relation to working with groups when devising theatre. My first impressions of Boal in 1985[8] were of a radical, political, charismatic man working with his Paris-based company on the techniques of the 'theatre of the oppressed'.[9] Working with him in 1988, 1989, and 1992[10] has developed my awareness and ability to address the potential, problems, and difficulties that can arise in a group devising theatre. Boal has developed these techniques, games, and exercises from the 'theatre of the oppressed'[11] as a way of challenging preconceptions, and illustrating quite radical ideas about power hierarchies and dynamics.

Boal's methods of working are useful for any group devising theatre. They enable an exploration of individual and group dynamics, relationships between people, sensitivity, trust, giving and taking, and listening skills. They can help establish those people in a group with a need to assert themselves, to be recognised, quick to intervene or criticise the work. Some techniques engage with the world of fantasy or imagination, whilst others encourage members of a group to become more open to new ideas, humble in opinions, observations or comments, to be able to distance themselves or stand back at times, to directly say what is felt, and to be more flexible or adaptable as appropriate.

The 'theatre of the oppressed' is both a method of working, and a language to analyse the interaction of group dynamics. Boal's techniques can be used in many ways, which is what attracts me to his work. I have used these techniques to dynamise or stimulate members of a group to show or see themselves in light of others. This is a learning process that cannot be forced, but comes from and with desire, choice, and recognition. Boal's techniques challenge a group to share and discover ideas practically with each other. In the same way, Boal's exercises and games for introductory group sessions stimulate members to build, develop, and communicate a group confidence and enjoyment of working cooperatively.

Boal divides preliminary exercises into four categories (to feel what we touch, to listen to what we hear, several senses, to see what we look at), proposing a range of activities that embrace the basics of initial group work. Here are some selected examples from each category:

1st category (to feel what we touch)

Hypnosis:

1 In pairs: One person holds the palm of their hand upright. The partner must focus and follow the palm of the hand with their nose and face as near to the palm as possible. Swop in turn as leader or follower.
2 In threes: The leader holds both palms upright for both others to follow. Swop in turn as leader or follower.
3 As a group: One person starts with palm of hand as leader of the exercise. All go in, one by one, locating a particular point of contact to follow on the next person. Try keeping as near to them as possible, or as far away as possible, and finally place the nose on the original point of contact.

Mimosas:

1 In pairs: One touches the other's body, so that the partner must immediately start shaking that part of the body in response to the contact. This is continued so that the partner is using the whole body in the end to spontaneously respond to different points of contact. Swop in turn.
2 Continue the exercise so that a sound is also made with each physical contact. Try and make the sounds as melodic as possible.

2nd category (to listen to what we hear)

Machine of rhythms:

1 As a group: Everyone stands in a circle with one volunteer in the middle. The person begins making a rhythmic movement and sound of a machine. One by one, everybody joins in, relating their movement and sound to a specific person or part of the machine. The group now operates as a rhythmic movement and sound machine.
2 Repeat the exercise as a 'Hate Machine'. The individual's focus is on a rhythmic movement and sound of hate that relates to another one observed in the group.
3 Repeat the exercise as a 'Love Machine'.
4 Repeat the exercise as an 'England Today Machine'.

Note: Once the group is working as a machine, speed up the rhythm very fast; slow down until the group finds a way to stop on its own.

(This exercise is about spontaneity, impulse and instinct. It is not about thinking of the various possibilities or interpretations of the theme.)

West Side Story:

1 As a group: Divide into two groups at either end of the space with a leader at the front. The leader makes a sound and movement, which is copied by other members of group one, as they advance towards group two. The leader of group two responds to group one's movement/sound, which is copied by group two. They advance on group one, who retreat

backwards. This pattern is then repeated in continuum, with a new leader stepping forward each time.

Note: The actions and sounds should become more complicated as the exercise progresses and both groups gain in confidence.

3rd category (several senses)

Noise:

1 In pairs: One is 'blind' and must move towards an agreed noise made by the partner. The partner explores making the lowest sound so that it is almost inaudible. Swop in turn.

Note: Boal suggests that at some point somebody else makes the sound to test if the 'blind' person is aware that it is not their partner.

4th category (to see what we look at)

Complete the image:

1 Using two people, start by demonstrating them shaking hands together. Encourage the group to comment on the image, saying the first things that come into their heads. Immediately respond to the image and as Boal says, 'Do not censor what you speak'.[12]
2 In pairs: Start by shaking hands. One drops out and looks at the image of their partner. That person returns and makes a new joint image in relation to their partner. The partner drops out, looks at the person, returns and makes a new joint image again.

Note: This exercise is about fostering the objective and subjective at the same time. The aim is to work spontaneously and instinctively, rather than thinking and interpreting the ideas of the image.

I have selected only a few examples to indicate the kind of exercises and warm-up activities available to a group, and suggest looking at Games for Actors and Non-Actors[13] for a more detailed description of these exercises, and further information about Boal's work. Other books that I have found helpful in terms of selecting and adapting warm-up exercises for a group are Moshe Feldenkrais' *Awareness Through Movement*,[14] Iyengar's *Light on Yoga*,[15] and Litz Pisk's *The Actor and His Body*.[16] What I must reiterate is the significant point that every group must decide on its own needs in terms of choosing exercises, games, or warm-up activities that will benefit those particular individuals, the project, and the initial objectives of the group. Explore what is relevant and appropriate in context of the specific circumstances.

This section ends with a selection of exercises that I have used with new groups to encourage a spirit of communication and cooperation, in order to develop skills of concentration, trust, and sensitivity to each other. They are drawn from a wide range of eclectic experiences and sources, proving of value in a number of diverse working situations. They can be incorporated together as an initial preliminary group session, or used independently as required.[17]

Introductory group exercises

1 Name game

Standing in a circle, each person introduces him/her self in any way they choose, moving and speaking within the centre of the circle. Everybody then goes in and imitates the presentation as accurately as possible. Repeat so that the movement/speech is more individually adventurous and inventive.

2 Getting to know each other

1 Within a time limit of two minutes, individuals introduce themselves through their name and one piece of chosen information to every member of the group.
2 Greet every member of the group with a particular physical gesture that is special to each new pairing or partnership. There is no discussion in this exercise, with every pair finding a gesture collaboratively without words. Each member of the group now has a repertoire of physical greetings.
3 Divide the group into two lines and number them individually. The left side line is numbered 1–6 left to right, and the

179

right side line is numbered 1–6, right to left, so that the 'ones' are diagonally opposite each other. One person calls out two numbers, for instance, 'left one' and 'right five', and those two people must physically greet each other in the central space. There is no discussion, and if greetings cannot be remembered, the pair must improvise.

3 Games

'Yes, let's!'

One person is elected to start, and makes a suggestion to the group, prefaced by 'Let's all. . .', to which everyone replies with huge enthusiasm, 'Yes, let's. . .'. The suggestion is then carried out by all the group, and continues until somebody says 'Let's all. . .', and so the activity continues.

Note: This is a fun game, but each suggestion should be carried out with serious intent.

'Zing, zing, zing and 1,2,3'

Standing in a circle, each person is numbered individually. The game opens with everyone chanting 'Zing, zing, zing and 1,2,3', followed by the person elected to begin, such as, 'number one', saying a number, for example, 'number six'. The person who is number six replies, 'Who me?', and number one says, 'Yes you!'; number six answers, 'Not me!', with number one questioning 'Then who?'. Number six suggests 'Number three', and so the pattern is repeated. Once the sequence is established, it is useful to play with the vocal presentation of the exercise in terms of pace, tone, and diction. If the game breaks down at any point, the group chant is spoken and the exercise starts afresh.

Note: Other useful group games are 'Killer', 'Grandmother's Footsteps' and 'Court of the Holy Dido'.

4 Cannoning

Standing in a circle holding hands, think of this exercise as creating a current of group electricity. One person starts by raising their left arm upwards, which immediately triggers off the raising of the next person's right arm, so that we witness a series of arms being raised around the circle. Back to the opening person again, and the arms are brought down in sequence. This is then followed by each person bending their knees in turn, and is finally completed with a straightening of knees sequence.

Note: This exercise demands high levels of group concentration, and should be neatly carried out with quick, crisp, concise movements that flow around the circle.

5 Group huddle

Divide into two groups or remain as one group. One person stays outside the group as members make a 'rugby tackle huddle', bodies interlocked with heads down towards the ground. The outsider has to climb over the 'huddle', experimenting with ways of travelling across the group. Each person has a turn at finding a way to cross the 'huddle'.

6 Movement game

1 Standing in a circle, the first person, for example, A, creates a movement inside the circle and takes it to B. B must 'pick up' the movement on the spot before moving off into the circle with the movement. Once inside the space, B must change the movement instinctively without stopping the flow or direction so that a new movement is created, and then given to C. This pattern is then continued by members of the group. (Note: The fluidity of movement is important, and each person must be encouraged to really explore and experiment when changing the movement before it is finally passed on to someone else. The exercise is about being inventive, creative, and accurate in imitation.)
2 Repeat the exercise using sounds as well as movement. Again, it is vital that there is a fluid continuity of sound development with each new experimentation and change of person.

Note: Let the movement and sound evolve naturally out of

exploration rather than intellectually planning and preparing in the head.

7 Concentration exercises

1 In a group: Standing in a circle, the person elected to start, A, looks at B and walks slowly across the circle to them. Meanwhile B looks at C, who must say B's name aloud before A reaches B. B is then free to look at D and move to them. D must look at E, who says D's name before B arrives and D is free to move. (Note: This is an excellent exercise for any group, and can be included as part of an introductory warm-up routine. Once established, the participants should be able to run across the space so that it becomes a fast-moving alertness exercise.)

2 '1,2,3' – for pairs: A and B stand about three feet apart, facing each other. Using a spoken number sequence of '1,2,3', A says '1', B says '2', A says '3', B says '1', and so on. Once the sequence is clearly established, then the person who says '1' stamps their left foot at the same time. This is continued until the pair is satisfied with the sequence. Finally, the person who says '3' hits their head with their right hand so that a rhythmic flow is completed.

3 'Hi-yee' – for pairs: A and B stand about three feet apart, with knees bent and one finger of each hand pointing up towards the ceiling. This is the opening ceremonial gesture for the exercise. Make sure that both people can touch each other's noses comfortably. When ready, the pair jump together into opening position whilst shouting out 'Hi-yee' as the start to concentration. The aim is to touch the partner's nose without being told to stop. 'Stop!' is spoken when one of the pair is aware of the finger coming towards the nose.

4 'Mirrors' – for pairs: A and B stand about three feet apart, facing each other. The exercise should start slowly as they aim to imitate every movement made, as if watching a mirrored reflection of themselves. Gestures should be slow and simple until a confidence/trust is developed between the partners. At a later stage, the pair can move together around the space, find another pair, and make a mirror reflection of four people. (Note: If movements are to be accurately imitated, a strong sense of concentration is required between

the two people, which can only be developed slowly over a period of time.)

8 Trust exercises

1 Everyone stands at one end of the room except for the teacher/leader/facilitator/director, who stands at the other end. In turn, each person walks the length of the room with their eyes closed, until the leader says 'Stop!'. The rest of the group observe individuals to see if they slow down in anticipation of the command to stop and open their eyes.
2 Repeat (1) at a jogging pace.
3 Repeat (1) at a running pace. (Note: The leader must pay particular attention to safety provision in terms of physically stopping the individual, and allowing plenty of surrounding space at this end of the room.)
4 In pairs: In turn, A and B practise falling backwards into each other's arms. It is best to start with one person standing closely behind the other until confidence and trust is established. Ideally, B should be some distance away from A, so that A falls backwards, and B steps forward to catch A. (Note: B should bend knees when taking the weight of A.)
5 In group(s): Divide into small groups with each person in turn standing with their eyes closed in the centre of the circle. The group should be sufficiently close to catch the falling person and gently pass them to and fro within the circle. There should always be two people working together to receive the falling person and pass them across the circle. (Note: This is a real test of group trust, and is also a relaxing experience for the person in the middle of the group.)
6 Group diving exercise: Six to eight people are needed to form two lines opposite each other, about three feet apart. Every-one stands with the palms of their hands facing upwards, ready to catch the person who will dive into the receiving group of people. The 'diver' runs up to the group, jumps and springs into a horizontal diving position, and is then caught by the group. (Note: With more confident individuals, be aware of the distance they may travel through the air.) Sometimes, it requires more or less people to stand together because of an individual's size, height, weight, or degree of confidence. Once everyone is happy with this exercise, there

are variations that can be developed; for instance, the group members face away from each other at the start, and turn together to receive the 'diver', or the 'diver' stands on a table or rostrum and dives from a height into the group's arms.

Note: Always be aware of safety precautions for any or all of these trust exercises.

9 Introductory improvisation

1 Standing in a circle, one person (A) volunteers to be in the middle. A further six volunteers are selected to participate in the exercise. In turn, each person must create a new situation for A to spontaneously respond to and improvise from as one volunteer enters and the other exits. With each new person there should be an immediate change of situation, which challenges A to relate to a new set of circumstances.

2 Standing in a circle, one person (B) volunteers to be in the middle. The first volunteer (C) enters the group and places B in a situation to improvise with C. At an appropriate point, another volunteer (D) enters the circle, creating an alternative context for B, C, and D to improvise. No one leaves the circle, so that the last volunteer will create a situation that involves all members of the group improvising together.

3 Standing in two circles (inner and outer), pairs are formed by the inner circle turning to face the outer circle. A series of different circumstances and contexts is given by the leader, so that each new pair can spontaneously improvise the situation. Examples are: one of the pair has failed to keep an important appointment with the other; one has borrowed something from the other and failed to give it back; one is interviewing the other for a specific job that the interviewee is trying to discover at the same time. (Note: It is important that the inner circle moves round each time, so that partners change with every new improvisation.)

Note: These introductory exercises can produce a tendency towards rather shallow improvisation at first, with unreal characters, conversations, and situations. It is important to address this as a group, using observations of the exercises as a basis for discussion about the process of improvising with others. Do not be afraid to repeat exercises in order to develop particular skills further.

10 Pairs work

1 Sitting opposite each other, look specifically at every feature of the partner's face. Examine every feature in detail. (Note: The leader may wish to question individuals after this exercise about the colour of eyes, shape of nose, and so on.)
2 In turn, try and move as many as possible features of the face separately and in isolation. Explore what you can do with the mouth or eyebrows. Try and avoid using the eyes to express feelings. (Note: The partner can alert the other to over-use of the eyes.)
3 In turn, say to your partner, 'I love you very much' with one part of the face only, for instance, with the eyebrows. Say, 'I dislike you intensely' with the nose. Communicate boredom with the mouth to a partner. Indicate excitement with the eyes. The observing partner comments afterwards as to whether the message was conveyed, using only one part of the face.
4 Facing a wall, one person creates a face mask of horror or joy so that every part of the face is expressing that particular feeling. Keeping the rest of the body as neutral as possible, walk in the space without indicating the action of the mask. The partner should observe if a neutral body stance is adopted, if the face mask remains consistent when encountering others, and the level of concentration achieved. Swop roles.
5 Standing opposite each other and using the person's first name as the only word to be used, convey an individual mood through vocal exploration of the name. When the partner's mood is understood, convey *their* mood through body movement whilst still expressing one's own mood vocally. (Note: This is a difficult exercise, which can be examined further through discussion.)
6 Lying down opposite each other, place feet together so that both are able to cycle in unison. Experiment with cycling very slowly or fast. Whilst cycling, establish a nursery rhyme to say together. Then cycle very slowly and say the rhyme fast.

Do the reverse, cycling quickly and speaking the rhyme slowly.

7 One person bends forward; the other lies backwards across their partner's back and says the nursery rhyme. Swop roles.

8 One person bends forward, relaxing the knees and making sure that the neck and head are free. The partner checks that there is no tension in the neck, gently massaging the neck in the direction of the head. Cupping the hands, the partner firmly massages the spine in a rhythmic up and down movement. The person hanging should feel no tension in the body and be able to make a relaxed 'ha' sound from this position. The sound should vibrate through the back easily, and any tightness in projection indicates tension or strain. Swop roles.

11 Relaxation

Lying down in a space, check that the back is as close to the ground or floor as possible. Become comfortable with eyes closed. Think of the left foot in isolation and flex it just above the floor. Feel the tension and relax. Think of the left kneecap, calf, and foot. Pull up the kneecap, stretch the calf muscles and raise the foot off the floor in one movement. Tense and release. Focus on the whole left leg; tighten and tense as much as possible; hold and relax. Repeat everything with the right leg. Check that the feet are now relaxed outwards and not still in a tense position. Think of the left arm; make a clenched fist with the left hand and lift the whole arm just above the ground in as tense and tight a position as possible. Hold and release. Repeat with the right arm. Check that the hands are not still clenched, but relaxed open with the palms facing upwards. Hunch the shoulders to the ears as tightly as possible, keeping the back and head on the ground. Hold and relax. Repeat this several times. Keeping the shoulders on the ground, arch the back in an upward direction, clenching the buttocks together and tensing the whole back region. Tense and relax. With shoulders on the floor, raise the head off the ground and hold in a tense position. Relax. Repeat several times. Gently move the head from side to side. Think of the left side as a whole; stretch through from the foot, calf, kneecap, thigh, hip, waist, arm, hand, and shoulder to the head with the aim of tensing the left side of the body completely. Hold and relax. Repeat with the right side of the body. Repeat with the whole body, stretching, tensing, and relaxing several times. The body should now be in a relaxed state. Alter the position as needed. Breathing should be natural and relaxed. Imagine lying on a bed of feathers, gently drifting through the air, staring into space. Clear the mind of all worries and concerns, focussing on breathing and relaxing. Allow several minutes of pure relaxation. Slowly stretch right through the body, wriggling the toes and fingers gently. Taking as much time as is needed, turn on one side and carefully come up to a sitting position, with the eyes still closed. Rub the hands together and cover the face. Open the eyes behind the hands and slowly become aware of the environment.

(Note: Wherever possible, make sure that the room is warm and comfortable, and that the lights can be turned off for the main part of the exercise. A blackout facility is useful with members of a group lying on blankets or rugs. Individuals should not fall asleep during the exercise, but should reach a deep level of relaxation. It is at the discretion of the leader how often different parts of the exercise should be repeated until the point of pure relaxation. A gentle, soothing voice should be adopted when leading and talking through the exercise.)

WAYS OF STARTING TO DEVISE THEATRE

It is quite clear that devised theatre can start from almost anything, and this book reveals selected examples of the diversity of professional theatre practice to support this fact. It is also my own experience that the same starting stimuli can be taken by any new group interested in devising theatre, and the work produced will always be unique for those particular people involved in the work. I will always remember an especially difficult fifth-year secondary drama group I taught in 1980, who created an extraordinary devised piece based on a surrealist painting of a pair of shoes,[18] which not only fully occupied and absorbed their attention, but became a crafted, polished, and memorable performance.

Resources are infinite when beginning to devise theatre together, and this is often one of the first problems encountered by a group. Where exactly to start from? Ideas and suggestions must come from the group concerned in the context of the nature of the intended project. When I was teaching 'A' level Theatre Studies to a group of lower sixth formers in 1981, we examined the ideas and theories of Antonin Artaud by devising a piece of theatre that started with an exploration of objects. We looked at ideas of dismemberment, experimenting with a wide use of materials to create object-characters, such as the upside-down man, who originated from a varied collection of cardboard boxes, or the chrysalis creature, which writhed within the folds of thick industrial plastic sheeting in a pool of pink light against a background of distorted sound effects. The audience sat in the middle of the drama studio space on swivel chairs turning their attention to whichever action or activity interested them most. Musical instruments became people, lighting and sound played significant new roles, whilst actors were employed as props, set, or facilitators of the next sequence.

Initial ideas

This experimental, non-narrative piece of work developed from a desire to place greater emphasis on the visual and sensory nature of the theatrical experience. Therefore, it is important to ascertain whether the choice of stimuli or starting points are for a specific purpose, for example, to fulfil a major objective, or are randomly chosen in order to point a way forward in one direction or another. Having experimented with various ways of devising from a range of starting points, I suggest a skeleton checklist that offers potential beginnings for any group devising theatre. Personal choice determines the details of each category within this list, which simply lays open a structure for particular individual or group decisions about where to start:

1 Poems: 'Telephone Conversation' by Wole Soyinka; 'The Castaways or Vote for Caliban' by Adrian Mitchell; 'Little Johnny's Final Letter' by Brian Patten.
2 Pictures: *The Red Model*, 1934, or *The Reckless Sleeper*, 1927, by René Magritte; *The Robing of the Bride*, 1939, by Max Ernst; *Extase*, 1967, by Pyke Koch.
3 Music: Songs written by Tom Waits, for instance 'Frank's Wild Years' from the LP 'Swordfishtrombones'; the music

of the Windham Hill record label, and the composer Philip Glass, including 'Songs from the Trilogy – Einstein on the Beach, Satyagraha, Akhnaten'.

4 Prose: Cooking recipes.
5 Stories: 'How the Camel got his Hump' from *Aesop's Fables*.
6 Play texts, extracts of: 'Storm from Paradise' by Claire MacDonald.[19]
7 Objects: Kettle; old boots.
8 Issues: Crime; abortion; equal opportunities.
9 Theme: From a play; general, such as 'Body images' or 'Goddesses'.
10 People: Their stories and personal experiences.
11 Documents: Historical; letters.
12 Design: Space; set; physical materials.
13 Movement: Sequence of movements observed in life situation.
14 Concept, question, statement: Newspaper headline.
15 Photographs.
16 Films.

Exemplification

In order to examine different ways of starting to devise theatre, I want to take two examples from my experience as a performer/deviser and teacher/deviser, illustrating how processes can begin and subsequently develop. In the first example – 'Women Imprisoned', devised by Workshop Theatre Women in Leeds during 1985 – the driving force came from the director (Carola Luther) with her passionate interest in the treatment of women in prison. Luther was keen for the seven-strong company of women to devote a significant preliminary period of time to research and interviewing ex-offenders.[20] As performer/deviser, my brief was to get to know two ex-offenders, researching their backgrounds and stories of crime. Additionally, we were all given separate research tasks that addressed the wider issues of women in prison, including strip searching, use of drugs, and medical facilities, as well as other known cases at the time.[21] This research involved me in two prison visits to Askcombe Grange, an 'open' prison near York, and Styal Prison in Manchester, where we talked to women prisoners, officers, and the Governor.

The company made up a long list of case-studies, biographies, and other reading materials, which we reported on weekly in early meetings together. Throughout this initial period of research, we compiled a huge file of resource material, which was shared out so that every company member read all the articles, pamphlets, and written reports. Individuals conveyed information through their contacts with the 'Women in Prison Campaign',[22] meetings with the probation service, and attendance at a conference on 'Crimes against Women' in Leeds.[23]

With a deadline in view, one of our first objectives was to make a tape recording of each ex-offender's life story. A second objective was to ensure that all those participants were invited to become actively involved in the devised project. The company wished to 'give a voice' to the ex-offenders, desiring as close a collaboration as possible with the women. Informal meetings and discussions took place to encourage relationships, which developed slowly over a number of weeks. An initial aim was to create a pool of researched source material as a starting point for the work, with the clear intention of producing seven life stories of ex-offenders.

In tandem to the research work, the company held preliminary workshops that explored crime, being a criminal, getting caught, and the issue of stealing, in some depth. Apart from an examination of content material, these workshops revealed a great deal about individual members and their various attitudes to the subject. There were differences of opinions, beliefs, and perceptions of crime, which had to be faced directly by the group if they were to work collaboratively with the ex-offenders. These were difficult, firey sessions on occasion, demanding honesty and clarity from seven strong personalities, who also had to keep in perspective the fact that none of them had been in prison.

The work that followed the initial research period, discussions, informal meetings, and workshop sessions developed out of the seven original stories, which were transcribed, edited, and shortened into six performers' monologues. Scenes were written out of 'workshopping' and improvisation around source materials. It was at this stage of devising that several of the ex-offenders attended sessions, contributing ideas, advice, and views on the content being devised. I vividly remember us trying to construct a scene in the police station where I was meant to feel intimidated by the police, which was heavily criticised by two of the women watching the session. Frustrated by the timidity of the playing, one woman intervened and gave a rendition of how the police officers would have acted towards my character. It was rough, violent, and real! I never felt satisfied with this scene, but their contribution pushed it forward, and changed it in a way that we could never have achieved ourselves.

The early devising process for this show became a mixture of improvising ideas or content material for potential prison scenes whilst transcribing, writing, and editing the seven stories of the women. Parallel to this had been an initial decision for one member of the company to write music for songs linked to the characters and their stories, or issues that seemed relevant to all women in prison. What generally followed was that each company member wrote lyrics for their character's song, and group songs were written by the individual with special responsibility for music and singing. Structuring the show into a cohesive whole was essentially the director's responsibility within a working context of group agreement. A first draft of the intended script became a new starting point for revision, editing, more writing, and the beginning of rehearsals. At this point the work moved into another phase, which is an appropriate place to leave this example of one way to start devising theatre.

Another approach

'Women Imprisoned' was devised from original, contemporary, researched source material, and based on the true stories of seven women in prison. The second example of a way to start devising comes from my experience of working with B.Ed. drama students training to be primary teachers, whilst I was lecturing at Portsmouth Polytechnic in 1987. These were first-year students focussing on the 'Creative Arts', and the overall aim of the term's project was to devise together a theatre-in-education programme for nine- to ten-year-olds in a middle school. What follows is a description of the early work, which was centrally concerned with learning and the process of devising, rather than the final product. Apart from my role as teacher/facilitator/deviser, I attempted to highlight the various

191

choices or decisions available to the group, as well as indicating the different stages of the devising process.

The major difference in this second example is that we started from ourselves as a theatre-in-education company, working within the known context of devising a theatre-in-education programme for nine- to ten-year-olds in a Portsmouth middle school. After a preliminary 'getting to know each other' drama workshop, I initiated a 'brainstorming' session to establish more about ourselves, our thinking, and beliefs, as well as issues important to us as a company. Members of the group were asked to respond to three questions:

1 What do children want to learn?
2 What do children need to learn?
3 What do I want to teach them?

The discussion that followed from the 'breakdown of the sheets' revealed clear differences of opinions, which were further explored through the question: Is there any commonality or shared ground within the group?

Another early discussion that took place centred on what the programme was to be about. A popular theme was 'the family', which produced the questions:

1 What do we want to look at about the family for nine-year-olds?
2 What is the notion of 'the family', and how important is it to a nine-year-old?
3 What does the family mean to *us*?
4 Are we multi-racial conscious?

This particular session helped to identify individuals' personal perceptions and experiences of the family, which in turn focussed on power relationships, status, and roles within families, as well as the various images of the family to be explored in different countries and cultures.

Questions to the group provided structure and focus for sessions, challenging everyone to respond to the work. Two key questions which were placed in permanent view throughout the term were:

1 What are we going to do, and why?

192

2 How are we going to do it?

It was agreed early on that we would explore the family in as many practical ways as possible. I find the construction of images a useful means of clarifying ideas, and asked the students to make three physical group images of support, security, and duty, which were their agreed answers to the question 'What does the family mean to *us*?'. This exercise illuminated the security image as being a central reference point for the development of the theme. Smaller group images of the family were explored, which led to a series of images about the 'perfect family' as projected in advertising, media, and television culture. The brief at the end of the day was to write a song about 'The Perfect Family'.

My interest in Boal's 'Image Theatre' was explored through a number of exercises and techniques with the students in relation to the family. I asked each member of the group to think of a personal experience of oppression within the family, presenting it first as a still image, and second as a sound. I also requested that they show an image of their oppressor. Students then swopped images so that they took on another physical form, analysing how they felt in an image, and becoming aware of the range of oppressions. In discussion, I asked them which image they identified with most, which led to a sharing of experiences and further personal investment in the company. There then followed some improvised work in pairs that illustrated the roles of oppressor and oppressed within a family relationship. Contradictions and feelings of duality were also considered, for example, the daughter who loves her mother but also feels oppressed by her.

Improvisation was an important aspect of practical work. One exercise that enabled a fuller examination of the family was for every individual to choose to play a member of a family talking about another member, such as a nine-year-old child talking about her father, or a daughter-in-law speaking about her father-in-law. This particular exercise produced many ideas for further exploration, one of which was for everyone to script a monologue for their character and read them aloud. An interesting group improvisation (again influenced by Boal's 'Forum Theatre' work) was to take a family situation and show how one member of the family is being oppressed by the

193

others. It is important to clearly establish the oppression, the oppressor, and the protagonist of the scene. This work revealed the domination of a grandmother over her family with particular consequences for her daughter-in-law, the mother in the group. This scene took place around a table whilst eating a meal, and demonstrated beautifully the issues of power, status, and roles within the family.

During this same period of practical theme exploration, the group visited a local Portsmouth Middle School to observe me teaching drama to a class of nine-year-olds, as well as talking to the children about their interests, hobbies, and work activities. As a company, we listed the areas of learning for nine-year-olds and attempted to articulate what it meant to be a nine-year-old child. The next stage of the devising process began with the two questions:

1 What *questions* has the work on the family raised for us?
2 What are we going to do, and why?

Following a discussion of the responses, I asked the students to take their characters from the earlier sessions (scripting of individual monologues), and work in pairs on an improvisation that explored one question from the list of interest through the two characters. Examples of key questions selected were:

1 How important are the relationships between parents and children?
2 Is the extended family important?
3 What do the children think about the family?
4 Do the tensions of family life affect your relationships with other people?

From the improvisations created, we then looked at what was relevant to the areas of learning for nine-year-olds, devising collectively a list of agreed questions that we would want to raise for nine-year-olds. We then considered specific aims for the programme that would be presented to one class, which addressed what we wanted to do as educators, and how we wanted to use theatre. In terms of the programme's content, there were three aims:

1 To bring awareness to the fact that every member of a family has their own set of problems.

2 To bring awareness to the children that every type of family has problems that are individual and unique to them.
3 To promote better communication between family members and an ability to express their feelings.

It was at this point that we also started to discuss the possibilities of form for the programme, based on a content decision to work through selected family members and related characters.

This devising project developed through the use of questions, discussion, 'brainstorming' techniques, practically related exercises, and improvisation. It was my intention that we should constantly challenge ourselves in every session to look at the different possibilities and avenues to be explored, rather than make early decisions about the proposed product. We were always learning, whether it was about the content theme of the family, or about how nine-year-old children think, feel, and operate within the classroom situation. The progress of the work was fully dependent on the cooperation, collaboration, communication, and contribution of every individual member of the group.

EXPERIMENTING WITH FORM, CONTENT, OR AUDIENCE

In chapter seven, I outlined a theoretical model of process to be investigated in terms of initial decisions related to form, content, or audience. What I want to suggest now is a series of mini-projects that offer structures for experimentation with form, content, or audience. These mini-projects were originally created for drama degree students in a learning situation, and are offered to the reader as potential frameworks to be adapted for group exploration. The aims of these mini-projects are:

1 To free the imagination.
2 To consider the possibilities of content or subject for devised theatre.
3 To encourage and find a 'voice' for a piece.
4 To look at a style of presentation or performance.
5 To identify a form for a piece.
6 To know who it is *for*, and why.

Mini-projects

1 Form – Structure

1 Physicalisation of ideas or physical beginnings.
2 Multi-images: use of sound, lighting, music, film, video, projections, montage techniques, multi-media.

Project (i): Devise ten minutes of physical, visual theatre. Suggested title – 'Strangers'. Use music, slides, dance/movement, masks, colour/spectacle, costumes, and any other resources.

Project (ii): Explore a theme widely over a prescribed period of time, for instance, 'Summer', and then discover the potential of different kinds of devised shows on this theme. Consider the theme in relation to a piece of outdoor, site-specific theatre, and/or to the presentation of a physical performance that includes text, projections, soundtrack, Super 8 film, or video.

2 Content – Group/Company – Audience

Devising theatre from a range of varied content beginnings, for example, the group or company, the intended audience, an issue, concept or theme.

Project (iii): Devise a ten-minute piece of theatre that focusses on the exploration of personal material and interests within the group. (Boal's work from the 'theatre of the oppressed', such as, Image or Forum Theatre, could be considered in light of this project.)

Project (iv): Devise a fifteen-minute piece of street theatre that takes into consideration its potential non-theatre-going audience, intended environment, and site-specific circumstances.

Project (v): Devise a ten-minute piece of theatre based on the theme of food.

Project (vi): Devise a ten-minute piece of theatre based on the issue of gender and sexual politics.

3 Research – Improvisation – Workshop

Various kinds of research to form the basis of devised theatre, for example, naturalistic improvised scenes, issue-based work. Research through reading, interviews, tape recordings, visits to museums, schools, and other places.

Project (vii): Devise ten to fifteen minutes of improvised scenes based on characters created from research, improvisation, and developing work. (Consider the approach taken by Mike Leigh in relation to this project.)[24]

Project (viii): Devise fifteen minutes of a theatre-in-education programme for secondary pupils, aged fourteen years. Research a specific topic that is historically or biographically based, and examine a variety of possible theatre-in-education programme packages to be devised. Plan and present ideas for a workshop, offering examples as part of the overall present-ation. Edit material prior to demonstration of project. Plan and prepare a teachers' pack alongside the intended programme.

Project (ix). Research contemporary material related to group interest that is based on meeting people, interviews, tape recordings, oral reminiscences, and so on. Consider the potential forms to be explored in light of the researched material, examining different ways that the same material might be presented, for instance, look at a documentary form and style of presentation.

4 Style – Adaptation

The adaptation of existing written materials, including play text, novel, short story, song lyrics, myth or legend, poem.

Project (x): Devise fifteen minutes of 'Storytelling Theatre', working from an adaptation of a source text, and using the resources of the actors only to create a particular style of presentation.[25]

Other practical suggestions for groups wanting to make or create a devised performance:

1 Devise a piece of theatre for a specific audience with particular aims and objectives, for example, a touring show

for young people to be performed at 'Youth Club' venues, or work in collaboration with a local Women's Refuge to devise a piece of theatre that examines the oppression of battered women.

2 Consider a variety of approaches to writing in relation to the process of devising, including:

(a) Workshopping ideas as a company that are observed by a writer, who then goes away and writes a script;

(b) Improvising scenes as a group that are then tape recorded, transcribed, and edited by one member of the group;

(c) Writing from ideas collectively, for instance, individual scenes are written by different members of the group;

(d) Every company member produces a written contribution as a stimulus for leading a devising session;

(e) Every company member writes a song about one aspect of the proposed theme or subject matter.

PROBLEMS, DIFFICULTIES, OR BLOCKS ALONG THE WAY

During any devising or rehearsal process, there are always difficulties or problems at some point in the proceedings. Probably the most frustrating period is when a group feels 'blocked' in terms of finding the most appropriate way forward to develop the content or form of the intended piece. Unfortunately, there are no magic solutions available. I can only suggest certain preparations in advance which may or may not make the group ready for this baffling experience, and which often leave individuals feeling thwarted, disappointed, or unsatisfied.

First, when organising and planning the work schedule, try incorporating deadlines for specific activities to be completed. Knowing that there is only a prescribed amount of time available for a particular section of the project may finally reduce the group to a state of inertia, or it may just push some members into a state of action. Either way, it is worth the risk!

Second, a planned 'work-in-progress' is often useful, in order to consolidate the work so far, as well as identifying specific problems with the product. A small invited audience is essential to test out ideas, and post-performance discussions can provide positive outside feedback to the proposed material or form. Again, it is a case of knowing that you have agreed to show something to an audience in two days' time, regardless of feeling frustrated, helpless, depressed, and without direction.

Scheduling

Try to allow adequate time for rehearsal, rather than devising up to the bitter end and learning lines the night before the first performance. (It happens to the best professional companies too!) Create planned opportunities within the schedule structure for re-writing, editing, and revision. It may take several days to incorporate individual and small group activities related to the show, such as one member re-writing a section of text, or two performers rehearsing a scene, whilst the remaining members participate in painting the set, completing costumes, or looking for additional props. This will all become entirely theoretical once the group is so far behind that these suggestions are totally inappropriate, or have no relevance to the group's particular way of working or operation.

Sometimes when a group is 'blocked' in the devising process, it just requires someone external to the company to look at the work as an 'outside eye'. Fresh ideas, advice, criticism or comments can trigger off a new momentum for the group concerned. It may simply be a case of needing to identify and focus on one question, concept, section, or area of decision in relation to the intended form, content, or audience. Perhaps the group has lost sight of the needs and interests of the audience, or the material is so generalised that it lacks any power, presence, or direct appeal to either the performers or observers. One practical suggestion when 'blocked' with decisions about the structure of the piece, is to lay papers on the floor (indicating different sections, scenes, or images) and move them around to appreciate the possibilities of all the material. It is also helpful to include blank pieces of paper so that 'links' can be written or notated as they are discovered through experimentation with the form. Somehow connections are made easier by seeing the pieces laid out in front of the group, which can be physically and visually juggled until the right decisions are taken.

Inevitably, being 'blocked' means dealing with a number of

theatrical hurdles, going off at tangents, and almost abandoning an idea that will not come right, until suddenly the group sees a way through. What is most important is to find something that prompts action in order to maintain the group's momentum, however slow! Select a way forward even if it leads the group to a cul-de-sac; someone can always turn round and try another direction. In my experience, it is never the planned attempt to motivate ideas that produces results, but rather some spontaneous discovery that turns everything upside-down, and reveals a glimmer of light on the devising horizon.

Devising theatre is a new experience in the making with every new group of people who come together at the start of an intended show or project. It can cause heartache, joy, frustration, and satisfaction. It can make an individual wonder why she or he ever had this notion of wanting to create work that is unique to a particular group and interests. How much easier to pick up an already written play text, and interpret how the play should be produced in performance. What is this constant appeal of wanting to begin from the germ of an idea, and develop it into a full-scale piece of theatre? It is the need to say something, to express oneself, to give a voice to ideas, thoughts, and feelings about the world; to capture the essence of a particular group of people making and creating theatre. It is extremely hard work, but the reward comes from partaking and participating with others in an attempt to define, articulate, and contextualise contemporary cultural and societal experiences. The reward is being involved in a group of individuals wanting to assert their particular view of the world. Despite the difficulties, there is the stimulation, excitation, and sheer pleasure of working with other people in the act of sharing and pooling ideas together. Its attraction is in the multifarious aspects of both process and product.

However much the group evaluates and assesses the final product, there is simply no guarantee that its members will be able to apply that wisdom to new circumstances, or to the next devised project. It is vital to be open and accessible to changing one's mind, moderating one's views, and compromising when necessary. Against this is the desire to push for specific ideas with a determined passion that reveals a total commitment and dedication to the work. The ultimate goal is to feel completely satisfied and excited by the final product. Learning to devise theatre opens up the possibilities and potential of such an experience, which is always an unhabituated territory at the start.

Writing this book has enabled me to explore and examine a number of questions related to the subject of devised theatre. As I come to the end of my exploration, I find I have come full circle and am faced with even more questions about the process and practice of devising theatre. Hopefully, this book will lay some foundations for further building, enquiry, and critical examination. I want to encourage others to offer their experiences, responses, and answers to such questions. As the next academic year approaches with a different group of full-time fourth-year 'devising' students, I experience familiar feelings of both excitement and fear as I anticipate first beginnings, further learning, understanding and enlightenment, an unknown set of problems or difficulties, and the potential enjoyment of working with another group of people on what will certainly be a wholly different and original experience to the last. This is where the work commences with a series of questions and some initial ideas for starting . . .

Where and how shall I begin?

APPENDIX I

A description of fourteen companies devising theatre

From: McGillivray, D. (ed.), British Alternative Theatre Directory 1990–1991, Conway McGillivray, 1990

BELGRADE TIE (TIE)

Policy We work with young people, their teachers and parents, providing a free service to all state schools in Coventry. Using theatre and drama techniques, we create original work designed to enable young people to question and change the world in which they live.

Origins Started in 1965 by Coventry Council as a pilot scheme; the first TIE team in the country.

Subsidy Coventry City Council, ACGB.

Personnel A core of twelve long-term members operating as a collective, 7 actor/teachers, resident designer, resident stage manager, schools liaison worker and two part-time administrators operating a job share.

Audience Between 8 and 35 people for a participatory programme in school. Anything up to 800 young people and adults for our annual YPT/community event.

GLORIA

Policy Gloria is a new production company set up to produce and promote the work of its members: Neil Bartlett, Nicholas Bloomfield, Annie Griffin, Leah Hausman and Simon Mellor.

Origins Founded June 1988.

Personnel Various, according to production.

Subsidy Project funding from ACGB, SAC, RAAs and local authority.

GREENWICH YOUNG PEOPLE'S THEATRE (TIE/YPTS)

Policy The aims are twofold: to provide a professional TIE service for the schools of S.E. London and to provide a comprehensive programme of theatre/arts activities for young people in their own time.

Origins Started in 1970 by Ewan Hooper, founder and director of the Greenwich Theatre, as part of the theatre's policy to provide as wide a range as possible of theatre/arts activities for all sections of its S.E. London community.

Subsidy 1989/1990: ILEA, ACGB (via Greenwich Theatre), London Borough of Greenwich, European Social Fund, GLA, EEC Youth Initiative Fund.

Personnel Management structure responsible to a board of management, but with an executive committee to safeguard full company participation. Responsibility for the work is shared among the 21 company members. Members' functions include director, administrator, secretary, caretaker, TIE team leader, centre activities team leader, liaison officer, production manager, stage managers, designers, musical director, actor/teachers, writer.

Tours Usually only in S.E. London, although exceptions have been made for special reasons. The Youth Theatre has toured widely, both in this country and abroad, eg. Poland and Czechoslovakia. We are open to suggestions for promoting our work, particularly internationally. Most venues are acceptable; we usually work in non-theatre venues. Special venue requirements depend upon the programme/play.

Audience Perform mainly to school pupils, some adult audiences. Additional areas of work include projects for the young unemployed and special needs groups.

Equipment Carry lighting, sound, musical instruments, photography, 1 van.

Activities TIE: Usually full-day participatory programmes either in schools or at GYPT for primary and secondary pupils. Meetings and workshops with teachers and the provision of teacher's notes to accompany programmes are integral to all schools work. INSET: INSET programmes in drama and theatre are provided on a regular basis for local teachers and are available nationally by negotiation. Arts workshops: Workshop sessions in drama, music and photography are held in the evenings for young people aged between 7 and 25. These sessions are open to all young people: there are no auditions. Several youth theatre groups give performances of both improvised and scripted work. 'Green Jam': The first national full-time training scheme in theatre arts for young adults with moderate and severe learning difficulties.

MAJOR ROAD THEATRE COMPANY

Policy Major Road is a theatre company committed to creating and commissioning work to the highest standard.
Origins Formed in 1973 in London; moved to Yorkshire in 1978.
Subsidy Revenue funded by ACGB, Yorkshire Arts Association and Yorkshire Grants.
Personnel Varies according to the programme of work. During 1989 the minimum was three, the maximum was 29.
Tours Throughout the UK, Europe and the United States.
Audience Vary according to the nature of the individual show.
Equipment Vehicles and technical equipment occasionally available for hire.

From: McGillivray, D. (ed.), The British Alternative Theatre Directory 1992–1993, Rebecca Books, 1992

AGE EXCHANGE THEATRE TRUST

A professional touring theatre company which specialises in producing reminiscence theatre for the elderly.

FORCED ENTERTAINMENT THEATRE CO-OPERATIVE

Policy Forced Entertainment has been working from Sheffield since 1984. The company is a permanent ensemble whose experimental theatre work is well respected both in this country and abroad. Live performances include specially commissioned sound tracks as well as increasingly complex use of

video. They support their theatre pieces by conducting work-shops, residencies, lectures, and after show discussions.
Origins Founded 1984.
Subsidy ACGB, Yorkshire Arts,* Sheffield City Council. 1990 production sponsored by Barclays New Stages.**
Audience Generally 16+, in any venue technically equipped to house current touring show. Preferred two nights.
(*Now Yorkshire and Humberside Arts.)
(**1991 production was also sponsored by Barclays New Stages.)

FORKBEARD FANTASY – THE BRITTONIONI BROS

Policy Mixing humour with living sets, intriguing gadgetry, visual surprise and extremely unusual tricks and interactive antics with film we take the excitement of theatre as far and wide as possible.
Origins Founded in 1974.
Subsidy Revenue funding from ACGB. Also Southern Arts (Theatre, Film and Visual Arts panels), South West Arts (Theatre and Film), and the British Council for work abroad.
Personnel Chris Britton, Tim Britton, Penny Saunders and Ed Jobling.
Tours All over and almost anywhere. We like to spread the net. Any venue is possible for one or other Forkbeard show, but we need booking well in advance to fix sensible tours. We also do cinemas, film clubs, galleries, around four residencies, and about two sessions abroad each year.
Audience Anyone.
Equipment Carry own, but not much lighting.
Other activities Workshops and educational residencies; free-lance set and prop design for theatre, film and TV; cartoons and extensive film work.

IOU

Policy To invent and develop a rich form of theatre where music, imagery and words can combine with equal status. To present the work in a wide range of venues, indoor and outdoor touring shows being balanced with site-specific productions.

IOU's work is characterised by vivid images, distinctive sets and original music with an emphasis on atmosphere rather than plot.

Origins Founded in August 1976 by a group of fine artists and musicians who wanted to work together exploring different ways of looking at paintings and sculpture and how these could be combined with music. Theatre was the most appropriate medium.

Subsidy ACGB.

Personnel Permanent staff comprising one artistic and technical co-ordinator, one administrator and one tour co-ordinator. Core of artists, musicians and performers plus freelance practitioners on a project by project basis.

Tours Britain and abroad. Large scale productions for theatres and indoor spaces, smaller scale touring shows both indoor and outdoor. Also theatre created for particular chosen landscapes; examples include castles, catacombs, beaches, rooftops, car parks, derelict houses, market-halls, and others.

Audience As wide as possible. Indoor shows are usually seen by a theatre-going audience in arts centres, studio theatres and colleges seating 100–300. Outdoor shows attract a mixed general audience of families, shoppers and holidaymakers.

LUMIERE & SON

Policy To produce new theatre in which language, music, choreography and visual aspects are equally evolved. Recent shows have developed a use of projected photography. The intention in all the work is to coalesce these elements with a mix of humour and spectacle to produce a seamless fabric of theatre. The work is non-naturalistic and frequently depicts people subjected to pressures which drive them into extraordinary and unexpected regions.

Origins Founded in 1973 by David Gale and Hilary Westlake, who wished to work together as, respectively, writer and director.

Subsidy ACGB 1973–1992.

Other activities Lumiere & Son welcomes commissions from venues, festivals, and producing managements. The company would like to develop collaborations with other artists.

PEOPLE SHOW

Celebrating their 25th birthday, the People Show continues to tour their new shows and cabaret with a professional ease that extends the imagination and overdraft.

Policy To continue developing and exploring a multi-disciplinary, collaborative, highly theatrical approach to theatre.

Subsidy ACGB.

RED LADDER THEATRE COMPANY

Policy Socialist, feminist theatre company, committed to taking artistically stimulating work to young people in youth clubs and other similar venues. The company's work encourages young people to ask questions and explore dilemmas and is always followed by a discussion/workshop with the audience in small groups. Red Ladder is a multi-racial company, which includes disabled performers. Much of the company's work is signed. We frequently commission new writers.

Origins Red Ladder was founded in 1968 as the Agitprop Street Players, performing at demonstrations, tenants' meetings, weekend schools, etc. In 1976 the company moved from London to Yorkshire, and since 1985 has concentrated on work for young people (14–25) and the adults working with them.

Subsidy Revenue funding 1990/91: ACGB £89,795.50; West Yorkshire Grants £10,700; Yorkshire Arts £10,700. RAB touring grants 1991/92 not supplied.

Personnel Full-time artistic director, administrator and tour co-ordinator/development worker. Others contracted for specific shows.

Tours Up to three tours a year, nationally and in West Yorkshire. Generally autumn and spring/summer.

Audience Young people in their normal meeting place, eg. youth club, Phab club, probation group. Not usually in schools unless to get to a particular target group, eg. Asian girls, young deaf people. An audience of up to 60 makes for the best discussions after the show.

Other activities Training projects, workshops, residentials for youth workers and young people. Summer school for youth workers. Follow-up workshops for young people, linked to our performing work.

STATION HOUSE OPERA

Policy To present work with a unique physical and visual style, combining in its view of urban life the funny, the spectacular, the obsessional, and the ingenious. The work varies widely in look, scale and location, from the studio theatre to the twenty-storey high outside event, but it retains throughout a use of spectacle to explore the intimate relationship between people and the environment they inhabit. It is work without parallel in Britain today, combining serious non-narrative themes with room for simple enjoyment. It has a challenging accessibility, and occupies a political as well as artistic context.

Origins Founded in 1980 by Julian Maynard Smith, Miranda Payne, and Alison Urquhart.

TRESTLE THEATRE

Policy Trestle seeks to broaden the appeal of mask, mime, and visual theatre by pursuing two main aims. First, to develop a rich, visual style without forsaking narrative, emotion or humour, that stimulates on both a personal and theatrical level and that concerns itself with everyday people and their lives. Second, through extensive touring we aim to reach as broad-based an audience as possible, across the geographical, age, and disability spread.

Origins Having worked together for three years at Middlesex Polytechnic the professional company was formed in 1981.

Audience Their work is enjoyed by any age except the very young.

Subsidy ACGB annual funding, touring subsidy from RABs and sponsorship.

Equipment Tour everything except lights.

Other activities Mask residencies undertaken.

WELFARE STATE INTERNATIONAL

Alongside its programme of live work WSI offers training opportunities for arts practitioners at its headquarters in Ulverston, Cumbria. There is a varied programme of practical courses across many art forms.

Courses offered Short 4-day courses offered in street music, shadow theatre, low-level fire technology, devising community events, carnival costume, and other skills – open to anyone. The Winter School and the Summer School are two, 10-day intensive courses for experienced artists, who need to apply for a place. Each course has 20 places and 3 or 4 tutors. Brochure available October.

Facilities The WSI headquarters offer a variety of well equipped making, meeting, and rehearsal spaces with facilities for people needing wheelchair access. WSI has a good specialist library and extensive audio-visual archive.

Accommodation is in local guest houses. Lunch and evening meals provided at WSI headquarters. Fees include all materials, accommodation, and food.

WSI is willing to discuss training packages to suit the needs of different organisations.

APPENDIX II

'The Edge of Reason' (1989–90) – Greenwich Young People's Theatre

Examples of two 'sheets' or wall posters displayed in Studio One on September 14th, 1989.

1 Exercise on September 12th, 1989

	Baker's Daughter
Feelings:	Protective
	Unbelieving
	Horror
	Injustice
	Anger
Actions:	Cries
	Head Moving
	Eye Contact
Attitude:	Heat rising
	Rush of feelings/emotions
	Betrayal
Physically:	Closes up
	then
	re-opens and
	Plunges on . . .
	and explodes

2 Exercise on September 13th, 1989
Baker's daughter's perception of the four characters:

	Baker	*Sister*	*Jacobin*	*Daughter*
Animal	Hyena	Cat	Alsation (*sic*)	Lion Cub
Fire Signs	Earth	Air	Fire	Water

Sound	Rasp	Hum	Sigh	Gasp
Food	Heavy Supper	Light Lunch	Sandwich	Nouvelle Cuisine
Material	Sacking	Velvet	Kid Leather	Starched Linen
Colour	White	Green	Purple	Pink

Monologues written for three characters, which were used as core material for visits to two secondary schools on September 14th, 1989.

THE WOMAN

'Everyday there's this Q. You have to be here earlier every day. This morning I got here at five o'clock. Five o bloody clock. For a loaf of bread that wouldn't choke a sparrow. Even so there were still twenty here before me. Twenty. A couple of months ago when all this started I used to be in the first three most mornings. We used to joke about it then "Two hours wait, we'll soon be dropping babies in this Q." We've had all that, and more. Fights. Q sitters is the problem. Pay em and when you get back they've buggered off, well you can't lose your money and your place so you try to get your place back and wham bam. It stinks down this street. Have you noticed how the first thing you want when you start to Q is a pee. Well, I'll tell you it don't go away when you've been here a few hours. The rumour today is they've put chalk in the flour. Bastards. If we've topped the king and all the rest of his scroungers and confiscated – yeh I know the words – confiscated, taken away, his property why is it there ain't no bloody bread? And don't say the war. The crops are still growing. These pricks couldn't run a piss house let alone a revolution. I'm fed up with this. Tell that bloody baker we're fed up with his Q's. You can bet he's hoarding flour till the price goes up. I'm fed up with Q's and promises and excuses. Give us bread or else.'

THE BAKER

'I've run this shop for what – 18 years now – since me father passed away. We've had five years of this revolution and I've seen some sights I might tell you, but nothing, nothing

211

compared to this morning. It takes the biscuit. Women used to be human beings. That's before they started letting em shoot their mouths off. Every time there's a problem it's a sod to a sous that a woman's at the back of it. Who marched from Paris and dragged the king back here to be killed (God rest his soul) women. They've been encouraging women to do things and think things they're not equipped to handle and this is the result – chaos. Equal rights – you have to earn equality not just demand it. All this equal pay, equal this, equal that, get people to look after babies in crowds instead of doing it yourself, changing words – citizen weren't no good for them – they had to be citizenesses. And where's it got us. Giving in to them. I don't ask my wife every time I go out and I don't hear her complaining. Look at that lot. Spitting and screaming, ransacking the place, pinching me stock, calling me a hoarder. Me! I'm a saint compared to most of the bakers round here. Its not my fault there's a bread shortage, I sell what I'm told to by the revolutionary committee (Load of leeches). If I step out of line I get it in the neck – and I mean in the neck. That's what's beginning to happen round here. Well someone's got to take control its getting out of hand. We need a strong bloke back in charge. Military rule, that'll sort them out. Bloody women. I've given her name in. Her that started it. Its got to stop.'

THE JACOBIN

'Citizens. You have heard the testimonies. France is at war. There have to be sacrifices. This woman puts herself above everything. *She* is hungry. *She* is impatient. *She* is the enemy of the revolution! Leading a mob against the interests of the revolution makes her a counter revolutionary. You shake your heads. No, you say, she did not intend to be that, she only wanted bread. She only wanted bread. Let us pursue her action, this innocent woman. She broke into the bakers, encouraged women to take all the bread and flour for their needs. So for today they have full bellies. Where will the bread come from tomorrow. And when the soldiers at the front hear about her example, why should they not throw down their weapons and say no more war for today, no more sacrifice for today, and where will the next day find them and France? Defeated. Defeated by counter revolution that she did not intend.

212

Whether she intends it or not the result is the same. We will be swallowed up and soon will be back in those days of hell where human beings were thought to be worth nothing by those who ruled them. That is why we fought the revolution – to be free. For us each human being is the revolution until their action places them against it. They then place themselves above others just as their old masters did. So we must deal with these as we did with them. Guilty. Guillotine. Next case.'

Story as agreed by the team and written on the blackboard on September 14th, 1989.

1st Jan 1794, France in Crèvecœur. Time of terror. Baker, widower, daughter, 16, he's an opportunist. *Arranged marriage.* Working for the English. *Sister from Paris*, secret revolutionary, daughter forms close relation and helps politicise daughter. Price of bread is going up, hoarder, forger, anti-revolutionary. *Jacobin sent to purge village of anti-revolutionary forces.* Ambitious & is a zealot, fancies the daughter, Prig. Baker shops his sister to cover himself. *Daughter shops her Dad* to protect Aunt and keep her integrity. *Jacobin rumbles them & picks his target. Daughter challenges the Jacobin.*

APPENDIX III

Code of Practice
(This is taken from a theatre-in-education company that wishes to remain anonymous.)

1 COMPANY POLICY AND OBJECTIVES

All the company's work presents complex issues in a dramatic way which challenges young people to ask questions and often make decisions about the world in which they live. The form and content of the work necessarily develops as the priorities and personnel of the company changes and as the needs of young people and the world in which they live also changes (*sic*).

The company operates an internal democratic management structure where every company member is expected to contribute fully to discussion and decision making.

2 COMPANY MEETINGS

a. Authority and sphere of influence

All artistic and other major policy shall be discussed and voted on at company meetings or planning meetings.

b. Constitution and procedure

(i)   Meetings should be held once weekly and shall normally constitute an evening call.
(ii) All long term company members shall attend company meetings unless prevented by bona fide commitments.

214

(iii)   Short term company members have the option to attend Company meetings and only have voting rights on the show/project they are involved in.

(iv)   The appointment of chair and minute taker shall be decided on a rota basis with each company member taking her/his turn.

(v)   The chair shall be responsible for ordering the items on the agenda prior to the meeting. This may be challenged by the meeting with normal voting procedures applying.

(vi)   Any company member may place items on the agenda.

(vii)   Any company member placing an item on the agenda shall be responsible for the presentation of appropriate information at the company meeting, beforehand if possible, and for opening the discussion. Wherever possible that person should have or put forward a proposal in advance of the meeting.

(viii)   Company meetings shall aim to reach resolutions on items under discussion.

(ix)   Resolutions are determined by vote.

(x)   Each company member has one vote. Proxy voting shall only be allowed at the discretion of the company.

(xi)   Resolutions are reached by overall majority.

(xii)   Special company meetings may be called by any single member of the company. All long term company members shall attend special company meetings unless prevented by bona fide commitments.

(xiii)   The quorum for a company meeting shall not be fewer than ⅔ of the long term company members. If a meeting is not quorate then discussion may be had but no vote taken.

(xiv)   The same quorum shall apply to special company meetings and every effort will be made to contact all members.

3 PLANNING MEETINGS

a. Authority and sphere of influence

Planning meetings may be called at such times as company meetings see fit. Planning decisions should be taken to the company meeting if they affect a programme in which short term company members are currently working.

b. Constitution and procedure

(i) Voting rules apply as for the company meeting.
(ii) All long term company members shall attend planning meetings unless prevented by bona fide commitments.
(iii) The appointment of chair and minute taker shall be decided on a rota basis with each company member taking her/his turn.
(iv) Any company member may place items on the agenda.
(v) Any company member placing an item on the agenda shall be responsible for the presentation of appropriate information at the company meeting, beforehand if possible, and for opening the discussion. Wherever possible, that person should have or put forward a proposal in advance.

4 ASSESSMENT

The programme assessment shall take place in three parts:

Part A

Personal assessment

Each member of the company shall be required to assess her/his personal achievement and development. There shall also be an opportunity for the company to discuss each company member's contribution at the assessment concluding a programme. The assessment meeting may begin first stages of the disciplinary procedure and can require an improvement in the standard or level of contribution.

Part B

Project analysis

Each of the following shall be discussed by the company at the assessment concluding a programme:

1 The Devising/Rehearsal process
2 The Script
3 The Workshop(s)
4 The Schools (problems or comments)

5 The Teaching Pack/Follow up material
6 Project Achievement/Lessons for the future

Part C

Each project shall have a teachers assessment timetabled at the end of each tour.

5 PROCEDURES FOR APPOINTMENT

ACTOR/TEACHERS: Applicants are shortlisted for workshop audition on the basis of their written applications. Every long term company member is involved in drawing up the shortlist. Following the workshop audition, all long term company members are responsible for determining who is to join the company.

Other appointments are made following shortlisting and interviewing of candidates. An interview panel will be decided by the company in advance and may include a member from outside. The final decision is taken by all long term company members following the report back of the interview panel members.

The administrator is responsible for contracting new company members, and ensuring that the necessary paperwork is dealt with, where possible, in advance of the member joining us.

New long term company members will join the company on open ended contracts. Their contributions will be reviewed eight weeks before the end of their first programme or within three months of joining at which point either party has the right to terminate the contract with eight weeks notice.

APPENDIX IV

Selected reading list

Artaud, A., *The Theatre and Its Double*, J. Calder, 1970
Ayers, R., and Butler, D. (eds), *Live Art*, AN Publications, 1991
Boal, A., *Theatre of the Oppressed*, Pluto Press, 1979
Bolton, G., *Towards a Theory of Drama in Education*, Longman, 1979
Brook, P., *The Shifting Point*, Methuen, 1988
Brook, P., *The Empty Space*, Penguin, 1990
Bruner, J., *Toward a Theory of Instruction*, Harvard University Press, 1974
Chambers, I., *Popular Culture – The Metropolitan Experience*, Routledge, 1990
Chekhov, M., *To the Actor*, Harper & Row, 1985
Craig, E., *On the Art of the Theatre*, Heinemann, 1968
Elam, K., *The Semiotics of Theatre and Drama*, Methuen, 1980
Esslin, M., *Field of Drama*, Methuen, 1987
Freire, P., *The Pedagogy of the Oppressed*, Penguin, 1990
Goldberg, R., *Performance Art*, Thames & Hudson, 1988
Goldman, W., *Adventures in the Screen Trade*, Futura, 1990
Goldman, W., *The Season*, Limelight Editions, 1985
Grotowski, J., *Towards a Poor Theatre*, Methuen, 1969
Halpern, J., *Conference of the Birds*, Methuen, 1989
Hebdige, D., *Hiding in the Light*, Routledge, 1988
Hewison, R., *Future Tense – A New Art for the Nineties*, Methuen, 1990
Holt, J., *How Children Fail*, Penguin, 1990
Holt, J., *How Children Learn*, Penguin, 1991
Jackson, T. (ed.), *Learning through Theatre, Essays and Casebooks on Theatre in Education*, Manchester University Press, 1980
Johnson, L., and O'Neill, C. (eds), *Dorothy Heathcote: Collected Writings on Education and Drama*, Hutchinson, 1984

Nairne, S., *State of the Art*, Chatto & Windus, 1990

O'Toole, J., *Theatre in Education: New Objectives for Theatre, New Techniques in Education*, Hodder & Stoughton, 1977

Robinson, K. (ed.), *Exploring Theatre and Education*, Heinemann Educational Books, 1980

Roose-Evans, J., *Experimental Theatre*, Routledge, 1989

Schechner, R., *Performance Theory*, Routledge, 1988

Tarkovsky, A., *Sculpting in Time*, Bodley Head, 1986

Templeton, F., *YOU – The City*, Sun & Moon Press, 1990

Wallis, B. (ed.),*Blasted Allegories*, MIT Press, 1987

Willett, J. (ed.), *Brecht on Theatre*, Methuen, 1978

Various articles in *Theatre Quarterly, Performance Magazine, Drama Magazine, New Theatre Quarterly, SCYPT Journal, Platform,* and *Dartington Theatre Papers.*

Interviews, biographies, autobiographies of artists and their work.

APPENDIX V

Contact list

AGE EXCHANGE THEATRE TRUST LIMITED
The Reminiscence Centre
11 Blackheath Village
London SE3 9LA
Phone: 0181–318 9105
Fax: 0181–318 0060
Contact: Pam Schweitzer

BELGRADE THEATRE-IN-EDUCATION COMPANY
Belgrade Theatre
Belgrade Square
Coventry CV1 1GS
Phone: 01203 256431
Fax: 01203 550680

FORCED ENTERTAINMENT
Unit 102 The Workstation
46 Shoreham Street
Sheffield S1 4SP
Phone & Fax: 0114 279 8977
Contact: Deborah Chadbourn

FORKBEARD FANTASY
Moor Cottage
Huntsham
Tiverton
Devon EX16 7NF
Phone: 01398 361329
Fax: 0117 949 1178
Contact: Tim Britton

GLORIA
The Lyric Theatre Hammersmith
King Street
London W6 0QL
Phone: 0181–563 9293
Fax: 0181–563 9294
Contact: Mavis Seaman

GREENWICH YOUNG PEOPLE'S THEATRE
Burrage Road
London SE18 7JZ
Phone: 0181–854 1316/0181–855 4911
Contact: Vivien Harris

IOU
Unit M10
Dean Clough Industrial Park
Halifax HX3 5AX
Phone: 01422 369217
Fax: 01422 330203
Contact: Maureen Jordan

LUMIERE & SON
36 Leander Road
London SW2 2LH
Phone: 0181–674 7177
Fax: 0181–674 4309
Contact: Hilary Westlake

MAJOR ROAD THEATRE COMPANY
29 Queens Road
Bradford
West Yorkshire BD8 7BS
Phone: 01274 480251
Fax: 01274 548528
Contact: Sue Cullen

PEOPLE SHOW
St James the Great Institute
Pollard Row
London E2 6NB
Phone: 0171–729 1841
Fax: 0171–739 0203
Contact: Jane Martin

PIRATE PRODUCTIONS
Clink Street Studios
1 Clink Street
London SE1 9DG
Phone: 0171–403 2007
Fax: 0171–403 2721
Contact: Parisa Taghizadeh

RED LADDER THEATRE COMPANY
Cobden Avenue
Lower Wortley
Leeds LS12 5PB
Phone: 0113 279 2228
Fax: 0113 231 0660
Contact: Kully Thiarai

STATION HOUSE OPERA
Artsadmin
Toynbee Studios
29 Commercial Street
London E1 6LS
Phone: 0171–247 5102
Fax: 0171–247 5103
Contact: Judith Knight

TRESTLE THEATRE
47 Wood Street
Barnet
Herts EN5 4BS
Phone: 0181–441 0349
Fax: 0181–449 7036
Contact: Penny Mayes

WELFARE STATE INTERNATIONAL
The Ellers
Ulverston
Cumbria LA12 1AA
Phone: 01229 581127
Fax: 01229 581232
Contact: Sue Gill

APPENDIX VI

Video availability list

AGE EXCHANGE THEATRE TRUST LIMITED
'Can We Afford the Doctor?' (Television History Workshop for Channel 4). Available from the company, price £40.

BELGRADE THEATRE-IN-EDUCATION COMPANY
'Take the Biscuit' – programme for five years plus.
'Lives Worth Living' – programme for fourteen years plus.

FORCED ENTERTAINMENT THEATRE CO-OPERATIVE
'Let the Water Run its Course (to the Sea that Made the Promise)'
'200% & Bloody Thirsty'
'Some Confusions in the Law about Love'
'Marina & Lee'
'Emanuelle Enchanted'
Archive collection of videos of all company productions.

FORKBEARD FANTASY
Compilation of 16mm *films* including 'The Bonehunter'(1984), 'Night of the Gnat'(1983), and 'Worm'(1986). Also various (in form of compilations) television appearances, cartoons, and so on.
No full shows available.

GLORIA
'Lady Audley's Secret', 'A Vision of Love Revealed in Sleep, Part 3', and 'Sarrasine' are kept at the National Sound Archive.

GREENWICH YOUNG PEOPLE'S THEATRE
'The Edge of Reason'
Most theatre-in-education programmes have been videoed by the company. Two videos use extracts of the company's work:

1 'From Coping to Confidence', produced by NFER/OU, featuring Special Needs work.
2 'The Longest Road' – programme for 9–11 year olds. Transmitted as part of Channel 4's Schools Broadcasts – Middle English, Spring 1991. Television programme produced by Thames Television.

IOU
'Just Add Water', 'Full Tilt', 'Weatherhouse', 'Windfall', and 'An Example of Zeal' are available from the company.

LUMIERE & SON
'Fifty Five years of the Swallow and the Butterfly'
'Panic'
'Paradise'
'Deadwood'
'War Dance'
'Senseless'
'Brightside'
'Vulture Culture'
'Nightfall'
'The Appeal' (for Channel 4)
'Circus Lumiere' (for Channel 4)

MAJOR ROAD THEATRE COMPANY
Archive collection of videos of all company productions.

PEOPLE SHOW
No. 53 – 'Guinness'
No. 88 – 'The George Khan Show' (4 different videos available)
No. 89 – 'Checkpoint'
No. 91 – 'A Romance' (3 versions)
No. 93 – 'Marooned'
No. 94 – 'Farrago: A Jazz Cabaret'
No. 95 – 'The Big Sweep'

No. 96 – 'The Mad Hatter Appreciation Society Centenary
        Dinner'
No. 97 – 'Burning Horizon'
'Starwashed' – Channel 4, 1983
'Polverigi' – 1985
'20th Anniversary Show'
'The People Show Cabaret' – 1982
'The Bologna Show' – 1988
'The Boxing Show' – 1987 (various videos)
No. 98 – 'The Solo Experience' – 1992

PIRATE PRODUCTIONS
'Skylark'
'Ariadne'
'The Deadly Grove'
'Almost Persuaded'
'Blackbeard the Pirate'
'How to Act Better'
'Headpieces' (5 short films for MTV Europe, commissioned
1992)

TRESTLE THEATRE
'Plastered'
'Top Storey'
'Ties that Bind'
'L'Amfiparnaso'
'Hanging Around'
'Masking Taped' (a residency performance)
A three-minute promotional video on Trestle Theatre.

APPENDIX VII

Publications featuring the work of companies – selected books, magazines, and journals

AGE EXCHANGE THEATRE TRUST LIMITED

Books published by the company:
Goodnight Children Everywhere
A Day at the Fair
What did You do in the War Mum?
Just Like the Country
A Place to Stay
Health Remedies and Healthy Recipes
The Time of our Lives
Can we Afford the Doctor?
My First Job
All our Christmases
Fifty Years Ago
On the River
Good Morning Children
When we Were Young
Many Happy Retirements
A Practical Guide to Reminiscence
Lifetimes
Across the Irish Sea
Our Lovely Hops

Oddey, A., 'Devising Theatre', *Music Theatre Dance*, No. 2, Summer 1990

BELGRADE THEATRE-IN-EDUCATION COMPANY

Belgrade TIE, *Killed: July 17th, 1916*, Amber Lane Press, 1988
Craig, S. (ed.), *Dreams and Deconstructions*, Amber Lane Press, 1980
Jackson, T. (ed.), *Learning Through Theatre*, Manchester University Press, 1980
Redington, C., *Can Theatre Teach?*, Pergamon Press, 1983
Redington, C. (ed.), *Six Theatre-in-Education Programmes*, Methuen, 1987 ('Lives Worth Living')
Schweitzer, P. (ed.), *Theatre-in-Education, Five Infant Programmes*, vol. 1, Methuen Young Drama, 1980 ('Pow Wow')
Schweitzer, P. (ed.), *Theatre-in-Education, Four Secondary Programmes*, Methuen, 1980 ('Example')
Swortzell, L., *et al.* (eds), *International Guide to Children's Theatre and Educational Theatre*, Greenwood Press, 1990

Oddey, A., 'Devising Theatre', *Music Theatre Dance*, No. 2, Summer 1990

Various articles about the company's work or written contributions by company members, published in *SCYPT Journal*.

The company has an archive containing scripts, teachers' notes, and photographs, which is available for reference by visiting students of the work.

FORCED ENTERTAINMENT THEATRE CO-OPERATIVE

Etchells, T., 'I've Been to this Country Before, in Movies', *Performance Magazine*, No. 50/51, November–January, 1987
Etchells, T., 'Theatre Preview', *City Limits*, February 9–17th, 1989
Etchells, T., 'Elvis Lives', *City Limits*, March 1st–8th, 1990
Etchells, T., 'You the City', *Music Theatre Dance*, No. 1, Winter 1990
Hewison, R., *Future Tense – A New Art for the Nineties*, Methuen, 1990
Hiley, J., 'Play from a Savage Nursery', *Observer Magazine*, March 4th, 1990
MacDonald, C., 'The Challenge of Experimental Theatre', *New Socialist*, April 1987

Oddey, A., 'Devising Theatre', *Music Theatre Dance*, No. 2, Summer 1990

Watson, K., 'New British Theatre', *Plays and Players*, May 1987

FORKBEARD FANTASY

'The Cloning of an Eccentric', *Performance Magazine*, No. 7, 1980
'Forkbeard Fantasy The Library Ssshow', *Performance Magazine*, No. 16, March/April, 1982

Various reviews of past productions in *Art and Artists*, September 1979, *Performance Magazine*, No. 17, May/June 1982, and *The Peninsula Voice*, No. 49, 1986.

GLORIA

Text of 'A Vision of Love Revealed in Sleep, Part 3', in Wilcox, M. (ed.), *Gay Plays, Volume 4*, Methuen, 1990.
Neil Bartlett has two books published by Serpent's Tail: *Who was that Man?* and *Ready to Catch him Should he Fall*, as well as a collection of theatre translations published by Absolute Press.

GREENWICH YOUNG PEOPLE'S THEATRE

Jackson, T. (ed.), *Learning Through Theatre*, Manchester University Press, 1980
Redington, C., *Can Theatre Teach?*, Pergamon Press, 1983
Redington, C. (ed.), *Six Theatre-in-Education Programmes*, Methuen, 1987 ('The School on the Green')

Oddey, A., 'Devising Theatre', *Music Theatre Dance*, No. 2, Summer 1990
SCYPT Journal, No. 12 – 'A Lesson in Learning' – Case Study
New Voices – *SCYPT Journal*, No. 15 – 'Theatre Memory and Learning' – The Long Term Impact of T.I.E. – an edited version of a study undertaken by Lynne Suffolk (T.I.E Team Leader for Greenwich Young People's Theatre, 1985–1989)

Various reviews, articles and press cuttings from *The Times Educational Supplement* and others are kept at the company address. Teachers' Packs are also available for all the theatre-in-education programmes.

IOU

Tufnell, M., and Crickmay, C., *BODY SPACE IMAGE Notes Towards Improvisation and Performance*, Virago, 1990

Van Riel, R. (ed.), *THERE'S A LOT MORE WHERE THAT CAME FROM - The Arts in Yorkshire 1969-1990*, Yorkshire Art Circus, 1991

Burt, S., and Barker, C., 'IOU and the New Vocabulary of Performance Art', *Theatre Quarterly*, Vol. X, No. 37, 1980

Eilash, M., 'Back to the Garden', *Performance Magazine*, No. 18, August/September 1982

Hiley, J., 'Mystery Plays', *Observer Magazine*, March 1st, 1987

Various reviews of past productions in *Performance Magazine*, Nos. 15, 40, 50/51, 58, January/February 1982 to Summer 1989.

LUMIERE & SON

Craig, S. (ed.), *Dreams and Deconstructions*, Amber Lane Press, 1980

Gale, D., and Westlake, H., 'Doff this Bonnet before it becomes a Tea Cosy!', *Performance Magazine*, Nos. 44/45, November/February 1986/87

McLeod, D., 'Mutually Hostile Species', *Performance Magazine*, No. 16, March/April 1982

Oddey, A., 'Devising Theatre', *Music Theatre Dance*, No. 2, Summer 1990

Rogers, S., 'Entranced by Butterflies', *Performance Magazine*, No. 43, September/October, 1986

PEOPLE SHOW

Craig, S. (ed.), *Dreams and Deconstructions*, Amber Lane Press, 1980

Itzin, C., *Stages in the Revolution*, Methuen, 1980

Long, M., 'About the People Show', *Drama Review*, Vol. 15, No. 4, Fall 1971

Long, M., 'The People Show', *Theatre Papers*, Fourth Series, No. 2, Department of Theatre, Dartington College of Arts, 1982

Numerous articles, press cuttings, and reviews to be found in the archive collection at the company address.

PIRATE PRODUCTIONS

Hiley, J., 'Nexus of Ariadne', *Observer Magazine*, November 26th, 1989

Hiley, J., 'Love Streams', *The Listener*, December 7th, 1989

MacDonald, C., 'The Challenge of Experimental Theatre', *New Socialist*, April 1987

Oddey, A., 'Devising Theatre', *Music Theatre Dance*, No. 2, Summer 1990

Pascal, J., Review of 'Ariadne', *Music Theatre Dance*, No. 2, Summer 1990

Rogers, S., and La Frenais, R., 'The English Dream', *Performance Magazine*, No. 44/45, November/February 1986/87

Watkins, J., 'The Deadly Grove', *Art Monthly*, September 1988

Various features, reviews, interviews and articles related to past productions in publications including *The Pink Paper, The Times, Guardian, Glasgow Herald, Los Angeles Times, Boston Globe, Boston Phoenix, Los Angeles Weekly,* and *Spare Rib.*

RED LADDER THEATRE COMPANY

Craig, S. (ed.), *Dreams and Deconstructions*, Amber Lane Press, 1980

Itzin, C., *Stages in the Revolution*, Methuen, 1980

STATION HOUSE OPERA

Maynard-Smith, J., 'Documentation', *Performance Magazine*, No. 22, February/March 1983

Rogers, S., and Maynard Smith, J., 'Showing the Wires', *Performance Magazine*, No. 56/57, December/January/February 1988

Thornton, M., 'Psychological Architecture', *Artscribe International*, September 1988

Various reviews of past productions in *Performance Magazine*, Nos. 12, 49, 59, July/August 1981 to Winter 1989/90.

TRESTLE THEATRE

Frost, A., and Yarrow, R., *Improvisation in Drama*, New Directions in Theatre, Macmillan, 1990

WELFARE STATE INTERNATIONAL

Coult, T., and Kershaw, B. (eds), *Engineers of the Imagination, The Welfare State Handbook*, Methuen, 1990 (revised edn); see Appendix 7, 'Bibliography' (pp. 271–72), for books, selected magazines, and journals featuring Welfare State International's work.

Itzin, C., *Stages in the Revolution*, Methuen, 1980

APPENDIX VIII
Chronology of theatre companies

NOTES

1 AN INTRODUCTION TO DEVISED THEATRE

1 For a detailed description of the origins and history of this company (and the beginnings of the theatre-in-education movement), see Redington, C., *Can Theatre Teach?*, Pergamon, 1983.

2 For a description of the Agitprop Street Players' early work, and development of Red Ladder Theatre Company, see Itzin, C., *Stages in the Revolution*, Methuen, 1980, pp. 39–50.

3 For a detailed description of Welfare State International's origins and history, see Coult, T., and Kershaw, B. (eds), *Engineers of the Imagination, The Welfare State Handbook*, Methuen, 1990 (revised edn).

4 For a general background to British alternative theatre, see Craig, S. (ed.), *Dreams and Deconstructions, Alternative Theatre in Britain*, Amber Lane Press, 1980.

5 Long, M., 'About the People Show', *Drama Review*, Vol. 15, No. 4, Fall 1971, p. 57.

6 From an unpublished interview with David Gale in September 1990.

7 From an unpublished interview with Mark Long in October 1990.

8 Long, M., 'The People Show', *Dartington Theatre Papers*, No. 2, Fourth Series, Dartington College of Arts, 1982, p. 19.

9 Itzin, C., *Stages in the Revolution, Political Theatre in Britain Since 1968*, Methuen, 1980; Wandor, M., *Carry on Understudies, Theatre and Sexual Politics*, Routledge and Kegan Paul, 1986; Ritchie, R. (ed.), *The Joint Stock Book*, Methuen, 1987.

10 Hanna, G., *Monstrous Regiment, A Collective Celebration*, Nick Hern Books, 1991.

11 Jellicoe, A., *Community Plays – How to Put Them On*, Methuen, 1987.

12 Gillian Hanna interviewed by Lisbeth Goodman, 'Waiting for Spring to Come Again: Feminist Theatre, 1978 and 1979', in *New Theatre Quarterly*, Vol. VI, No. 21, February 1990, p. 53.

13 The Arts Council of Great Britain operates a system of 'Annual' funding to cover a yearly programme of work in a specific financial year. At the same time, it offers 'Revenue' funding which recurs annually and is expected to continue subject to review. Companies

are freely moved between both 'Annual' and 'Revenue' funding, in order to take account of those companies in crisis, such as, managerial or local authority problems, and as a strategy for rescue. Non-building based companies may apply for a 'Three year franchise' which becomes 'Annual' funding after two years, so that the position can be reviewed. 'Project' funded companies can apply for franchise funding (based on a long track record of artistic achievement), and are evaluated against long-standing franchise companies. Although traditional companies receive more funding overall than those devising theatre, it is interesting to note that since 1986 there are seventeen devising companies who have come on to franchise funding (including Trestle Theatre, Forkbeard Fantasy, and Gloria), against six companies who have lost revenue or franchise funding status on primarily artistic, but also managerial and financial, grounds (such as Joint Stock and Lumiere & Son). For further information, see *47th Annual Report and Accounts, 1991/ 92*, The Arts Council of Great Britain, October 1992.

14 For 1992/93, Belgrade Theatre was allocated £420,000 Arts Council funding. From this allocation, Belgrade Theatre Trust contributed £50,550 to Belgrade Theatre-in-Education Company, leaving a remainder of £369,450 for other theatre activities. The theatre-in-education company received £148,940 from Coventry City Council in 1992/93.

15 *47th Annual Report and Accounts, 1991/92*, The Arts Council of Great Britain, October 1992, pp. 60–61.

Selected examples of 'Annual Clients':
Forkbeard Fantasy	£ 54,500
Lumiere & Son Theatre Company Ltd	£ 95,500
Red Ladder Theatre Company Ltd	£ 96,000
Trestle Theatre Company Ltd	£110,000

Selected examples of 'Three year franchise clients (touring)':
IOU Ltd	£ 98,000
Major Road Theatre Company	£100,500
The People Show Ltd	£ 65,500

Selected examples of 'Projects':
Forced Entertainment Theatre Co-op	£ 38,400
Gloria Theatre Ltd	£ 20,000
Pirate Productions	£ 23,900

16 This budget was not grant aid, but made available from Age Exchange reserves. Otherwise, this project would have been unfunded.

17 £4,040 does not include salaries, and was solely for set construction, hardware, and other production costs. The total production budget for 'Some Confusions in the Law about Love' was £6,561, which included the costs of hiring rehearsal rooms, lighting, and making the soundtrack.

18 £800 was dedicated to costume, set, lighting, music, and other

related production costs. It did not include salaries, or company running costs.

19 Impact Theatre started as a group of ex-students of Leeds University in 1978. The original members were Tyrone Huggins, Graeme Miller, Lesley Stiles, Pete Brooks, and Claire MacDonald. In the period 1981–86, the company produced a huge amount of devised theatre, including three to four major shows a year, residencies in colleges, and children's performances. Impact Theatre did not receive Arts Council funding until 1982 with 'Damnerungstrasse 55', which toured widely. One of its most influential productions was 'The Carrier Frequency'(1984–85), which was concerned with the physical language of people in a mythical, fictional environment. It was created through a collaborative process with Russell Hoban, which resulted in his writing a specially commissioned script/text. (The text was also used in his novel *The Medusa Frequency*.) See Hoban's description of the working process of 'The Carrier Frequency' in 'Working with Impact', *Performance*, No. 32, November/December 1984, pp. 12–14.

2 BEGINNINGS: HOW AND WHERE TO START

1 From an unpublished interview with Mark Long in October 1990. All subsequent quotations cited are taken from this interview.

2 Introduction by Sandars, N., *The Epic of Gilgamesh*, Penguin Classics, 1960.

3 Opie, I., and Opie, P., *Classic Fairy Tales*, Oxford University Press, 1974.

4 Eliot, T.S., *The Complete Poems and Plays of T.S. Eliot*, Faber & Faber, 1969, pp. 115–26.

5 Waits, T., 'Christmas Card from a Hooker in Minneapolis', from the musical album *Blue Valentine*, WEA Records Ltd, 1978; Waits, T., 'Frank's Wild Years', from the musical album *Swordfishtrombones*, Island Records Ltd, 1982.

6 Stories retold by Williams-Ellis, A., *Tales of the Arabian Nights*, Blackie & Son, 1957.

7 Alfreds, M., 'A shared experience: The actor as storyteller', *Theatre Papers*, Third Series, No. 6., Department of Theatre, Dartington College of Arts, 1979.

8 From an unpublished interview with Pam Schweitzer in June 1990. All subsequent quotations cited are taken from this interview.

9 From an unpublished interview with Pam Schweitzer in November 1989.

10 From an unpublished interview with Annie Griffin in August 1989. All subsequent quotations cited are taken from this interview.

11 Brennan, M., review of 'Ariadne', *Glasgow Herald*, April 5th, 1990.

12 From an unpublished interview with Terry O'Connor in July 1990. Unless otherwise indicated, all subsequent quotations cited are

taken from unpublished interviews with Terry O'Connor and Tim Etchells in July 1990.
13 From an unpublished interview with Hilary Westlake in May 1990.

3 PROCESS: WAYS AND MEANS OF MAKING THEATRE

1 From an unpublished interview with Mark Long in October 1990.
2 Ibid.
3 Long, M., 'The People Show', *Theatre Papers*, Fourth Series, No. 2, Department of Theatre, Dartington College of Arts, 1982, p. 7.
4 From an unpublished interview with Tim Etchells in August 1989. Unless otherwise indicated, all subsequent quotations cited are taken from unpublished interviews with Tim Etchells and Terry O'Connor in August 1989 and July 1990.
5 McGillivray, D. (ed.), *British Alternative Theatre Directory 1990–1991*, Conway McGillivray, 1990, p. 122.
6 From an unpublished interview with Sarah Westaway in March 1990. All subsequent quotations cited are taken from unpublished interviews with members of the 'Monkey' sub-company in March 1990.
7 From an unpublished interview with Gail McIntyre in July 1990. All subsequent quotations cited are taken from this interview.
8 McGillivray, D. (ed.), *British Alternative Theatre Directory 1990–1991*, Conway McGillivray, 1990, p. 129.
9 From an unpublished interview with Viv Harris in November 1989. Unless otherwise indicated, all subsequent quotations cited are taken from unpublished interviews with Viv Harris, John Wood, and other company members in 1989 and 1990.
10 Goodman, L. (ed.), 'Devising as Writing', *TDR*, No. T126, Summer 1990, p. 17.
11 Goodman, L. (ed. and intro.), 'The (Woman) Writer and T.I.E. Part II', *MTD*, No. 4, Summer 1991, p. 25.
12 Wandor, M. (ed. and intro.), *Strike While the Iron is Hot*, Three Plays on Sexual Politics, Journeyman Press, 1980, p. 63.
13 Churchill, C., 'Light Shining in Buckinghamshire', in *Plays: One*, Methuen, 1985, p. 184.
14 Gooch, S., *Altogether Now*, Methuen, 1984, p. 55.
15 Davis, J. (ed. and intro.), *Lesbian Plays*, Methuen, 1987, p. 52.
16 From an unpublished interview with Annie Griffin in May 1990. All subsequent quotations cited are taken from this interview.
17 From an unpublished interview with Hilary Westlake in April 1990. All subsequent quotations cited are taken from a series of unpublished interviews with Hilary Westlake, David Gale, Simon Corder, and Jeremy Peyton-Jones in 1990.
18 Hiley, J., 'Nexus of Ariadne', *Observer Magazine*, November 26th, 1989, p. 69.

19 From an unpublished interview with John Wright in July 1990.
20 From an unpublished interview with Pam Schweitzer in July 1990. Unless otherwise indicated, all subsequent quotations cited are taken from this interview.

4 FROM PROCESS TO PRODUCT: RELATIONSHIP AND PRACTICE

1 The author is aware of Living Memory Theatre based in Newcastle-upon-Tyne, whose policy is to 'use reminiscence as a basis for theatre that is relevant to the life experience of our audience'. McGillivray, D. (ed.), *British Alternative Theatre Directory 1991–1992*, Rebecca Books, 1991, p. 84.
2 'Making Memories Matter', *Age Exchange Annual Report*, 1988/1989, p. 1.
3 From an unpublished interview with Pam Schweitzer in July 1990. Unless otherwise indicated, all subsequent quotations cited are taken from unpublished interviews with Pam Schweitzer in November 1989 and in July 1990.
4 Coveney, M., 'Forced Charm', *The Financial Times*, March 14th, 1987.
5 MacDonald, C., 'The Challenge of Experimental Theatre', *New Socialist*, April 1987.
6 From an unpublished interview with Tim Etchells in August 1989. Unless otherwise indicated, all subsequent quotations cited are taken from unpublished interviews with Tim Etchells and Terry O'Connor in August 1989 and March–July 1990.
7 Unpublished company pamphlet of 1988 is lodged with Forced Entertainment Theatre Co-operative at Unit 102, The Workstation, 46 Shoreham Street, Sheffield S14 5P.
8 Etchells, T., 'Forced Entertainment, You and the City', *Music Theatre Dance*, Winter 1990, p. 34.
9 For a description of The Wooster Group and its work, see Savran, D., *Breaking the Rules: The Wooster Group*, Theatre Communications Group, 1988.
10 Gale, D., 'Forced Entertainment', *Guardian*, March 8th, 1990.

5 FROM PROCESS TO PRODUCT: THE PARTICIPATORY THEATRE-IN-EDUCATION PROGRAMME

1 From an unpublished interview with Viv Harris in November 1989. All subsequent quotations cited are taken from unpublished interviews with company members in 1989 and 1990.
2 Since abolition of ILEA in 1990, the Inspectorates of neither principal funding body (London Boroughs of Greenwich and Lewisham Education Departments) have included a post with exclusive responsibility for drama. Both inspectorates have

reduced considerably during 1990–93, with contacts maintained via the English Inspectors. There are two continuing teacher advisory groups (for primary and secondary sectors), plus additional groups created for specific projects (for example, HIV Education programmes) comprising teachers, users, and other specialists.

3 Since April 1990, Greenwich Young People's Theatre has undergone various changes in its funding situation and company structure. In Spring 1993 (with grant aid from both London Boroughs further reduced by 45%), the company is currently re-organising staff structure again, with a commitment to continuing an in-house company of actor-teachers. The company is also identifying targets for increase in earned income, and new audiences as appropriate.

Staff at April 1993:

3 actor-teachers; technical stage manager; education liaison officer; youth arts worker; business development director; artistic/educational director; administrative director; administration secretary; accounts assistant; caretaking, reception, and cleaning.

4 See Appendix II for full version of the Jacobin's monologue written by John Wood for the pre-school visits in September 1989.

6 SPACE: SITE-SPECIFIC THEATRE

1 McGillivray, D. (ed.), *British Alternative Theatre Directory 1991–1992*, Rebecca Books, 1991, p. 64.

2 From an unpublished discussion document with IOU in 1991. All subsequent IOU quotations are taken from this document, and are agreed by the company as representing one collective voice.

3 Eilash, M., 'Back to the Garden', *Performance Magazine*, No. 18, August/September 1982, p. 19.

4 From an unpublished interview with Graham Devlin in December 1990. All subsequent quotations cited are taken from this interview.

5 The 'Feast of Furness Festival' in the summer of 1990 was the result of Welfare State International's three-year residency in Barrow-in-Furness. It was a spectacular community celebration using plays, music, songs, images, stories, and pageant. Central to the Festival were the 'Shipyard Tales', written by local writers and performed by hundreds of local people drawing on the town's own skill and resources.

6 Neumark, V., 'The Lake Lake Lake Show', *The Times Educational Supplement*, No. 3659, August 15th, 1986.

7 From an unpublished interview with Tim Britton in December 1990. All subsequent Forkbeard Fantasy quotations in this chapter are attributed to Tim Britton from the same interview.

8 This has also been the case for other company members, such as David Gale and Jeremy Peyton-Jones. (See chapter 3, pp. 56–58 and

pp. 59–60 for additional views on the difficulties of local involvement and working with amateurs.)
9 From an unpublished interview with Hilary Westlake in May 1990. All subsequent quotations cited are taken from this interview.

7 THEORY AND PRACTICE

1 Graeme Miller: 'A Girl Skipping' (1991), 'The Desire Paths' (1993); Gary Stevens: 'Name' (1992–93); Annie Griffin: 'How to Act Better' (1993); Steve Shill: A Trilogy of Interiors (1993), including 'Face Down', 'A Fine Film of Ashes', and 'A Little Theatre'.
2 The University of Kent offers a B.A. Single Honours degree in Drama and Theatre Studies over a period of four years. Students must choose one of three specialist courses offered in Devising, Directing, or Theatre Administration for full-time study in the fourth year.
3 Enterprise Kent is a government-funded scheme through which the University of Kent has been able to develop a Drama 'Professionalisation Project' from 1990 to 1993. From July 1990 to July 1991, £12,500 was allocated to the Drama Board of Studies to enable a series of different theatre projects to be set up between staff, students, and professional theatre practitioners. 1991–93 has seen a continuation of further financial support with £7,100 being given to additional projects.
4 See chapter one, note 19 for further information about Impact's 'The Carrier Frequency'.
5 McGrath, J., A Good Night Out, Methuen, 1981, pp. 5–6.
6 The Cardiff Performance Research conference on 'Devising and Documentation' was held in Cardiff on February 26–28th, 1993. Companies attending included: Anna O; Bodies in Flight; Brith Gof; Clanjamfrie; Clock; Desperate Optimists; Emergency Exit Arts; Forced Entertainment Theatre Co-operative; Forkbeard Fantasy; IOU; Man Act; Pants; The People Show; The Practice; Triangle.

8 LEARNING TO DEVISE: PRACTICAL IDEAS AND SUGGESTIONS

1 Ritchie, R. (ed.), The Joint Stock Book, Methuen, 1987; Coult, T., and Kershaw, B. (eds), Engineers of the Imagination, The Welfare State Handbook, Methuen, 1990 (revised edn); Savran, D., Breaking the Rules: The Wooster Group, Theatre Communications Group, 1988; MacLennan, E., The Moon Belongs to Everyone, Making Theatre with 7:84, Methuen, 1990.
2 The London International Festival of Theatre originated in 1981 and is a biennial festival that presents some of the most significant international companies in contemporary performance work. In

1993, the Lift Festival hosted 150 different performances from 22 world companies at venues across London; these included: the first performances in England of The Wooster Group's 'Brace Up!'; a world premiere of 'A Guerra Santa' (performed in Portuguese and Italian) and directed by Brazilian Gabriel Villela; a 'work-in-progress' of 'Sarajevo', performed by artists of former Yugoslavia in Serbo-Croat, Turkish, Yiddish, Swedish, Slovenian, and Macedonian; Platform's 'Homeland' (an installation in a house that will travel through London); and the British premiere of Bobby Baker's 'HOW TO SHOP'.

3 Particular productions that inspired and influenced me as an undergraduate included:

'The Great Caper', performed by the Ken Campbell Roadshow at Exeter University in 1974;

A promenade production of 'The Speakers' by Heathcote Williams, performed by Joint Stock in a Plymouth hall in 1974;

Monstrous Regiment's 'SCUM – Death, Destruction and Dirty Washing', and 'Vinegar Tom' by Caryl Churchill, at St Luke's College, Exeter in 1975/76;

Gay Sweatshop's group-written 'Mister X', at Exeter University in 1975;

'England Expects' by The Belt and Braces Roadshow, at St. Luke's College, Exeter in 1976;

Shared Experience's trilogy 'The Arabian Nights or Recitals of Mystery, Violence and Desire', at St Luke's College, Exeter during 1976/77;

Foco Novo's 'A Seventh Man' by Adrian Mitchell, at St Luke's College, Exeter during 1976/77;

7:84's 'Wreckers' by David Edgar, at St Luke's College, Exeter during 1976/77;

Nola Rae and the London Mime Theatre.

4 Hunt, A., *Hopes for Great Happenings: Alternatives in Education and Theatre*, Eyre Methuen, 1976, pp. 167–75.

5 Johnstone, K., *IMPRO Improvisation and the Theatre*, Methuen, 1981.

6 Barker, C., *Theatre Games*, Methuen, 1977, p. 1.

7 Tufnell, M., and Crickmay, C., *BODY SPACE IMAGE Notes Towards Improvisation and Performance*, Virago, 1990 (Introduction).

8 I attended a 4-day course on 'The Theatre of the Oppressed', at Goldsmiths' College in March 1985.

9 See Boal, A., *Theatre of the Oppressed*, Pluto Press, 1979.

10 I attended a one-day workshop with Boal at Trent Polytechnic, Nottingham (now The Nottingham Trent University) in 1988; a week's course on 'Image Theatre', 'Forum Theatre', and some 'Cop in the head' techniques at Trent Polytechnic on August 20–26th, 1989; and a week's course on 'The Rainbow of Desires' at the London Bubble on January 20–25th, 1992.

11 See Boal, A., *Games for Actors and Non-Actors* (trans. Adrian Jackson), Routledge, 1992.

12 This is a verbal quotation from Boal, frequently used by him at 'The Rainbow of Desires' course at the London Bubble, January 20–25th, 1992.

13 Ibid. Boal's description of the selected exercises is as follows:

Columbian hypnosis, pp. 63–64;
Bolivian mimosas, pp. 98–99;
The machine of rhythms, pp. 90–91;
West Side Story, p. 93;
Noises, p. 107;
Complete the image, pp. 130–31.

It is interesting to note that Boal placed 'mimosas' in the first category of exercises in August 1989, but it is now in the second category of exercises in his book *Games for Actors and Non-Actors*.

14 Feldenkrais, M., *Awareness Through Movement*, Penguin, 1980.

15 Iyengar, B.K.S., *Light on Yoga*, George Allen & Unwin, 1966.

16 Pisk, L., *The Actor and His Body*, Harrap, 1975.

17 At the beginning of an introductory session with a new group, I stress the importance of each individual being able to choose not to participate in an exercise if it seems uncomfortable or inappropriate. This is particularly relevant in relation to gender, race, or religion.

18 The painting is 'The Red Model' by René Magritte, 1934, Sussex, Edward James Foundation. It is reproduced in Wilson, S., *Surrealist Painting*, Phaidon, 1975.

19 Levy, D. (ed.), *Walks on Water*, Methuen, 1992, pp. 158–81.

20 Research for 'Women Imprisoned' was completed over a six-month period. The show was devised in three weeks.

21 On February 22nd, 1985, Annie Maguire was released from Cookham Wood prison after serving more than nine years for a crime that she did not commit. She was convicted of explosives offences at the Old Bailey on March 4th, 1976.

22 For further details about the Campaign for Women in Prison, contact Women in Prison, Highbury Grove, London.

23 The 'Crimes Against Women' Conference was organised by Leeds Women's Committee at Civic Hall, Leeds, on January 26th, 1985.

24 See Clements, P., *The Improvised Play – The Work of Mike Leigh*, Methuen, 1983 for a description of Leigh's approach to improvisation and character.

25 See Alfreds, M., 'A Shared Experience: The Actor as Storyteller', *Theatre Papers*, Third Series, No. 6., Department of Theatre, Dartington College of Arts, 1979, for one approach to 'Storytelling Theatre'.

BIBLIOGRAPHY

1 AN INTRODUCTION TO DEVISED THEATRE

Books

Coult, T., and Kershaw, B. (eds), *Engineers of the Imagination, The Welfare State Handbook*, Methuen, 1990 (revised edn)

Craig, S. (ed.), *Dreams and Deconstructions, Alternative Theatre in Britain*, Amber Lane Press, 1980

Hanna, G., *Monstrous Regiment, A Collective Celebration*, Nick Hern Books, 1991

Itzin, C., *Stages in the Revolution, Political Theatre in Britain Since 1968*, Methuen, 1980

Jellicoe, A., *Community Plays – How to Put Them on*, Methuen, 1987

Redington, C., *Can Theatre Teach?*, Pergamon Press, 1983

Ritchie, R. (ed.), *The Joint Stock Book*, Methuen, 1987

Wandor M., *Carry on Understudies: Theatre and Sexual Politics*, Routledge & Kegan Paul, 1986

Articles

Hanna, G., 'Waiting for Spring to Come Again: Feminist Theatre, 1978 and 1989', *New Theatre Quarterly*, Vol. VI, No. 21, February 1990

Hoban, R., 'Working with Impact', *Performance*, No. 32, November/December 1984

Long, M., 'About the People Show', *Drama Review*, Vol. 15, No. 4, Fall 1971

Long, M., 'The People Show', *Dartington Theatre Papers*, No. 2, Fourth Series, Department of Theatre, Dartington College of Arts, 1982

Other

47th Annual Report and Accounts 1991/92, The Arts Council of Great Britain, October 1992

2 BEGINNINGS: HOW AND WHERE TO START

Books

Eliot, T.S., *The Complete Poems and Plays of T.S.Eliot*, Faber & Faber, 1969
Opie, I., and Opie, P., *Classic Fairy Tales*, Oxford University Press, 1974
Sandars, N.K. (intro.), *The Epic of Gilgamesh*, Penguin Classics, 1960
(Stories retold by) Williams-Ellis, A., *Tales of the Arabian Nights*, Blackie & Son, 1957

Articles

Alfreds, M., 'A Shared Experience: The Actor as Storyteller', *Theatre Papers*, Third Series, No. 6, Department of Theatre, Dartington College of Arts, 1979
Brennan, M., review of 'Ariadne', *Glasgow Herald*, April 5th, 1990

Other

Waits, T., 'Blue Valentine', WEA Records Ltd, 1978
Waits, T., 'Swordfishtrombones', Island Records Ltd, 1982

3 PROCESS: WAYS AND MEANS OF MAKING THEATRE

Books

Churchill, C., *Plays: One*, Methuen, 1985
Davis, J. (ed.), *Lesbian Plays*, Methuen, 1987
Gooch, S., *Altogether Now*, Methuen, 1984
McGillivray, D. (ed.), *British Alternative Theatre Directory 1990–1991*, Conway McGillivray, 1990
Wandor, M. (ed. and intro.), *Strike While the Iron is Hot*, Three Plays on Sexual Politics, Journeyman Press, 1980

Articles

Goodman, L. (ed.), 'Devising as Writing', *TDR*, No. T126, Summer 1990
Goodman, L. (ed.), 'The (Woman) Writer and T.I.E. Part II', *MTD*, No. 4, Summer 1991
Hiley, J., 'Nexus of Ariadne', *Observer Magazine*, November 26th, 1989
Long, M., 'The People Show', *Theatre Papers*, Fourth Series, No. 2, Department of Theatre, Dartington College of Arts, 1982

4 FROM PROCESS TO PRODUCT: RELATIONSHIP AND PRACTICE

Books

McGillivray, D. (ed.), *British Alternative Theatre Directory 1991–1992*, Rebecca Books, 1991

Savran, D., *Breaking the Rules: The Wooster Group*, Theatre Communications Group, 1988

Articles

Coveney, M., 'Forced Charm', *The Financial Times*, March 14th, 1987

Etchells, T., 'Forced Entertainment, You and the City', *Music Theatre Dance*, Winter 1990

Gale, D., 'Forced Entertainment', *Guardian*, March 8th, 1990

MacDonald, C., 'The Challenge of Experimental Theatre', *New Socialist*, April 1987

Other

'Making Memories Matter', *Age Exchange Annual Report*, 1988/1989

6 SPACE: SITE-SPECIFIC THEATRE

Books

McGillivray, D (ed.)., *British Alternative Theatre Directory 1991–1992*, Rebecca Books, 1991

Articles

Eilash, M., 'Back to the Garden', *Performance Magazine*, No. 18, August/September 1982

Neumark, V., 'The Lake Lake Lake Show', *The Times Educational Supplement*, No. 3659, August 15th, 1986

7 THEORY AND PRACTICE

Books

McGrath, J., *A Good Night Out*, Methuen, 1981

8 LEARNING TO DEVISE: PRACTICAL IDEAS AND SUGGESTIONS

Books

Barker, C., *Theatre Games*, Methuen, 1977

Boal, A., *Theatre of the Oppressed*, Pluto Press, 1979

Boal, A., *Games for Actors and Non-Actors* (trans. Adrian Jackson), Routledge, 1992

Clements, P., *The Improvised Play – The Work of Mike Leigh*, Methuen, 1983

Coult, T., and Kershaw, B. (eds), *Engineers of the Imagination, The Welfare State Handbook*, Methuen, 1990 (revised edn)

Feldenkrais, M., *Awareness Through Movement*, Penguin, 1980

Grotowski, J., *Towards a Poor Theatre*, Methuen, 1969

Hunt, A., *HOPES FOR GREAT HAPPENINGS Alternatives in Education and Theatre*, Eyre Methuen, 1976

Iyengar, B.K.S., *Light on Yoga*, George Allen & Unwin, 1966

Johnstone, K., *IMPRO Improvisation and the Theatre*, Eyre Methuen, 1981

MacLennan, E., *The Moon Belongs to Everyone, Making Theatre with 7:84*, Methuen, 1990

Pisk, L., *The Actor and His Body*, Harrap, 1975

Ritchie, R. (ed.), *The Joint Stock Book*, Methuen, 1987

Savran, D., *Breaking the Rules: The Wooster Group*, Theatre Communications Group, 1988

Tufnell, M., and Crickmay, C., *BODY SPACE IMAGE Notes Towards Improvisation and Performance*, Virago, 1990

Wilson, S., *Surrealist Painting*, Phaidon, 1975

Articles

Alfreds, M., 'A Shared Experience: The Actor as Storyteller', *Theatre Papers*, Third Series, No. 6, Department of Theatre, Dartington College of Arts, 1979

Other

Levy, D. (ed.), *Walks on Water*, Methuen, 1992

INDEX

246